Technology, Education—Connections
The TEC Series

Series Editor: Marcia C. Linn.
Advisory Board: Robert Bjork, Chris Dede, BatSheva Eylon,
Carol Lee, Jim Minstrell, Mitch Resnick.

Electric Worlds in the Classroom:
Teaching and Learning with Role-Based Computer Games
BRIAN M. SLATOR AND ASSOCIATES

Meaningful Learning Using Technology:
What Educators Need to Know and Do
ELIZABETH A. ASHBURN AND ROBERT E. FLODEN, EDITORS

Using Technology Wisely:
The Keys to Success in Schools
HAROLD WENGLINSKY

ELECTRIC WORLDS
in the Classroom

Teaching and Learning with Role-Based Computer Games

Brian M. Slator

and

Richard T. Beckwith
Harold Chaput
Lisa M. Daniels
Phil McClean
Bernhardt Saini-Eidukat
Bradley Vender

Lisa Brandt
Jeffrey T. Clark
Curt Hill
John Opgrande
Donald P. Schwert
Alan R. White

Additional material contributed by

Otto Borchert
Michael Lee
Chin Lua

Lura Joseph
Mei Li
Max Pool

TEACHERS
COLLEGE
PRESS

Teachers College, Columbia University
New York and London

Published by Teachers College Press, 1234 Amsterdam Avenue, New York, NY 10027

Library of Congress Cataloging-in-Publication Data

Electric worlds in the classroom: teaching and learning with role-based computer games / Brian M. Slator and Richard Beckwith...[et al.] ; with additional material contributed by Otto Borchert...[et al].
   p. cm. – (Technology, education—connections, the TEC series)
   Includes bibliographical references and index
   ISBN 13: 978-0-8077-4676-9 (cloth)
   ISBN 10: 0-8077-4676-2 (cloth)
   ISBN 13: 978-0-8077-4675-2 (pbk.)
   ISBN 10: 0-8077-4675-4 (pbk.)
   1. Education—Computer network resources. 2. Teaching—Computer network resources. 3. Simulated environment (Teaching method). 4. Educational games. I.Title. II. Series.

LB1044.87+
2006040404

ISBN 13: 978-0-8077-4675-2 (paper)   ISBN 10: 0-8077-4675-4 (paper)
ISBN 13: 978-0-8077-4676-9 (cloth)   ISBN 10: 0-8077-4676-2 (cloth)

Printed on acid-free paper

Manufactured in the United States of America

13 12 11 10 09 08 07 06   8 7 6 5 4 3 2 1

Contents

Preface:
Welcome to Our Worlds

This book is about learning and experiences, and about virtual world software that provides experiences. And it is about our experience with creating that software. We build our virtual worlds so players can play a game and, if they want to win, learn how to act—in other words, assimilate a role within a context. That context might be a gigantic imaginary plant cell, where they learn the role of a biologist, or it might be a shallow valley, where they learn to act like a geologist.

In all cases, players explore a computer-based simulated environment populated with a variety of "things" that make these virtual spaces lively and engaging. Things such as the tools, instruments, and reference libraries needed to successfully operate in the environment. Things such as software agents that create atmosphere or provide infrastructure—or, especially important, the intelligent software tutors that teach and guide. And perhaps most important, "things" like other people, friends or strangers, who might give help; need help; provide cooperation, collaboration, or competition; or simply offer companionship along the way.

The central idea is fairly simple. Students log into a computer simulation and are assigned a sequence of goals. To achieve the goals, they need to learn about the structure of the environment and the processes it supports—in the plant cell example, this means processes like respiration and photosynthesis. They also need to learn about conducting experiments, analyzing results, and drawing conclusions. Along the way, they write their own story, the story of their experience.

These stories are accounts of enculturation—the process of passing ideas and behaviors through a social group. We call this "role-based learning" in order to stress the belief that learning is measurably better when students are given authentic goals and afforded the opportunity to learn through experience. Experience is how they practice to become citizens in our culture of learning.

Meanwhile, we have built many worlds, as you will see. Some worlds are very big, as in planet-sized, and some are microscopic. Some are earthly, and others are not, but all are built with a common set of ideas in mind.

We are developing a range of virtual environments for education spanning a variety of disciplines, from earth science to anthropology, and from business to biology. All of these projects, however, share a strategy, a set of assumptions, an approach to assessment, and an emerging set of tools. This sharing allows each individual to leverage from the insights and advances of the others.

Meanwhile, the value of play in learning can hardly be overemphasized. Students quickly tire of rigid tutorial systems designed to teach at any cost and at some predetermined pace. However, since simulations can be adaptive and responsive, playing a role in a simulation can be fun. Players will throw themselves terrier-like into an environment if it feels like a game. Our claim is that, insofar as possible, educational software should be game-like: engaging, entertaining, immersive, attractive, interactive, and flexible.

Our software capitalizes on the opportunities afforded by virtual environments. For example, they:

- control virtual time and collapse virtual distance,
- create shared spaces that are physical or practical impossibilities,
- support shared experiences for participants in different physical locations,
- share agents, tools, resources, and pedagogical strategies,
- support multi-user collaborations and competitive play.

Each software environment has a range of properties in common. They are role-based and goal-oriented; they are immersive simulations intended to promote learning-by-doing; they are spatially oriented, exploratory, and highly interactive; they are multiuser and collaborative; and they employ software agents for atmosphere, infrastructure, and intelligent tutoring.

ABOUT THIS BOOK

You may have noticed there are quite a number of authors on this book, and there is a good reason for that. It turns out that building role-based virtual worlds for education requires a fairly vast range of knowledge and skill—more than any individual is likely to possess. Thus, these projects almost always turn out to be collaborative efforts, combining the talents of computer programmers, subject matter experts, graphic designers, education specialists, and cognitive scientists. The authors of this book reflect that diversity.

This book comprises three conceptual sections. The first three chapters establish the context and background by describing the goals and objectives of our role-based virtual environments for education—the thesis being that quantitative and qualitative educational advantages arise from these software systems—and the rationale and strategy for assessing and evaluating the systems. The next five chapters cover in some detail a range of the systems we have developed for geology, biology, computer science, microeconomics, and archaeology. The final four chapters describe what could be termed "related work"—including the concentrated effort to implement software tutoring agents and the controlled studies of learning and usability that demonstrate the effectiveness of our systems, as well as a somewhat scholarly review of our and others' efforts in this arena, a digression into technical detail, and our views on the future and where it will lead us.

Welcome to our worlds.

PART I

THE BIG BANG
OF OUR WORLDS

Everything starts somewhere. This book started with ideas about changing the way computers are used in school. These ideas are mostly simple, and arise from home-spun observations. Stuff your grandmother could tell you:

- The best way to learn French is well known. Get your parents to pay your way to France. There you can immerse yourself in French language and culture, and before too long you will begin to "think" in French.
- Humans are a playful species, by and large. Learning can be fun if you make a game out of it.
- Much of what we learn, we learn from our peers, or, out in the street, as they say. And much of what we call education is apprenticeship in one form or another. Yogi Berra says you can see a lot just by watching, and Charles Colton said imitation is the sincerest form of flattery.

Taken all together, these humble observations have directed our thinking toward the ideas in this book. Whatever else may be true, this is a book about computer games, where players are immersed in a cultural context, and where they learn by modeling the expertise of others.

This part of the book is about that—the inception of our worlds. The chapters discuss research and design strategies, the academic evidence supporting your grandmother's home-spun observations, and the agent-oriented implementation of these simulated worlds.

Chapter 1

Introduction

The World Wide Web Instructional Committee (WWWIC) at North Dakota State University (NDSU) is a group of faculty with a strong, active interest in applying information technology for instructional purposes. This faculty group is using the next wave of Internet and multimedia tools to develop sophisticated, but user-friendly, courseware, with the continued goal of improving student learning by engaging in research and development of active simulations within virtual environments, including the Geology Explorer, the NDSU Virtual Cell, Dollar Bay, and the ProgrammingLand MOOseum of Computer Science, as well as others.

On one level, these projects are all the same. They are multi-user computer games where players explore a virtual space in order to learn about it. These spaces are designed to be informative, and players are assigned the first of a sequence of goals the minute they arrive. In the course of achieving their goals, the players learn things. For example, if they are exploring Planet Oit (the scene of the Geology Explorer), they will begin by learning how to use instruments to perform simple experiments in order to identify rocks and minerals. Once the players achieve the first set of goals, more advanced goals are assigned.

The individual projects are described in detail later in this volume. They are at varying levels of "maturity"—meaning some are more completely developed than others. Most have undergone formal testing in classroom settings, some extensively so—a few are not ready for that just yet. All the projects tested in classrooms were introduced through first-year college courses. However, increasingly, the aim is to re-deploy these systems in middle school, junior high, and high school settings.

WWWIC RESEARCH GOALS

WWWIC projects have both shared and individual goals. Shared goals include the mission to teach science structure and process: the scientific method, scientific problem solving, diagnosis, hypothesis formation and testing, and experimental design. The individual goals are to teach the content of specific disciplines: geoscience, cell biology, computer science, and so on. In addition, WWWIC is applying techniques learned in science education to new domains such as history, microeconomics, and anthropology. Further, WWWIC has active research projects in other highly related areas: assessment of student learning and intelligent software agents.

WWWIC designs and develops educational media by employing a coherent strategy for all its efforts. This strategy is to develop systems that share critical assumptions and technologies supporting each project's efforts. In particular, systems are designed to employ consistent elements across disciplines and, as a consequence, foster the potential for intersecting development plans and common tools for that development. Thus, WWWIC has identified discrete but related approaches for innovative design of role-based educational simulations, which are both highly technical and highly promising in terms of broad applicability for the development of courseware.

Designing educational simulations is an exercise in balancing trade-offs. Educational content should be foremost, but should not occlude playability and simple fun. Students who learn through simulations should acquire content-related concepts and skills as a consequence of playing the game, and this learning should transfer to knowledge contexts outside the game. Simulated situations should be familiar, or at least easily recognizable, but should not slavishly replicate all the tedious details of "real life." Experience in the simulated environment should be authentic but not utterly predictable. Further, we believe that educational technology should capitalize on the natural human propensity for role playing. Students are willing to assume roles if the environment makes it easy to do so, and if the environment reinforces role playing through careful crafting of the explicit tutorial components of the game.

Finally, to support student learning through playing roles, the tutorial components of a simulated environment should present conceptual and procedural instruction on how to succeed only within their strategic contexts. In other words, the approach in a role-playing environment should mirror the mythical law school professor who says, "You are not here to learn the law, you are here to learn to think like a lawyer."

Each WWWIC project emphasizes active student interaction with course materials. Because each game depends on some form of simulation, students modify parameters (by deciding to conduct a particular experiment, for example) and choose their own route to learning. This active engagement with the course materials promotes the learning experience. Thus our virtual role-playing simulations are designed to meet the following criteria:

- The role (geologist, biologist, etc.) of the players is explicit from the outset from the nature of the game and the goals assigned.
- The players' success at learning their role in the environment translates directly into their success at playing the game.
- Player actions have a "real" effect on the simulated environment, and the environment reacts in authentic ways.
- The simulated environment is unintrusively proactive—the system is watchful and active, but the players are always in control of the experience.
- The simulated environment is rich, complex, and filled with interesting yet plausible detail.
- Complexity in the environment is limited to those tasks and functions that relate directly to the teaching goals of the system—other elements are trivial, or used for diversion and entertainment purposes.
- Interfaces are easy to use and obviously representative of the environment being simulated in order to promote the players' "willing suspension of disbelief" (immersion) and further their acceptance of a role in the environment.

- Finally, players are able to receive context-sensitive help and advice at literally any point in the game as determined by the task they are pursuing.

A virtual role-playing environment can be a powerful mechanism of instruction, provided it is authentic, that is, constructed so that learning how to play and win the game contributes to a players' understanding of real-world concepts and procedures. To succeed in a virtual world and effectively play the game, learners master the concepts and skills required to play their part. To win, they learn the domain, and they learn their role in it. The challenge, then, is to construct a game with sufficiently interesting complexity that is true to its premise. When players act in the simulated environment, the environment must react in consistent and plausible ways. This requires content expertise on the design team. Without this authenticity, the games will fail the ultimate test—players will not play them.

Despite all this, and the many interesting side questions that arise, the central research questions are about learning—pure and simple. How can our designs promote learning? How can we assess what is being learned?

WWWIC DESIGN STRATEGY

Ongoing WWWIC research work involves the construction of educational technology applications for tutoring and training. These applications are of a particular type: synthetic, multi-user environments, spatially oriented and designed on a model that promotes learning-by-doing, collaboration, exploration, and positive role playing. Systems of this sort capitalize on the advantages inherent in game-like educational media. Participants in a role-based environment are immersed in a sustained problem-solving simulation. Therefore, WWWIC designs have the following overarching characteristics.

Role-Based: Simulated environments enable learners to assume roles in particular contexts and have meaningful, authentic experiences. WWWIC promotes a learning strategy based on the ancient idea of apprenticeship where, in modern terms, the student progresses by "modeling the expertise" of the master. These environments allow the student access to the tools of the scientist, and these tools embody the practices of science. Role-based learning is learning-by-doing, but not the mere goal-oriented "doing" of a task. Rather, it is learning-by-doing within the structure of playing a role in context. Instead of simply teaching goal-based behavior and tactical task-oriented skills and methods, the role-based approach communicates a general and strategic manner of practice. Authentic role-based instruction allows students to participate in the practices of working scientists and engage in the cognitive apprenticeship needed to succeed.

Goal-Oriented: Goals are important, because they provide problems to be solved within the context of roles. It is through goals that obstacles leading to problem solving are encountered. Techniques and methods are learned and rehearsed within the local goal framework. Practice and repetition in problem solving is how apprentices learn the master's craft.

Based on Learning-by-Doing: When experiences are structured and arranged so that playing a role in the environment illustrates the important concepts and procedures of the simulated domain, students are able to "learn-by-doing." Experiences are the best teachers.

Immersive: The combination of role-based scenarios and spatially oriented simulations promotes an immersive atmosphere—sometimes described as spatial locality, or a sense of place. The concept of immersion has long been shown to be valuable in foreign language learning (where, it is anecdotally understood, the key moment arrives when learners succeed in reaching the point where they are "thinking in X," where X is French, German, Farsi, or whatever). Immersion, then, is elemental to the concept of role-based learning where it is the strategic thinking of the master, within an authentic context, that the apprentice eventually learns to model.

Spatially Oriented: WWWIC simulations are spatially oriented to leverage the natural human propensity for authentic and physically plausible context. In this way, simulations promote immersion, which in turn reinforces the role-based elements of the environments.

Exploratory: Exploratory simulation means students are able to control their own experience and pursue their own interests. This approach, sometimes referred to as user-centered, promotes a pedagogical environment where learners are self-directed, in control, and given the freedom to structure, construct, and internalize their own experience.

Game-Like: Games have the capacity to engage the player/user. Humans are naturally playful, and learning how to play is a part of every child's early development. Learning-by-playing is as ancient and time-honored as "pretending"—we can imagine Neanderthal children pretending to hunt, as well as we can remember playing house, and even playing doctor, in our own childhood.

Interactive: One major challenge for science educators is to develop educational tools and methods that deliver the principles but also teach important content material in a meaningful way. At the same time, the need for computer-based education and distance learning systems has become increasingly obvious. Additionally, the value of active versus passive learning has become increasingly clear.

Multi-User: One challenge is to craft role-based, goal-oriented environments that promote cooperation and collaboration as well as the more easily conceived competition. The answer lies in designing systems in which students/players have multiple roles to choose from and in carefully constructing the simulation so that these roles are inherently complementary. WWWIC educational systems are uniformly multi-user, and all are hosted on a particular client–server architecture that supports multiple simultaneous users. This adds a powerful new dimension to the concept of simulation, allowing the introduction of cooperation, competition, delegation, trust, and specialization into the worlds. This is a new dimension rather than a feature because multiple players can change the simulation in many different ways.

Include Software Agents: The term *software agent* is somewhat ambiguous but generally refers to a program that performs what usually is thought of as a human activity—a digital assistant of sorts. In terms of WWWIC systems, software agents are implemented to exhibit a range of authentic behaviors designed to assist with learning.

Unintrusive Tutoring: A key feature of educational media is the ability to tutor students. In WWWIC environments, tutoring is done through unintrusive, but proactive, software agents. Agents monitor students' actions and "visit" students when the need arises. Tutors give advice, but they do not mandate or prevent student actions.

WWWIC RESEARCH ON ASSESSMENT

A central element of the WWWIC research effort is developing methods for the assessment of student learning. The assessment goal determines the benefit students derive from their learning-by-doing experiences.

The WWWIC assessment strategy rejects the notion of standardized multiple-choice tests as an adequate instrument in this pedagogical context. While, indeed, facts and concepts, which are neatly packagable and testable with objective instruments, are acquired in the course of exploration, we would expect the effect on student learning in that arena may not be significant.

Therefore, the main assessment protocol is qualitative and seeks to measure how student thinking has improved. To do this, players are given a pregame, narrative-based survey in which they are told short problem-solving stories and asked to record their impressions along with any questions that occur to them. These surveys are analyzed for the presence of what could be considered important domain or problem-solving concepts or procedures. These are contrasted with a posttreatment survey in order to measure effects on student maturity within the problem-solving domain.

Science educators, interested in teaching basic concepts, look to both the Benchmarks for Science Literacy of the Advancing Science Serving Society (AAAS, 1993) and the National Science Education Standards (National Academies Press, 1995) for a solid, high-level research agenda for improvement and reform. As laid out in these standards, virtual environments should:

- Challenge students to accept and share responsibility for their own learning (NSES Teaching Standard B)
- Nurture collaboration among students (NSES Teaching Standard E)
- Demonstrate the value of evidence, logic, and good arguments (AAAS Benchmark: Scientific Inquiry)
- Show that science disciplines share a common purpose and philosophy (AAAS Benchmark: The Scientific Enterprise)
- Actively engage students in science methodology (AAAS Benchmark: Blueprint for Reform)
- Provide a student-centered learning environment (AAAS Benchmark: Blueprint for Reform)

CONCLUSION

Virtual classrooms and virtual laboratories will help solve many of the problems facing modern schools: Distance learning will become a reality, learner diversity will be accommodated (in terms of both learning styles and life-styles), and in many cases the curriculum will become more active, more role-based, more self-paced, and more learn-by-doing than learn-by-listening.

It is not hard to imagine a day when the curriculum will be taught in both real and virtual laboratories—or to foresee a time when students will take virtual field trips in order to prepare for the real thing. We also can imagine a curriculum that combines physical classrooms with virtual ones: where some lecture material is delivered at the same time and place, and other material, employing time shifting and place shifting, is not.

Chapter 2

Roles, Goals, Authenticity, and Assessment

The premise of the systems described here, where learning is achieved through experiences, is as old as can be. The underlying idea is that learning is a cultural phenomenon, embedded within problem-solving contexts. The world we live in, and the virtual worlds we create to simulate it, are places where opportunities for learning are constantly presented. The issue for virtual world developers is to invent the spaces in a way that is both engaging and authentic.

This chapter describes the anthropological underpinnings that motivate the development of virtual worlds for education, and the thinking that leads to the resulting departures from tradition. This entails a discussion of what is called "authentic instruction" and a cognitive apprenticeship model we call role-based learning, including an example from the Geology Explorer system that operates on the mythical "Planet Oit."

The key distinction in any simulation exercise is the trade-off between realism and authenticity. This leads to a number of questions that involve the age-old decision about what to teach and what to pass over. Every teacher makes this choice every day: What is important to cover, and what is less so?

Virtual role-based learning research during the past decade has transformed our understanding of human–machine and cognition–culture impacts on college-level learning (Collins, 1997, 1998; Farrell, 2001; Linn, 1995; Piringer, 2001; Reimer & Edelson, 1998, 1999; Slator et al., 2002; Slator, Clark, et al., 2002; UkeU, 2002; Vaupel & Sommer, 1997). Powerful new technologies for visual worlds and multi-user interaction, combined with sciences of learning and education, have resulted in a new subfield of scientific knowledge: a science of learning in immersive virtual role-based environments. Although these new multidisciplinary research teams have increased our understanding of many aspects of human and machine learning, the scattered and uncoordinated research has left us with large knowledge gaps and little public–private sector coordination to meet the social mandate of educating students for current and future challenges in science and the workforce. Especially complex but fundamental issues, such as the difference between learning in single-user worlds and multi-user worlds, the difference between visual- and non-visual-world learning, and the use of real-world learning simultaneously with virtual-world learning, remain largely unexplored by virtual learning scientists. Not only do we know very little about the long-term impacts of virtual learning; we know even less about how sociocultural experience within and outside the virtual world sculpts the learning process (Rogoff, 2003a).

Furthermore, a principal concern in education is student motivation. Uninspired students often create difficulties for instructors and themselves. However, recent studies indicate that the use of technology in the classroom not only increases student motivation, but also improves achievement (Blume, Garcia, Mullinax, & Vogel, 2001). Yet simply incorporating technology into traditional, teacher-centered instruction will not accomplish the goal of either motivation or achievement. Moreover, this approach to "technology in the classroom" actually has contributed to the "digital divide" between socioeconomic groups. Low-income students are frequently limited in their technological savvy as they often use computers for simple rote exercises, creating roadblocks to their process of "social inclusion" in a digital society (Warschauer, 2003). We address this problem with a focus on immersive apprenticeship.

The tradition of immersive apprenticeship (i.e., learning in context) as a means of transmitting culturally relevant learning is both time-honored and supported by modern research, but the actual processes involved in contextual learning came to be studied vigorously only in the past 20 years (D'Andrade, 1995; LeVine, 1984; Rogoff, 2003a, 2003b). The basic premise of constructivist learning theory is that individuals piece together their own understanding by reference to their own comprehension of materials and to their own individual experience (Dede, 1996; Duffy & Jonassen, 1992). Constructivist approaches to education hold that true learning occurs when learners construct their own meaning about a given topic. Consequently, instruction needs to be focused on the learners; it needs to be student-centered. The use of immersive virtual environments (IVEs) in instruction promises to be an exceptional way of incorporating student-centered technology. Studies indicate that students are more attentive while working in virtual environments (Mikropoulos, 2001), and that immersion in a virtual environment provides students opportunities for authentic learning (Winn, 1999).

We find that the catalyst that transforms the virtual world into a cultural learning experience can be understood as enculturation effected within the virtual conditions (Brandt, 2003). Enculturation classically refers to the processes by which cultural ideas and behaviors are passed from one generation to the next (Dix, 2000; Harris, 1968; Spindler & Spindler, 2000). Enculturation, in contemporary anthropological usage, refers to cultural learning in general (Ortuno, 1991). Enculturation is an intrinsically social process relying on material and symbolic context and content of experience to bridge the gap between cognizance of new ideas and practice relying on those ideas (Rogers & Shoemaker, 1971).

ANTHROPOLOGY AND CONTEXTUAL LEARNING ACTIVITIES

The anthropological contribution to a science of IVE learning involves understanding how student engagement of problems in a cultural context engages the learning process and produces outcomes in individual and group knowledge. Using examples from ethnographic studies in education (Wolcott, 1985, 1991), the immersive virtual role-based environments we study can be described as cognitive artifacts for education, that is, as tools for learning. Cognitive artifacts are fundamental to most of humanity's learning processes (Bidney, 1947; D'Andrade, 1989; Norman, 1993). As cognitive artifacts, virtual role-based worlds for education are constructed purposefully for student immersion in scientific and humanities problems, where immersion entails plunging into a virtual world in the role of a particular persona, as distinguished from student presence in a classroom or other traditional learning environments (Slator et al., 2002).

Scientists and scholars working with IVEs as worlds for learning, refer to these immersive contexts as "authentic" (Lave & Wenger, 1991; Naidu, Ip, & Linser, 2000). Anthropology defines these virtually authentic worlds as cultural in the sense that the world is made up by selecting traits from a universe of possibilities (Batteau, 2000). Specifically, the world is designed to offer a limited set of facts in a rich context of scientific practice (Edelson, Pea, & Gomez, 1996).

The resulting virtual world has an effect on students that can be characterized, in part, in terms of the linguistic relativity principle developed by Sapir and Whorf (see Swoyer, 2003, for an overview of the principle in its current form). Simply put, the virtual world is limited, and hence it constrains, through language and symbolic communicative experience and behavior, students' understanding of the virtual reality. Because the virtual reality is an archetype of real-world reality, students' understanding of the virtual problem is transferable to real-world problems, using the same class of psychological and social processes as are associated with individual learning through problem exposure (Spindler, 1955), unceremonious social coaching (D'Andrade, 1981), and innovation diffusion found within a cultural system (Rogers, 1962). Current study of simulation learning theory argues from anthropological participant observation of simulation studies among college students (e.g., D'Andrade 1981, 1987; Owen, 2002), and transference of these arguments to analogous situations in the virtual world (Brandt, 2003). We find that the student, by taking the role of scientist, scholar, or artist, advances in the problem scenario by learning disciplinary content and, more significantly, by learning to think in patterns appropriate to that discipline, as shown through the use of methods, tools, and analytical approaches learned in the virtual world and demonstrated in both the virtual world and the real world (Clark et al., 2002; Slator & MacQuarrie, 1995). This is the goal of IVE learning: that what counts is not so much the work produced by students in the environment, but the students' enhanced ability to produce work in an appropriate way (to think "scientifically") by way of contextual reasoning (Sidorkin, 2002).

Virtual role-based worlds are specially constructed to engage students at theory and method levels. As a role-based participant, the student appears in the virtual world to self and others as an individual and unique persona (an avatar in the visual virtual worlds), capable of engaging objects and others through language and virtual physical behavior. The role may be a scientist, or businessperson, or engineer, depending on the discipline involved and the goals built into the simulation. Regardless of the environment, the pattern of engagement with theory and method in the virtual world is driven by individual experiences and "other-dependent learning" in both the virtual and real worlds.

Other-dependent learning involves "conditions of informally guided discovery" (D'Andrade, 1981, p. 186). We learn best not on our own but through engagement with others. Student engagement in the virtual world is both formal and informal, made possible through interaction with things, software agents, and other people online in the virtual world. These other people include instructors whose virtual behavior takes the form of "powerful hints and occasional correction," so important to other-dependent learning. Similar learning theory is found among business management theoreticians, who emphasize the role of people who are "third party brokers" and "go-betweens" (Nooteboom, 1999, 2000). The interaction of the instructors with the students in the virtual world is deliberately patterned and part of the selection of the traits (elements) of the world. The patterns of theory and method constructed into the virtual world are recognized at various levels of cognizance by the students as they work with the problems presented in the scenarios (seemingly similar to processes of cognizance and learning reported by D'Andrade, 1984). Student recognition of the patterns in the world is indicative of learning stages, and increasing comprehension requires many rearrangements of understanding. Hence, as students learn, so the understanding of the virtual world changes for them. Learning is both accumulative and transformational, whether the learning environment is constructed for science (e.g., Van Haneghan, Barron, Young, Williams, & Bransford, 1992) or the workplace (e.g., Clancey, 1995).

To interact and learn in the virtual world students must engage virtual objects, virtual avatars (software agents), and real-time personas of real people co-resident in virtual space. Formal teaching of virtual engagement learning can reach only rudimentary levels. Students are given a vocabulary and interaction etiquette guidelines. Once students have a handle on the basic tools of engagement, they are given goals and the reasons for being in the virtual world. They are given simple tasks at first, while they learn to use the technology that is the mechanism of physical engagement in the virtual world. Students are encouraged to work together. But they have no real experiential understanding of the virtual world until they are in it.

Invariably, some students have experienced virtual worlds and virtual role-based interaction previously. These experienced students explore the world with confidence and act as informal mentoring agents to newer students. The more experienced virtual students teach others how to get along in the virtual world, usually through various informal behaviors and discourse. In this, we see that there is an ordering of interaction through a complex set of formal and informal rules of a category described by Sapir (2002). Specifically, the virtual worlds represent a diversity of learning levels. Hence, the culture of the virtual world is shared unequally among the members of the group, much like what occurs in the real world (Bailey, 1983; D'Andrade, 1992). The culture perpetuates itself, however, through a significant reliance on informal other-dependent learning and the advancement of knowledge in new generations of learners. This can be explained as enculturative context (Harris, 1968) affected by diffusion processes (Rogers & Shoemaker, 1971). This pushes forward the question, how does learning proceed among different levels of students as the students encounter each other in the virtual world? We find the answer, in part, to be connected to performative action.

In immersive virtual environments, there are performative social interactions that directly affect learning processes (Guimarães, 2001). Performative interactions are social interplay that produce effects either on the performers or on the other social actors. Specifically, there is reflexive behavior as categorized by Turner (1987), where the students learn by observing or engaging in social interactions generated by other people. Their sense of self and knowledge is changed through these reflexive cognitive performative encounters. At the textual discourse level, performative behavior occurs when students are self-conscious of their language interaction and use and perceive their role as "displaying for others" a certain grasp of specialized concepts and language. This is self-conscious proactive shifting of the language-style presentation of self to others (Schilling-Estes, 1998).

For the virtual learner, performative social interaction develops and changes as the student progresses through levels of understanding and learning. These various developments are salient where the students display increasing levels of communicative competence (similar to that described by Bonvillain, 1997). That is, as the students expand knowledge and confidence in the information and interactions encountered in the virtual environment, their learning is reflected, in part, in the ability to deal with stylized speech and presentation forms specific to the virtual scenario discipline. Today, an anthropology of performance focused on virtual environments is concerned with "the way by which the multimedia resources . . . are appropriated and resignified by the users through the analysis of the interactions that take place inside it" (Guimarães, 2001, p. 1).

Performance for learning is associated with studies of the cultural meanings associated with the physical behaviors of the avatars representing users. The performance approach is related to a conception of culture as a process, a flux of facts embedded in a web of meanings that flow through time. The culture, hence, is not considered as homogeneous or fixed, but as being in continuous movement and change. Indeed, all the virtual social interactions are innovations derived from the fundamental set of instructions given to students prior to their entrance into the virtual world.

However, the virtual world reflects archetypes of communication processes extant in the real world; consequently, activity in the virtual world, no matter how open-ended, will find itself reflecting hegemonic rules of interaction from the real world. Therefore, as in the real world, learning through social interaction in the virtual world is encased in rules of interaction similar to those described by Moerman (1987). This pushes research to ask, how does the individual's commitment to virtual social interaction support or undermine the individual's learning?

Furthermore, anthropologists observe that individual learning is affected by the degree of commitment of an individual to interaction with others and the environment (Morris, 1994), especially interaction with change agents (Rogers, 1962). Thus, in the role-based scenario of the virtual world, the amount of social role-based interaction bears on the effectiveness of the learning environment for students. In other words, the more students interact with objects, agents, and persons, the more possible is engagement of other-dependent learning and, through that, diffusion of knowledge. In the authentic scenarios of the virtual world, study of learning processes affords research on the degree of commitment students have to virtual interaction with others.

ASSESSMENT TRADITIONS

Historically, the primary assessment of student learning has been achieved by testing student recognition of sets of individual facts. The economics of assessment provides a simple explanation for this. There is a need to test students on what they have learned, and the easiest thing to do is survey their responses using a multiple-choice exam. Thus, the economics of assessment drives teachers to teach individual and largely disconnected facts.

Multiple-choice exams ask each student to look over an identical set of questions. These questions are "facts" that have been presented. Often the questions can be seen as a virtual mad-lib that presents an incomplete sentence and offers various words to complete it. To select the correct answer from the list of potential completions, students must recognize the fact that was presented in the course materials. If students can complete a number of these sentences, we assume this is a good heuristic for understanding the subject.

Essay tests are another assessment strategy available to the instructor. These tests can be designed so that students must recall some information about the field. Here, students must recall something more complex, perhaps even something about the tools or practices of the field.

However, when there are large numbers of students to contend with, grading many, many essays stretches the realm of possibility. Instructors (i.e., modern education institutions) cannot afford to spend the time to read through and evaluate students' answers. Consequently, instructors with many students typically have been forced to use multiple-choice tests, which, we argue, can get at only disconnected facts, which can be only a heuristic for understanding the content domain.

Therefore, the economics of assessment drives, to a large extent, the practice of inauthentic assessment. What may be less obvious is that the economics of instruction also determines the practice of inauthentic instruction. In the past, when students were taught some domain of science, an instructor often had to lecture the students rather than require them to adopt the practices and tools of the working scientist. Monitoring students in practice has been too costly except in small-group settings.

Consider the most common method of teaching, the lecture. While ubiquitous, and economical, this method has many drawbacks. Lectures are very much teacher-centered; the teacher is essentially elevated as the only one who has something to share. Communication is typically unidirectional; the instructor speaks and the students listen. If well done, in a small-group setting, with student involvement and interaction among all members of the group, it can lead to a sense of ownership. Yet the practical realities are that small groups are an expensive luxury. Typically, the lecture model treats students as passive information sponges. But by using large lecture sessions, teachers are able to give out information in a cost-effective way.

In a lecture setting, students are to be quiet, hanging on every word and carefully copying every mark recorded on the chalkboard. There is time for little or no comprehension or reflection; if students consider an item for too long, the instructor is on to a new topic and they will have missed something in the meantime. The role of the student is to faithfully record every bit of information and, while outside of the classroom, attempt to make sense of it. In rare cases, a student might ask a question during a lecture, but self-consciousness prevents most of this. The problem, except in rare small-group settings, is that the experience is more passive than active (Reid, 1994).

The content of a lecture can be communicated by a number of means to make it even more cost-effective. Instead of students assembling in a single class-room, the use of broadcast media, such as television, can disseminate the image and sound to a much wider audience. This still has the disadvantages of occurring at a single time and the expense of broadcasting, but it can communicate nearly as effectively as a live performance. A videotape can capture the performance but may be harder to distribute than a video signal. It does have the notable advan-tage that students now have control over the time of presentation. Some of the power has been wrested from the instructor and given to the students; however, the presentation itself is very much linear. Students must start at the beginning and proceed sequentially. The fast forward, rewind, and pause buttons give them some options not available in a real lecture, but the format is still essentially linear and, again, almost totally passive.

AUTHENTIC INSTRUCTION

Authentic instruction allows students to participate in the practices of the work-ing scientist. Students are a part of laboratory research or fieldwork, have access to the tools of the working scientist, and are shepherded through the scientific process. Concepts—the beliefs of the scientist—are introduced in this naturalistic context.

During the 1980s and 1990s, much changed in the way that educators ad-dressed science instruction. During this period and earlier, much changed also in the way science itself was viewed. In order to explain the rationale for the peda-gogy suggested here, we will review some of these changes.

Every field of science has a set of correlative beliefs and a set of canonical beliefs, which constitute the science. To know science requires an understanding of what the science holds true, and this knowledge is what the science is about. However, recent work in the philosophy of science and, more interestingly, an-thropology has given us a deeper understanding of what a science really is.

Every field of science is a rich network of beliefs and practices. Thomas Kuhn (1962) introduced the concept of a paradigm shift within a field of science. At the same time, the model of science that he proposed is one in which a field is defined by an interdependent set of beliefs that are supported by (and support) the over-arching paradigm in the field. More recently, philosophers of science have argued that scientific facts are given coherence by the context of other facts and practices. For example, Thagard (1989) says, "But there is much more to the development of science than belief change, for we can ask why conceptual changes took place involving the introduction and reorganization of whole conceptual systems" (p. 435). Simply put, current views of science hold that a field consists of an inter-connected set of things we know and things we do.

Every field of science can be understood as a community defined by the practices of its members. Rather than say that a science is some body of knowl-edge, we now say that a particular science is defined by practicing scientists. These scientists are seen as a community or culture whose members share a set of beliefs and practices. Science, in this view, is seen as a "community of practice" (e.g., Pea, 1993). Typically, the practices—for example, the methods used in the laboratory or field—determine which beliefs are accepted by community members. The knowledge and acceptance of these practices give meaning to the beliefs. In this view, the practices of scientists are fundamental to a science.

This view of science points to a new way of teaching science. When science is viewed as interdependent beliefs, practices, and tools, the failure of students to learn science when presented as sets of disconnected facts is easily understood—because the connections and relations between concepts are missing in that model.

Science isn't just facts. More than anything else, a science is an internally consistent and coherent set of beliefs, practices, and tools. We have been instructing students to remember facts (i.e., beliefs) outside of the context in which those facts are understood. History has shown (e.g., Schmidt, McKnight, & Raizen, 1997) that teaching some subset of a science's beliefs devoid of their belief context has been unsuccessful in helping students to learn science.

We need to embed science facts in an authentic context. The focus on embedding science facts in a context of scientific practice is reflected in much current educational practice. This move often is billed as teaching science in an "authentic" context, meaning that students learn a set of facts in a context that is an analog of the context in which scientists do their work. Therefore, many have moved from a focus on teaching a broad set of specific facts to a focus on embedding a more limited set of facts in a richer context of scientific practice (Edelson, Pea, & Gomez, 1996). This is seen as a way to teach students how to think like scientists. Many resist this move because of what Randy Bass (Bass, Clinch, Reeves, Slator, & Terhune, 1999) calls "anupholsteraphobia": the fear of not covering everything. The strategy is to get more deeply into the material, thus revealing more of the structure of the discipline and how it works, trading breadth for depth.

To understand science is to understand the activities of scientists. Authentic science is what scientists do. Scientists not only know that certain things are true; they also know how to show that those things are true. Scientific beliefs are embedded in a context of what scientists do. Scientific thought, then, is a type of "situated cognition" (Lave & Wenger, 1991). The "situations" of what is called situated cognition are the contexts in which scientists do their work. These situations describe how the scientists discover knowledge. In other words, "Situations might be said to co-produce knowledge through activity" (Brown, Collins, & Duguid, 1989, p. 32). To understand science is to understand the tools and methods of scientists, which embody the practices of the community (Lave & Wenger, 1991).

ROLE-BASED LEARNING

Immersive virtual education involves role-based interaction. Roles are multiplex social statuses or identities to which are attached culturally shared and agreed-upon sets of rights, duties, obligations, and levels of expected specialized knowledge and ability (Gluckman, 1963). People live in cultural groups, and culture perpetuates itself by providing models of role behavior for society members to integrate and assimilate (Harris, 1968, 1979). Enculturation is the process of cultural learning that transmits knowledge and skills from one generation to the next through observation, memorization, and performance in learning ("encul-turative") contexts (Harris, 1968; Ortner, 1984; Peacock, 1986). Enculturation has been examined routinely in countless sociological and anthropological studies of culture change in both industrial and traditional groups and societies (e.g., Rogers & Shoemaker, 1971; Spradley, 1987; Swidler, 1986; Tishman, Jay, & Perkins, 1993; Voget, 1975), and, more recently, in terms of educational learning (e.g., Hagge, 1995).

One illustration of learning and cultural perpetuation through enculturation is provided by Like-A-Fishhook Village in what is now north-central North Dakota (Smith, 1972). Like-A-Fishhook Village was an earth-lodge settlement established by three sedentary tribes, who, after centuries of internecine feuding, banded together in the 1840s in the aftermath of a smallpox epidemic. The village was located on a strategically defensible bluff in the shadow of a trading post (later an army fort) as a defense against the predations of ancient enemies.

According to Smith (1972), Like-A-Fishhook Village was the last great earth-lodge village and the scene of fascinating cultural continuity and change as the three tribes learned to co-exist for mutual protection. During the time of the vil-lage, the individual tribal groups worked to preserve their own identities while both absorbing and resisting the modern influences of the White traders and con-quering soldiers. There are accounts of heartbreaking struggle and uplifting ac-commodation, shared recollections of children crossing tribal lines for the sake of marriage and adoption, movements to preserve cultural integrity along with re-luctant adaptive reliance on jobs as traders and scouts for the White government, and a remarkable account of early adoption of a certain specific new rifle that was bartered and swapped from hand to hand, passing from North Dakota to New Mexico in a week's time.

It was an era of change, marked by fluidity, absorption, adaptation, accom-modation, and ultimately transition to a new synthesized culture. Throughout all of this there was learning through enculturation. The children of the tribes did not, for example, attend lectures on hunting and trading. Instead, the children went out into the world and experienced hunting and trading for themselves. They watched, they asked questions, they tried it for themselves, they failed in various ways, they received additional advice, and because they had seen it done all their lives, they learned how to hunt and trade. In the process of learning, this next generation accumulated new skills and new technologies, and learned new ways of surviving in their contemporary world. Later, with varying levels of success, they passed the knowledge and practices to their own children through the same enculturation processes.

This is a story of learning through enculturation. The main features are that the learner is informed by context as well as verbal or textual content (in a man-ner similar to that described by Kay, 1997), and the learner develops skills and conceptual understandings that come with practicing a discipline (involving both behavior and dialogue) under the watchful eye of more experienced practitioners, eventually learning both new and old concepts and techniques. The learner pro-ceeds through various spiraling and semi-reiterative phases of learning, from knowledge function (akin to those described by Rogers & Shoemaker, 1971) to schema (re)construction (similar to that described by D'Andrade, 1987).

For the contemporary virtual environment learner, enculturative learning occurs in role-based immersive experiences and cognitive apprenticeship. Teaching by fieldwork in geology and anthropology, by laboratory exercise in biology and chemistry, by residency in medicine and psychology, and by cases in business and law are all examples of role-based learning—that liminal performance zone at the threshold where concept is put into practice and learning passes from memorizing and reciting facts to experiential knowledge shared by a specific community (Turner, 1977, 1987), developing what mathematicians call intuition.

Research in Authentic Instruction and Role-Based Learning

WWWIC uses immersive virtual environments to create an authentic experience of science for students. These environments allow students access to authentic virtual versions of the tools of the scientist, and these tools, as noted by Lave and Wenger (1991), embody the practices of science. Students are given these virtual tools in a simulated context of that in which scientists work. Students interact with a virtual world that offers them an analog of the situations in which scientists use these tools. This is the context in which scientific beliefs are presented, and this is the context in which students learn the science. Assessment is, likewise, in the virtual world. Just as scientists are judged by their ability to use tools to uncover facts in the world, students use similar virtual tools to uncover facts in similar virtual worlds. What is assessed in this context is the ability to practice what the scientists practice. Students learn not only to talk the talk, but also to walk the walk.

The Geology Explorer Example

Classroom instruction in geology is difficult. Students often are required to go into a large lecture hall and then asked to listen to a geologist describe various beliefs about the field. Instructors typically are restricted in the extent to which they actually can bring students out into the field and have them engage in geology. Day-long field trips or week-long field camps put considerable requirements on both students—to give up a day of other instruction—and the instructor—to both give up other instruction and supervise the students. Such fieldwork usually is restricted to advanced college level courses where the course sizes are smaller and the students are more motivated to spend the time.

Unfortunately, this means that introductory students, who are committing several hours a week for many weeks, may be exposed only to facts presented from the front of a lecture hall. Presenting an authentic experience to these students has been all but impossible and their understanding of geology naturally suffers.

The Geology Explorer project implements an educational game for teaching the geosciences. This takes the form of a synthetic, virtual environment, Planet Oit, where students are given the means and the equipment to explore a planet as a geologist would. The world and the activities undertaken within it are as close to the experience of fieldwork as is possible. Students are asked to explore this world and to begin to determine where certain minerals are found. As they navigate through the world, they are given rich descriptions of their environment and are given tools with which to test various minerals. The minerals are deposited in geological formations similar to those found on Earth. These minerals can be tested using tools functionally identical to those used by working geologists. Students' ability to use these tools—to engage in the practices of working geologists—determines their ability to reach their goals within the virtual space. Thus, the students are given an authentic—albeit virtual—experience of the science of geology. Furthermore, their ability to succeed in this space is determined by their ability to engage in the practices of geologists, using the tools of geologists.

Assessments are embedded. The assessment of the task promotes authenticity because assessment is the completion of the task.

DESIGN PRACTICE: AUTHENTICITY VS. REALISM

Developing any sort of curriculum is an exercise in trade-offs; teachers constantly are required to decide which details to explore and which to gloss over, and in which order to present material. Designing virtual worlds for education is no different. Yes, we want to accurately capture reality but not by minutely replicating it. Rather, we seek to choose the best level of description so that important concepts are revealed against the noise of excessive detail. In our case, these trade-offs are magnified on one hand by the need to promote game-play (which is an important element of our approach) and on the other by the ability to control virtual time and space.

Our experience with developing other virtual worlds, and other pedagogically oriented software, prepared us to deal with these issues in the design of the Geology Explorer. In every case, we addressed these issues from a theoretical perspective, to ensure that students have an experience that promotes their understanding, and assimilation, of the role of a geologist, pursuing goals of geologists, and using the tools of geologists. These are the parameters that guide our design decisions.

Some examples will help illustrate this distinction between authenticity and realism and how our design is consistently motivated to find the right margin between them.

Example #1: In real life, a rock pick is primarily a tool for striking rocks in order to retrieve samples, although a rock pick also can be used to scratch samples in order to test for hardness, or smell, or to listen for the quality of "ring." Naturally, the virtual rock picks in the Geology Explorer on Planet Oit are implemented to perform these functions as realistically as possible. However, a rock pick also can be a lethal weapon, and hitting another person with a rock pick, in real life, might result in injury or even death. On Planet Oit, no such thing occurs. There is little pedagogical value to implementing this realism, and so when a player on Planet Oit hits another player with a rock pick, nothing happens.

Example #2: In real life, a geologist might travel long distances in pursuit of a goal. In the course of the trip they experience hunger and fatigue, and their return journey is almost equally arduous. On Planet Oit, the players' characters do not get hungry or tired—although we discussed this element as a way of promoting the necessary decision making for expedition planning, and there are good game-play arguments on either side. Similarly, there is little pedagogical benefit to having players retrace their footsteps across the planet, particularly since we control virtual distance and easily provide students with a way to "beam around" the environment. On the other hand, we do not permit students to carry enormous room-sized analysis equipment around the planet, but rather require them to journey to the virtual laboratory to use such machinery. We could do it either way, but we choose to preserve this element of reality in the interest of plausibility.

While we do place certain restrictions on the players' ability to transport themselves across vast distances, we do not fear they will be misled into believing that geologists have fantastic teleportation abilities. Rather, we provide teleportation because there is no pedagogical reason not to, given our theoretical framework.

One particular strength of virtual environments is the ability to replicate experiences and instrumentation at a fraction of the normal price. The Chemical Composition Instrument (CCI) on Planet Oit is an excellent case in point. There is such a machine, costing $500,000, called the ICP–MS (Induced Current Plasma–Mass Spectrometer), which can analyze for dozens of elements simultaneously over a large dynamic range (from percent to part per million) on the same sample. However, instruments of this complexity present us with a range of design problems. On one hand, we are acutely sensitive to the "tricorder temptation": the impulse to provide imaginary virtual instruments that can provide answers to all questions. On the other hand, the procedures for operating the CCI in real life are enormously complex, and the level of granularity and specificity at which the CCI should be represented is an open question in the Geology Explorer context. The same is true for much of the advanced instrumentation of geoscience.

For our purposes, therefore, the design of the CCI is approached from both a pedagogical and theoretical viewpoint. Is it important, within our curriculum, that the detailed workings of the CCI be apparent to students? At what level will this knowledge promote students' learning to assimilate the geologist's role? And at what expense will this content be stressed, in terms of other concepts that necessarily will receive less detailed treatment? These are the questions we face in each of these design opportunities.

In the case of the CCI, we have developed a staged plan, where students first will present their samples to a laboratory assistant implemented as a software agent. This agent will provide a running account of the process of operating the CCI and will return results in report form. This agent also will be armed with a conversational network for answering questions about the process and interpreting the results.

If the CCI should become a key element in our pedagogical scheme, then additional realism will be implemented, and players will be required to learn to operate the CCI for themselves. If, however, the operation of the CCI is less important to our goals, while the results of the CCI contribute to the implementation of another pedagogical module, then the focus will remain on the main goal, and the possible noise of the CCI details will be glossed over. This is the sort of scaffolding decision (Applebee & Langer, 1983) that crops up repeatedly.

Our investigative tools are constructed to prevent potential confusion by students. It is important to note that with regard to the CCI's potential to return the answer for a geologist, a simple chemical analysis of a rock is usually just the starting point for an interpretation. It is part of the data set that, combined with mineralogical identification and the larger geologic context, becomes part of hypothesis formation and testing. In our simulations, we pursue a strategy that allows us to implement the level of detail appropriate to our instructional goals, balancing realism against pedagogy, according to our theoretical framework, exactly as every other educator does.

MANAGING AUTHENTICITY

One time we had a grant proposal review ask, "Is there really an option for a player in the Geology Explorer to use the rock pick to hit another player?"

The short answer is "Yes."

Why? Because the issue, especially when striving for authentic learning experiences as we do, is to balance authenticity against "spurious realism." On one hand, we want user-centered environments where learners have control and can do pretty much what they want, in any order and manner they choose. This user-centered control is quite important. On the other hand, we must exercise our best judgment about what functions to support.

The rock pick example arises because it can cross the margin between desirable authenticity and undesirable realism. It's a fact of the world that, given the freedom to do so, young people in virtual environments are going to try things "for the heck of it," and hitting—another student or anything else—is one of the many options they can try. However, we are wise to this and have precluded the possibility—the student moves away before he or she can be struck. We control for and guard against antisocial behavior.

In summary, if an action has pedagogical value, we try to support that action. If an action has entertainment value, we probably will try to support it. If an action is objectionable, we try to block or otherwise prevent it.

CONCLUSION

Authentic assessment is often discussed but rarely defined (AAAS, 1994; NSES, 1995). Given the preceding discussion, it stands to reason that authentic assessment requires that students be asked to use knowledge about a scientific domain (in both tools and practices) and to perform a task that makes sense within that domain. Students should be able to demonstrate that they not only "know what" but also "know how." Furthermore, authentic assessment means that students must be judged by the same criteria as scientists are judged.

Scientists typically are judged by their ability to use the tools of their field to answer questions of relevance within their field. An authentic assessment in science occurs when a scientist's work is judged by other scientists to be acceptable within the domain of that field; that is, that using the tools and practices of the field, the scientist was able to determine some fact within that field.

The goal of the WWWIC approach, like the goal of all work that attempts to offer authentic experiences to students, is to present students with a more valid representation of science.

Chapter 3

Simulating Virtual Worlds

Virtual worlds require software simulations that provide the exploratory environment and the interactive objects that populate the worlds. The simulated worlds must be designed carefully so as to represent the phenomenon being studied in a reasonable, plausible, and authentic manner—the "physics" of the simulation must be consistent and coherent; otherwise, the simulation may baffle, or confuse, or, worse yet, mislead. The objects within a simulation might be seemingly simple things like plants or rocks, but even these require software implementation—when a rock is hit with a virtual hammer, it must react (by a chunk breaking off). More complex objects also are built into virtual worlds, the most important of which are software agents.

Software agents are programs that perform human-like tasks. Three kinds of software agents are implemented in WWWIC virtual worlds: atmosphere agents, which lend local color; infrastructure agents, which contribute to game play; and tutoring agents, which monitor progress and attempt to give assistance.

In order to create the virtual learning environments we are describing, and to support virtual experiences that are both plausible and authentic, it is necessary to build a certain kind of software application known as a simulation. A simulation is most commonly thought of as a series of equations that model a complex phenomenon; for example, a simulation of global weather patterns, or the stock market, or the workings of a jet engine. Often, this sort of simulation takes enormous data sets of input values, and is designed to produce a sequence of "snapshots" over a period of time, intended to show how something, such as the weather, might change from day to day.

Simulating a virtual world is similar, in many respects, but differs by being far more interactive in nature. When actions are taken in the world, there should be immediate feedback, and it should be the right kind of feedback: plausible and authentic.

All simulations, indeed all software applications, are designed to be microcosms—little conceptual universes with a set of consistent rules for how things work. They all have (or should have) consistent user interface and functionality to allow the user to understand and even predict how the application will work. This is the purpose that the Macintosh Human Interface Guidelines serve (usually credited as the first such document): technical notes for creating applications that are true to the physics of the Macintosh.

The first consequence of this consistency and predictability is a greatly reduced learning curve. Thus, to continue the example, with a Macintosh application, users know right away they can cut and paste with Command-X and Command-V. With this bit of knowledge, users understand what cut and paste mean, that they can cut and paste nontext objects, even if they are new and unfamiliar, and they can cut and paste across applications. This knowledge is so fundamental to the use of a Macintosh that if any part of this schema fails, it could be said the application is functioning incorrectly.

The second and most important (although least recognized) benefit gained from consistency and predictability is that an application with a simple but powerful user interface constitutes a system that lends itself to understanding. By using certain cues, usually visual, we can look at the state of an application, tell whether the state is what we want, and know how to change it.

A simulation is just like any other application, except that its physical rules also are designed to be consistent—to some degree—with the real world. One classic example is SimCity, a computer game where the player acts as a mayor of an urban landscape. The mayor deals with zoning and transportation rather than characters. When a city block is riddled with crime, the mayor can try to fix the problem in one of several ways: increase the land value by building roads or parks, or put a police station near the property in question, or raise police funding, or increase the land value of the surrounding zones (the implausibility of this last type of operation is the principal source of criticism against SimCity, by the way). While these specific operations are meaningful within the context of the SimCity application—like cut and paste—they also have meaningful analogies to operations in the real world. This approach adds leverage to what is gained by simulating real-world actions familiar to users. Modeling such actions allows users to more easily adapt to the "rules" of the "universe" being simulated.

The key motivation for simulating virtual worlds is to implement a learning environment where a program that models some aspect of the real world well enough, will enable users to transfer knowledge gained from the software and apply it to domains found in the real world. This, by the way, is the flip side to virtual reality, where the sensory input (user interface) is sufficiently real to compensate for the lack of realism in the application content—"seeing is believing," as opposed to the simulation approach, "believing is seeing." In the case of SimCity, the system uses familiar user interface paradigms—like menus, windows, and point-and-click—to accomplish otherwise difficult real-world tasks, like building an airport.

SOFTWARE AGENTS IN VIRTUAL WORLDS

Over the years, the term *software agent* has become more and more generalized. Today it refers to any software displaying a kind of intelligence in accomplishing a task. In the systems described here, multi-user simulations of virtual worlds for education, the term is used slightly more narrowly—software to simulate roles that normally would be carried out by humans. In our systems, there is a fairly large number of these tasks, which are described below. In addition, the agents usually take on a human appearance (e.g., an avatar) while performing their tasks.

A common problem with simulations is that, as in the real world, players can foul things up and not know why. Unlike in the real world, though, all of the information for the simulation is readily available and can be used to generate explanations or warnings. The idea is that intelligent tutoring agents are looking over the players' shoulder as they play. The agents should be there when players need them, but when players know what they're doing (or think they know), they can ignore the agent. There should be no penalty for ignoring the agent's warnings, other than the inevitable failure to succeed, a penalty imposed by the simulation on players as a consequence of a failure to learn their role in the environment. In all cases, it is up to the players to decide how the warnings and advice will apply to them.

Tutoring agents are based on the design and information in the model and are triggered by user actions. When an agent is activated, the players see a warning; they can ask for more information (possibly bringing them a "visit" from an intelligent tutoring agent) or they can ignore the warning and carry on at their own risk. The simulation allows the players to win or lose in any way they choose. It is important that the environment be an active one, where players are stimulated by the events occurring in the game. The environment is not just a passive/reactive one; it seeks opportunities to interact and tutor.

The overall goal is to develop and employ intelligent agents within our multiuser simulations to help provide effective learning experiences. From the perspective of intelligent tutoring systems, the agents of interest fundamentally must support models of the knowledge of a domain expert and an instructor.

Three kinds of agents are implemented in our simulations.

- *Atmosphere software agent*: an agent that simply adds to the texture of the simulation by providing entertaining or diverting interactions. For example, in an urban simulation there might be a street magician, a street vendor, a beat cop, a street sweeper, and so forth; in a museum simulation there might be visitors wandering through the exhibits or vendors selling popcorn; on a planet, perhaps animals are roaming the countryside.
- *Infrastructure software agent*: an agent that, in some substantial way, adds to the game-play by taking actions that can affect the success of a player. For instance, in an urban simulation, perhaps a banker, an employee, or an advertising consultant may affect the financial health of the player; in a museum or on a planet, the agent may be a guide, or a laboratory assistant that operates machinery on behalf of the player.
- *Intelligent tutoring software agent*: an agent that monitors player moves and visits players to give them advice, sometimes in the form of expert stories and cases, sometimes in the form of hints and advice. These represent either domain expertise or past experiences of other players.

INTELLIGENT TUTORING SOFTWARE AGENTS

We implement three different approaches to intelligent tutoring, based on the knowledge available to the tutoring agent.

- Diagnostic Tutoring
- Case-Based Tutoring
- Rule-Based Tutoring

Diagnostic Tutoring

Diagnostic Tutors provide assistance to players in the course of their reasoning within the scientific problem solving required in order to accomplish their goals.

An example is the intelligent tutoring agents in the NDSU Geology Explorer, an educational game for teaching the geosciences. Planet Oit is a synthetic (or virtual) environment where students explore a planet as a geologist would. While on the planet, students are assigned goals related to rock and mineral identification.

The tutors work from knowledge of the rocks and minerals, knowledge of the experiments needed to confirm or deny the identity of a rock or mineral, and the students' history. Three opportunities for diagnostic tutoring are:

- an equipment tutor that detects when students have failed to buy the equipment necessary for achieving their goals
- an exploration tutor that detects when students have overlooked a goal in their travels
- a science tutor that detects when students make an incorrect identification report and why (i.e., what evidence they are lacking); or when students make a correct report with insufficient evidence (i.e., a lucky guess)

The Equipment Tutor. The equipment tutor is called in a number of circumstances. The tutor checks whether the players possess the instruments necessary to satisfy their goals. This is possible because each of the tasks necessary to achieve a goal is described by the system in terms of the tools necessary to complete the task. For example, if the goal is to locate calcite, which requires an acid reactivity experiment, and they have not acquired an acid bottle, the students are unlikely to achieve their goal.

The equipment tutor is called when players first start exploring, and immediately reminds them to visit the store and procure what is needed. The equipment tutor also is called when they leave the store, to determine whether they have all of the instruments needed to satisfy their goals. If not, the tutor remediates on the need to buy instruments that serve to satisfy goals. For the interested reader, the equipment used on Planet Oit is fully described at http://oit.ndsu.edu/oit/gui_usercard2.html.

The Exploration Tutor. The exploration tutor is called every time students move from one location to another on the planet. The tutor checks whether the students are leaving a location that might satisfy a goal; for example, if their goal is to locate kimberlite, and there is kimberlite in the location they just left. The tutor informs them they have walked past the goal they are seeking.

The Science Tutor. The science tutor is called when a player makes a report identifying a rock or mineral. Suppose the student is given the goal of locating and identifying graphite used in the production of steel and other materials.

To confirm that a mineral deposit is indeed graphite, they should test the deposit with a streak plate and observe a black streak, and scratch a deposit with a glass plate to determine whether its hardness is less than 5.0 on the standard (Mohs) scale. Assuming these experiments succeed, the student should report the sample as graphite.

Depending on the results of the reporting analysis, the tutor may decide to remediate on the spot, or to defer remediation until the student begins to show a pattern of behavior. The Science Tutor works from knowledge of the rocks and minerals, and of the experiments needed in order to confirm or deny the identity of a rock or mineral.

The tutor checks the players' history and determines which of the following cases pertain:

- *wrong tests*: they guessed incorrectly and their history indicates they have not conducted the necessary tests to identify the rock/mineral in question
- *wrong answer*: they guessed incorrectly but their history indicates they have conducted the necessary tests to identify the rock/mineral in question
- *lucky guess*: they guessed correctly but their history indicates they have not conducted the necessary tests to identify the rock/mineral in question
- *good work*: they guessed correctly and their history indicates they have conducted the necessary tests to identify the rock/mineral in question

The system encodes the necessary and sufficient experiments for each rock and mineral, as well as the expected results. The tutor checks these facts against the students' history whenever they report a deposit's identity. The tutor remediates, as appropriate, according to the four cases listed above by suggesting an experiment that will provide evidence leading to another conclusion or referring to the results of an experiment that is being misinterpreted.

Case-Based Tutoring

Case-Based Tutors provide assistance to players by presenting them with past examples of relevant experience (Bareiss & Slator, 1993; Hinrichs, Bareiss, & Slator, 1993; Slator & Bareiss, 1992). This is accomplished by:

- creating a library of prototypical cases of success and failure,
- capturing a record of the students as they play and creating a case to represent that experience,
- matching the new student case against the library of cases and retrieving the most similar, relevant match for use in remediation.

For example, intelligent tutoring in the NDSU Dollar Bay Retailing Game (Regan & Slator, 2002) is designed to assist players with identifying problems in a retail business and to expose them to potential solutions to those problems. The tutor provides advice based on the success or failure of previous players who resemble the current player. These agents act as subtopic experts who have access to problem-solving experiences, context-sensitive help and advice, conceptual and procedural tutorials, and stories of success and failure within their particular subtopic. The agents monitor progress and visit when their particular help is needed. The agents coach players by sharing expertise in the form of prototypical case studies, problem-solving dialogues, and prepackaged tutorials.

Tutoring agent behavior is adaptive in two senses. Each agent is the owner of a small set of subtopics and related cases. As players operate in the synthetic environment, they are building their own case, and the relevant agent is alerted for remediation whenever a learner case becomes similar and relevant to a case under the agent's control. As players' behavior changes, so do their profiles and the nature of the cases they match against. In this way, agents gain and lose interest in players according to the changes in their profiles.

Player states are preserved throughout the course of their involvement with the synthetic environment. As they leave the game, either as successful or unsuccessful players, their state and experience are saved as a new case. These saved cases, according to their profiles, become part of the inventory assigned to one or more of the tutorial agents. As later players enter the synthetic environment, the tutorial agents will have these additional cases of success and failure to present as part of their remediation package.

In other words, case-based tutoring agents begin the game armed with prototypical case studies, but they accumulate additional student case studies as players enter and leave the game over time.

Rule-Based Tutoring

Rule-Based Tutors provide assistance by

- encoding a set of rules about the domain,
- monitoring student actions looking for one of these rules to be broken,
- visiting students to present an expert dialogue, a case-based tutorial, or a passive presentation (in, say, video).

One example is the NDSU Virtual Cell (White, McClean, & Slator, 1999), simulating an active biosystem, which requires all relevant assay experiments be performed before giving credit for an organelle identification. Another example is the Dollar Bay game mentioned earlier, where players may decide to try to maximize profits by pricing their products at ten times the wholesale price. This is a naive strategy that says, "I might not sell very many, but each sale will be very profitable."

This breaks the simple rule: Don't set prices unreasonably high. The intelligent tutoring agent recognizes this as a losing strategy and knows the players are unlikely to sell anything at all. When the agent detects a strategic mistake, it sends a message to the players saying, "You may be setting your prices too high." At that point, the players can decide to ignore the message or act upon it.

The drawback with this rule-based approach is that rules of this sort are relatively rare (and relatively obvious) in a complex domain. Therefore, the rule-based method does not afford as many opportunities as other approaches. Finally, breaking the rules is not always the wrong thing to do (as many experts will tell you), which can create problems in all but the most elementary teaching systems.

TUTORING STRATEGIES

All of these approaches to tutoring preserve one consistent theme: unintrusiveness. These unintrusive methods of tutoring are implemented to be consistent with the educational game principles of leaving the players in control and letting them make their own mistakes. However, besides the approaches to tutoring described above, there still remains the question of tutoring strategies, which in large measure get reduced to a question of timing. The following questions remain:

- How often should students be remediated?
- What should trigger a tutor's decision to remediate?

To answer these questions, we unfailingly resort to the following heuristic.

- How do human experts/mentors make these decisions?

Our approach takes the form of tutoring scripts that shape the interaction in general terms. Our tutoring scripts array different combinations of questions, examples, cases, remedial exercises, and canned presentations to engage different students at different times.

As a consequence, we design all tutors on an authentic model: a geologist supervising a field course. For the exploration tutor, we asked ourselves, "If we have given them a goal to find some calcite, and we observe them walking past their goal without noticing it, what would we do, as a teaching geologist?" In this case, we decided the authentic and plausible course would be to steer the students back toward the goal. Similarly, if students have a goal of calcite, and we observe them embarking on their search without an acid bottle in hand, the plausible and authentic course is to gently remind them to acquire the necessary equipment. In these cases, the tutoring is designed to steer students toward their goals.

The science tutor, on the other hand, provides an interesting counterpoint. In this case, we asked ourselves, "If students with a calcite goal misidentify an unknown sample, do we have them drop the sample and continue the search for calcite? Or, do we tutor the students on the analysis of the sample being held?" The answer, in this case, is again informed by the field experience of teaching geologists; that is, the teaching geologist most plausibly would defer the calcite goal and use the unknown sample as a pedagogical starting point. In the field, tutoring would proceed by contrasting the unknown sample with calcite and leading the students through the diagnostic reasoning exercise that has presented itself.

TASK VS. STUDENT MODELS

It is important to note that the tutoring in these systems is not predicated on student modeling of any usual sort. Students are tracked, but only in terms of their goals and success or failure in achieving them. There is no attempt to count things about students (e.g., their attempts at a particular task, or the number of times they reference a particular help file); instead, the tutoring interventions depend on the students' particular failures on a given attempt.

In other words, tutoring depends on task-oriented errors and a well-formed model of the task. So if students make a report based on insufficient evidence, tutors are dispatched to remediate based on their knowledge of the task. This approach avoids the problem of trying to guess the students' misconceptions based on their actions.

History has shown student-modeling research to be relatively expensive in relation to the perceived benefit. Besides, if the constructivist theory (Duffy & Jonassen, 1992) is remotely plausible, then student models will tend to be unique, with two seldom the same, rendering the modeling problem computationally unattractive.

In a classroom, instructors often can gauge which students are grasping correctly the concepts being taught by in-class discussions. Although this same evaluation is possible in a virtual environment, it is more difficult for the students to obtain. Not all students log into the system at the same time, and those who are logged in simultaneously may have completely different goals. Having an agent evaluate the actions of players and invite collaboration between them helps the students who are having difficulties with their given tasks. Of course, there are problems with such an implementation. Students who excel in the exercises may receive multiple requests to help other students. A solution may be to have the tutoring agent contact a player only a set number of times before it starts to contact another player. Another solution would be to have the tutoring agent contact the instructor of the course for assistance. A dynamic online help system, involving human agents with an intervening software agent, is yet another way to extend virtual worlds to create a better learning environment.

CONCLUSION

This chapter surveys the range of strategies we have employed in simulating our worlds. The principal tool has been the implementation of software agents that perform a large number of roles in the simulated environments and provide services that range from entertainment to tutoring.

PART II

THESE ARE OUR WORLDS

This part explores our worlds in more detail. Each chapter concentrates on an individual world, with an emphasis on how the game is played and what it is designed to teach.

There are many similarities among our educational games. They are all multiuser simulations hosted on the Internet, so anyone with a computer and an Internet connection should be able to visit using a standard web browser (although some of the games employ special features that require the user to also download a browser plugin or other software). They all employ software agents in some fashion, often several different agents depending on the game. And, they are all supposed to be fun.

Each chapter in this part contains at least one URL that interested readers can follow to learn more.

These are our worlds.

Chapter 4

The Geology Explorer

The Geology Explorer is a system for geoscience and earth science education. Students using the system explore a simulated world, seeking to achieve their goals by performing experiments, interpreting results, and building representations of the structure of geologic terrains. The experience is modeled after the idea of a field camp where students operate under the direction of a mentor as a way of learning how to function as a geologist. The site of these discovery-based experiences is Planet Oit, a role-based, goal-oriented, distance learning simulation hosted on the Internet, where players pursue the goals set for them, interact with one another, and are visited, when necessary, by intelligent software tutor agents. Students learn by assimilating their role in this simulated environment and are engaged in real science activities as they explore the world.

The Geology Explorer Planet Oit can be visited at http://oit.ndsu.edu/.

In many respects, physical geology is an ideal course for a role-based environment. Unlike many other sciences, physical geology is highly visual, with landscapes ranging from mountaintops to ocean floors, from arid badlands to intensely leached tropical soils, from gently flowing streams to violent volcanic eruptions. The Geology Explorer (Saini-Eidukat, Schwert, & Slator, 2001; Schwert, Slator, & Saini-Eidukat, 1999) is an educational research project that implements a virtual world for geologic exploration and role-based learning—Planet Oit.

Planet Oit is designed to emulate the geologic features and processes of Earth and is based on a realistic planetary design. The geography consists of a single super-continent composed of roughly 50 locations (see Figure 4.1) arranged so as to be both diverse and coherent. A variety of Earth-like environments, ranging from tropical coastlines to volcanic calderas to glaciated peaks, allows for multiple geologic terrains to be explored. A museum of rocks and minerals is available at the landing site for use as a standard reference collection. Coordination of navigation on the planet is made possible by using directions relative to Earth-like geographic poles (North, South, etc.).

Implemented as well are almost 40 scientific instruments and geologic tools (streak plate, acid bottle, magnet, etc.), nearly 100 different rocks and minerals, and over 200 boulders, veins, and outcrops. In an earlier text-based version, students used a command language, which allowed for navigation, communication, and scientific investigation while on the planet. Commands were typed to apply instruments

Figure 4.1. Map Displaying the Geography of Planet Oit

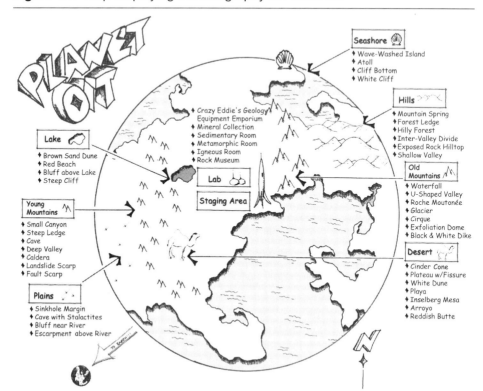

("streak," "scratch," "hit," etc.) and senses ("view," "taste," "touch," etc.). These functions have since been replaced by graphical point-and-click controls. Students can communicate with one another through typing into "speech balloons."

Once the layout and artifacts of Planet Oit were implemented, the rules of the game were imposed over the top. Specifically, we created an environment where students, after being transported to the planet's surface, automatically are assigned an initial exploratory goal and can acquire whatever equipment they wish. The goals are intended to motivate students into viewing their surroundings with a critical eye, as a geologist would. Goals are assigned from a principled set (i.e., the goals gradually get more difficult as the player gains experience), so as to leverage the progressive role-based elements of the game—as students gain experience, they gain confidence.

In order for students to achieve a goal (and therefore earn points), they must address a multitude of tasks that are virtually identical to those faced daily by field geologists. These include the selection and use of proper field tools, navigation across the planet to the correct region, and interpretation of the experiments applied to the problem.

Students are given a series of authentic geologic goals. The first goal is to locate and report the position of potentially valuable mineral deposits. Accomplishing these goals entails mastering several geologic concepts and procedures, and demonstrates student mastery of the material. The first module involves mineral exploration, where students are expected to embark on an expedition, locate mineral deposits, and navigate the somewhat vast virtual environment in order to report their findings. Later modules build on the first module through an exercise in geologic mapping that in turn leads to modules on strike-and-dip and true thickness.

As each goal is completed satisfactorily, students automatically are assigned new goals requiring progressively higher levels of expertise and decision making. Learners participate in field-oriented expedition planning, sample collection, and hands-on scientific problem solving. Through this practical application of the scientific method, students learn how to think, act, and react as geologists (Duffy & Jonassen, 1992).

LOCATIONS

Planet Oit is built on a hub-and-spoke model, with a central location that represents the expedition's landing and staging area. From there it is possible to travel toward each of the compass directions. There are seven main areas adjacent to the staging area, plus a "spaceship" (explained below).

- To the north is a glistening, azure, ocean seashore.
- To the northwest is a sparkling inland lake.
- To the west is a majestic range of chiseled mountains.
- To the southwest is a vast expanse of open prairie.
- To the south is a blistering desert.
- To the east is the soft outline of a mountain range.
- To the northeast is a broad area of rolling hills and valleys.

On Planet Oit, navigation is achieved by clicking on "compass icons" so, for example, a player in the Plains clicks on the icon marked "east" to get to the Cave with Stalactites.

The Lab and Staging Area (center, Figure 4.1) is the first place students find themselves. From there they can explore in various directions, toward the Seashore, Hills, Old Mountains, and so on, or enter the spaceship and visit the Rock Museum and Crazy Eddies, where they can get equipment.

PLAYING THE GAME

The "back story" is that Planet Oit is a recently discovered planet that is very similar to Earth. It is in our solar system and in the same orbit as Earth, but it is directly opposite the Sun from us—and so has been undetected until now. Some readers may recognize this premise as borrowed from low budget, black-and-white, science fiction movies filmed in the 1950s. Our spin on this time-worn premise is that, because of this "startling" discovery, the governments of Earth collectively are asking the world's geology and earth science students to join in a massive internationally sponsored exploration of this new planet.

Thus it is that Geology Explorer students are flown into outer space where they soon "land" on Planet Oit and find themselves in the Staging Area. They are met by a software agent who greets them and offers to answer questions. Software agent "guides" of this type are located in a variety of strategic locations around the planet. The other notable feature of the Staging Area is a spaceship that students can visit. Entering the spaceship brings them to a Laboratory where they find another software agent guide, and doorways leading to the Rock Museum and Crazy Eddie's Emporium.

The Rock Museum has a rare collectible guitar hanging on the wall (as a joke) and doorways leading to exhibits of igneous, sedimentary, and metamorphic rocks, as well as an exhibit on minerals. The players can inspect these exhibits, which provides an opportunity to visualize specimens of the rocks or minerals they have been assigned to locate on the planet. In Crazy Eddie's, the students are able to acquire a standard set of field instruments: rock pick, acid bottle, magnet, glass plate, and so on.

The moment they arrive, students are issued an "electronic log book" to record their findings and, most important, are assigned an initial exploratory goal. The students make their field observations, conduct small experiments, take note of the environment, and generally act like geologists on a field expedition as they work toward their goals. A scoring system has been developed so that students can compete with one another and with themselves.

Other resources available to the students are a set of "sensory input devices," including a "nose" to smell with, a "fingernail" to scratch with, a "tongue" to taste with, and so forth. They also start out with a map and a "bookcase" that contains their logbook as well as a help system and other reference materials.

Students on the planet are able to communicate with one another, which affords the opportunity to cooperate and collaborate. This is accomplished through speech balloons that appear when students click on their avatar/character. When they type into their speech balloon, the message becomes visible to everyone else in the same location (see Figure 4.2).

The Geology Explorer interface displayed in Figure 4.2 includes a "tool panel" (upper left) for choosing instruments to employ. The magnifying glass is currently selected, but a number of other functions are available, including the nose tool, for smelling a sample. Directly below the tool panel, on the left, is the bookcase, containing a number of useful reference materials—the Goals tab is currently selected. The main window is in the upper right, showing two players discussing their goals, displayed in speech balloons, and the results of various experiments, which also are displayed in speech balloons. Below and behind the main window is a magnified view of a mineral specimen, and just to the right of that is the map used for navigation around the planet.

Students automatically are assigned an initial exploratory goal in the identification game module. They are required to achieve a minimum number of points (usually 500) in order to meet the minimum expectations of the first planetary exercise. Upon achieving these points, the students "graduate" to more advanced modules. In some cases they eventually are given an invitation to an end-game scenario: an advanced setting of the game involving a fanciful integration of geologic investigations and riddle solving.

Figure 4.2. The Geology Explorer Graphical User Interface

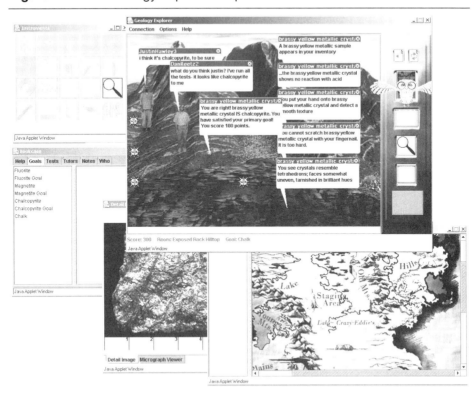

SOFTWARE TUTORS, GUIDES, AND OTHER AGENTS

A key feature of the Geology Explorer, indeed of all the systems described here, is the ability to tutor students. On Planet Oit, tutoring is done through nonintrusive but proactive software agents. These agents monitor student actions and visit students when the need arises. Tutors give advice, but they do not mandate or insist on student actions, nor do they block or prevent student actions. On Planet Oit, the equipment tutor tries to detect when students have failed to acquire the equipment necessary to achieving their goals. The exploration tutor warns students when they have overlooked a goal in their travels. The science tutor is implemented to detect when students make a mistake in identifying rocks and minerals. In addition, more advanced tutors are implemented in later modules to assist students with interpretive mapping exercises.

There are also a number of software agent guides that give directions and answer questions. In addition, there are a number of atmosphere agents that lend to the texture of the game without affecting game-play: a deer that wanders the hills, a scorpion in the desert, and so forth.

One recent innovation is the pop quiz agent that will drop in on a student and ask a relevant content question. For example, if the player has been assigned the goal of finding graphite, the pop quiz agent might visit and say, "For ten quick points, what is the color of graphite. You have 60 seconds to answer." This is an example of an infrastructure agent, since students are able to change their scores with a correct answer. The quiz questions are always chosen based on the current goal in order to be useful to the students' quest.

THE INTERPRETIVE DIKE MODULE

Once students have successfully learned how to identify rock outcrops, they are asked to build on this knowledge. They are assigned a goal that directs them to the Rolling Hills, where they are met by a software guide agent. They are supplied with a second map, this one an aerial/topographic view of the Basaltic Dike region, and are given instructions on how to begin their work.

The Basaltic Dike region is a hilly area where a ridge of volcanic material has been pushed up (i.e., has intruded) through layers of sandstone and limestone. Because of the awesome forces at play in a geologic event of this kind, the rock directly adjacent to the dike has been transformed from sandstone and limestone to quartzite and marble. Thus, sedimentary rocks (sandstone and limestone), through the application of terrific heat and pressure, became metamorphic rocks (quartzite and marble).

This is the back story of the Interpretive Mapping Module—but this is not a story the students are told. On the contrary, the overall goal in this module is for the students to discover this story for themselves. They demonstrate their understanding by creating a geologic map, which is the method used by geologists to create a model of subterranean structure based on evidence found on the surface.

In the center of the region stands another spaceship. Inside are a series of graphical displays explaining the concepts of geologic mapping and true thickness. The students are directed to identify the rock outcrops in the region. These identifications are added to their maps automatically, in the form of small color-coded triangles. Based on the location of these outcrops, students are required to create a geologic map by "coloring in" with a painting tool supplied by the game.

Students submit their completed maps for scoring by pressing a button. The system compares the maps with a small set of "school solutions" provided by professional geologists. A software tutor agent then provides feedback on their maps, including the regions that require more work (Figure 4.3, lower right, shows a square at 74% that needs improvement) and giving hints and advice relative to whatever problems they may have encountered. When a student map is within 80% of the school solution, the student is given credit for the work and graduates from the module.

ANCILLARY MATERIALS

Like most projects of this type, the Geology Explorer has a number of associated resources and materials to assist users with game-play. These typically come in two forms: assistance with using the software, and assistance with winning the game (where winning the game entails learning the geology). The Geology Explorer is fairly mainstream in this regard. There is a graphical user manual online

Figure 4.3. Geologic Map in the Interpretive Mapping Module

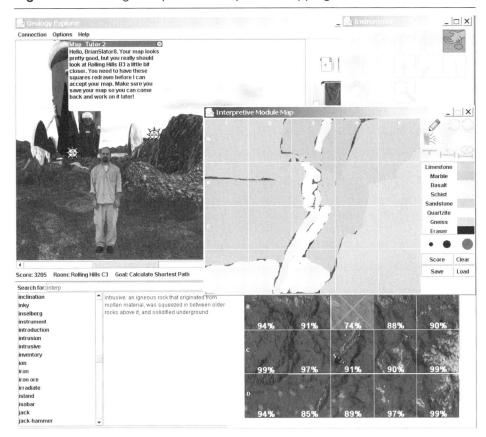

to explain the controls of the game software, and a "How to Play" slideshow. There is a page of frequently asked questions (FAQ), and there is a message board where players can post questions (and read other questions, and answers posted in response, sometimes by other players, sometimes by game administrators). There is also a well-developed help system within the game, available through the bookcase. These are all things that software users have come to expect from systems like this one. In addition to these systems, the Geology Explorer project has developed two innovations: lesson plans and Planet Oit Comics.

LESSON PLANS

In order to assist teachers with integrating the Geology Explorer into their classrooms, an initial set of lesson plans have been written. These are all developed with reference to national science teaching standards and provide a range of activities for teachers to employ, both in preparation for visiting the planet and afterward.

Among these materials are a memory game, a scavenger hunt, workbook exercises, quizzes with answer keys, and so forth. All this information is located online in a "teachers only" area that can be visited at http://oit.ndsu.edu/resources/.

PLANET OIT COMICS

It is a fact of life and of software games that users do not tend to want to read instruction manuals before embarking on game-play. It is also commonly observed that players often prefer to experiment rather than take advantage of the online help systems, and, further, routinely avoid reading text on-screen whenever possible. To alleviate these problems, we have developed Planet Oit Comics, a "graphical novel" telling the story of a group of students exploring Planet Oit and the adventures they encounter.

The story begins with the discovery of Planet Oit and the international effort devised to explore the new world with the help of geology and earth science students. A group of seven students volunteer to go on the exploration, and they are packed off to a sort of boot camp where they learn how to operate their virtual equipment device (VED). The VED, which is presented as a hand-held device, has a keypad interface that is strikingly similar to the controls of the Geology Explorer game. The student volunteers are taken through a series of boot camp exercises that familiarize them with the general ambience of the game and the specific workings of the VED.

Once their training is complete, the story continues with the students boarding a spaceship and flying to Planet Oit, where they land in the Staging Area. Up to this point in the story, the surroundings have been drawn in comic book style. However, from this point forward (which we think of as the "Land of Oz" moment in the story), the surroundings and backgrounds to all the panels are adapted from screen captures of the Planet Oit environment.

The story continues on the planet surface with the student volunteers being assigned goals that map directly to the goals assigned by the Geology Explorer: from rock and mineral identification to geologic mapping. Along the way, one of the members of the party gets lost, and the group works together to "save" him.

The idea for Planet Oit Comics was inspired by the same general motivation for developing educational games in the first place—to make learning fun. By disguising a user manual as a comic book, we promote user understanding of the game before students play it. By carefully conceiving of the story line and graphic art for the comic book, we promote visualization of the Planet Oit environment and provide examples of how to operate within the environment and how to go about solving problems while immersed there. Lastly, the story shows players working together to achieve goals, a positive aspect of multiplayer gaming. Thus, Planet Oit Comics address a range of issues relating to the use and acceptance of the Geology Explorer, and do so in a whimsical, entertaining manner.

IMPLEMENTATION ISSUES

The game, which teaches principles of geology, is an implementation of a networked, multiplayer, simulation-based, interactive, educational environment. The Geology Explorer was originally a text-based game, but because of the highly visual nature of geology, we soon implemented an interactive graphical interface to replace the text-based simulation. Despite the arguments of Multi-User Domain (MUD) "purists," described below, that the existing text-based game provided a suitably imaginative environment, we remain convinced that graphical visualization of space and objects has enhanced the quality, authenticity, and pedagogical value of geologic experiences on the planet. For example, the differentiation between hand specimens of quartz (a mineral), chert (a sedimentary rock), and obisidian (an igneous rock) requires overly lengthy descriptions in the text-based version, but becomes instantaneous with the introduction of an image of the specimen.

The software needed to play the game is quite mainstream—any web browser that supports Java applets. The Geology Explorer home page keeps an up-to-date list, along with suggested system configurations, and so on. In addition, a CD has been created containing the software and graphics—for the convenience of users with low-bandwidth Internet connections, as Planet Oit is graphically intensive and download times can be an issue for this class of user.

As of this writing, the Geology Explorer system and the Planet Oit simulation are hosted on a Unix server located on the campus of North Dakota State University. As the system gains popularity and traffic increases, we plan to distribute servers to other locations to balance the load.

CONCLUSION

The first module of the Geology Explorer (like most of the virtual worlds described here) can be characterized as an "identification game," or "ID game." Introducing the worlds using this style of game serves several purposes. First, it familiarizes the players with the basic tools and entities of the environment—the items and objects with which they will be operating. Second, the ID games are relatively easy, especially at first, and this allows the players to have early success—an important motivational device. Third, the module serves to acquaint players with the user interface, which helps them to understand how to expect the controls to work in later phases of the game.

Building the Geology Explorer on the model of a geology field camp has been of substantial benefit to the project. This strategy simplifies the design and implementation decisions by allowing us to fall back on the experience of geologists. There have been innumerable occasions where we settled design questions by asking, "Well, how would you handle this in the field?" This may not seem like much, but it has been a constant source of inspiration for project planning.

The decision to create a mythical planet instead of replicating Earth has been slightly controversial at various times over the years. Critics observe that we are teaching the geology of Earth, but not using Earth as the object of study. We chose this path in order to create an idealized planet, rich in necessary detail, but free from the "messy" complexities that might serve to distract or confuse students. In other words, we have created a planet with the level of detail we believe best suited to the topics that need to be covered. We argue that our planet differs from Earth in a way that makes it "better" than Earth.

Chapter 5

The Virtual Cell

The NDSU Virtual Cell (VCell) is an interactive, three-dimensional visualization of a bioenvironment designed to teach the structure and process of cellular biology. To the students, the Virtual Cell looks like an enormous navigable space populated with 3D organelles and other biological structures. Students explore this space using a "fly through" interface, conducting experiments and interpreting them in order to achieve their goals. The goals begin with identifying organelles, then move on to more challenging tasks and question-based assignments that promote diagnostic reasoning and problem solving in the authentic visualized context of a cell body. A software agent guide hands out the assignments, and software tutors assist when students struggle.

VCell can be visited at http://vcell.ndsu.edu/.

Student understanding of the concepts related to the structure and function of the cell is an essential feature of the pedagogy of modern biology. Learning the physical components of the cell, how these components interact, and how these interactions are regulated, has largely replaced the traditional organismal approach to teaching biology. The cell, though, is a complex, multidimensional environment where time and space are critical factors that determine when and where cellular events occur. It is very difficult to capture this multidimensionality in the 2D space of the printed page, chalkboard, or web page.

The NDSU VCell is a virtual, multi-user space where students fly around a 3D world and practice being cell biologists in a role-based, goal-oriented environment (White, McClean, & Slator, 1999). Working individually, or with others, students learn fundamental concepts of cell biology and strategies for diagnostic problem solving. This pedagogical approach provides students with authentic experiences that include elements of practical experimental design and decision making, while introducing them to biology content.

The goal in building VCell is to provide an authentic problem-solving experience that engages students in the active learning of the structure and function of the biological cell. To do this, the VCell simulation implements a virtual cell and a cell biology laboratory providing an experimental context for students in an interactive environment. Within the simulation, a virtual avatar acts as a guide and gives out assignments, and intelligent software tutor agents provide content and problem-solving advice. In addition, VCell supports multi-user collaborations, where both students and teachers from remote sites can communicate with one another and work together on shared goals.

The first module of the VCell is an identification game populated with subcellular components: nucleus, endoplasmic reticulum, Golgi apparatus, mitochondria, chloroplast, and vacuoles. Each of these organelle structures is rendered as a 3D object using the Virtual Reality Modeling Language (VRML), a computer language for specifying three-dimensional worlds that can be displayed and manipulated over the Internet.

The VCell consists of a 3D laboratory, a cell body, and subcellular structures. The initial point of entry is the interior of a virtual laboratory. Here the learner encounters a scientific mentor (a software agent guide) and receives a specific assignment. From there, students visit the interior of the Virtual Cell itself, where they perform simple experiments (assays) and learn the basic physical and chemical features of the cell and its components. As students progress through the levels of the module, they revisit the laboratory to receive more assignments. Periodically, students bring cellular samples back to the virtual lab for experimentation.

USER INTERFACE

The interface is technically a Java applet that is launched from a common web browser. It interacts with the server and consists of four regions (see Figure 5.1). The Virtual Cell Client Region (upper right) contains a fully interactive 3D world—note the presence of a "submarine," indicating another player is in the cell. Depending on the module and level, students will find themselves in either the laboratory, the cell, or the interior of an organelle. The upper left is the Reference Region, which provides structure and function information about the components seen in the Virtual Cell Client Region. Information is returned to the user from the server and database when a drop-down menu is activated. The Tool Region (lower left) contains the tools necessary to perform experiments on the items in the 3D panel. The MUD Region (lower right) provides textual interactivity with the server. In this region, the upper box is used to type in commands, and the lower box contains textual output specific to the actions occurring in the 3D region. For example, if students are conversing with a person in the lab, that "speech" will be seen in the dialog box. If they perform an experiment using items in the Tool Region, the experimental output will be displayed in the dialog box.

This functionality is extended as needed to support the learning goals of the project. In response to user activities, the server can instruct the client to display regions containing informational text, regions for selecting actions to perform on various objects, and so on.

THE VIRTUAL CELL EXPERIENCE: THE LABORATORY

In the laboratory, the learners receive specific assignments. This is a hallmark of these systems—learners are always in possession of a goal, and there is never any doubt about the goal on which they are supposed to be working. To achieve these

Figure 5.1. The Virtual Cell User Interface

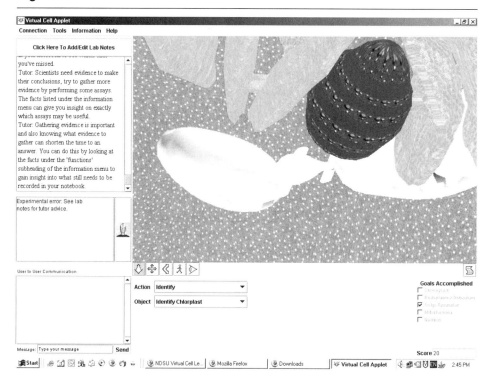

goals, students perform the experiments necessary to learn the physical and chemical features of the cell and its components. The virtual laboratory procedures invariably require a voyage into the 3D cell, where experimental science meets virtual reality. The learners are supplied with a toolbox of measuring devices that assay various cellular processes. These tools include such things as an O2 meter, CO2 meter, pH meter, sugar assay, protein assay, various stains, and enzyme assays. As students progress, they revisit the laboratory, perhaps bringing cellular samples back for experimentation, and subsequently receive more assignments (see Figure 5.2).

THE CELL

The Virtual Cell contains 3D representations of the important components and organelles of a cell (nucleus, mitochondria, chloroplasts, etc.). The user flies among these organelles and uses virtual instruments to conduct experiments. All navigation is learner-directed; there is no predetermined exploratory path. This feature empowers students to direct their own learning. As they progress through the modules, the students also are able to travel into linked 3D worlds that represent the interior of selected cellular organelles. Further experimentation inside each organelle allows students to learn about its specific functions (Y. Wu, 1998).

Figure 5.2. The Virtual Cell Laboratory

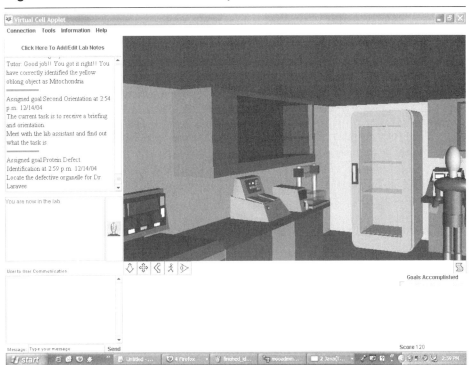

For example, learners may confront the nucleus and perform several simple experiments. Suppose the nucleus is not consuming or generating O_2 or CO_2; it has a positive Fulgen stain reaction and it demonstrates a negative luciferase enzyme reaction. The students must put these results into a context. They may learn from a lecture, a textbook, or a tutoring agent that a positive Fulgen stain means DNA is present, and a negative luciferase reaction means ATP is absent. In the cell, this general information is contained in the 3D representation and offered via touch-sensitive points. Putting this and information from additional experiments together, they infer that the object is the nucleus and that DNA is contained there. Additional pertinent data about the nucleus and other cellular organelles are collected in the same manner.

More advanced levels of this module include the introduction of cellular perturbations and the investigation of the functions of various cellular structures or processes. In the second level, the simulation changes the cell by either introducing a mutation or adding an inhibitor that disrupts a cellular process. An alarm might sound, some cellular process will malfunction, and the learners are given the goal of diagnosing the problem. Using the same tools as in the previous level, the learners navigate through the cell, make observations, and perform measurements and experiments. The learners attempt to identify the affected area, the perturbed process, and the nature of the mutation or inhibitor that is causing the problem. As a result, they will learn details of cellular processes and functions, and become familiar with the importance of various mutations and inhibitors for cell biology experimentation.

In the third level of this module, the learners are given a set of goals to investigate a specific cellular structure or process. They have at their disposal the tools from the first level and the mutations and inhibitors from the second level. Using these tools in various combinations, the students will form hypotheses, design experiments, and employ their toolbox items to perform the experiments. For example, the learners might be given the goal of determining how a membrane vesicle buds off from one compartment and is specifically targeted to fuse with another compartment. Using the tools from previous levels, and their experience with designing and performing experiments, the learners could determine that proteins from two compartments recognize each other, bind in a specific fashion, and promote the fusion of a vesicle to the target compartment.

RESPIRATION AND PHOTOSYNTHESIS

More advanced modules of the Virtual Cell are designed for the study of the "electron transport chain" within the mitochondria, and photosynthesis within the chloroplast, as well as others. The approach taken is the same in every instance.

The students, having graduated from a module, report to the laboratory, where the lab guide software agent gives them a new assignment. At the same time, behind the scenes, their reference library and help menus are updated with information relevant to the new goal.

The students are given a short reading assignment from within the new material (see Figure 5.3 for an example). Then they are directed to an area within the Virtual Cell where they review an annotated illustration of the process. Once they indicate they are finished looking at the illustration, they are directed to another area where they watch an animated movie of the process in action.

Once the overall goal has been defined and the process has been explained and demonstrated, the students are directed to enter a 3D simulation of the process and are assigned a sequence of experimental tasks aimed at providing them with experiences to assist in their understanding of the process. For example, in the Electron Transport Chain Module, they first search the Virtual Cell looking for

Figure 5.3. Virtual Cell Reference Entry for ATP Synthase

ATP SYNTHASE

ATP Synthase consists of a bulb-shaped protein complex that spans a biological membrane. ATP Synthase is found in the inner membrane of mitochondria, the thylakoid membrane of plant chloroplasts, and the plasma membrane of aerobic bacteria. ATP Synthase complexes are embedded in organelle membranes that separate two cellular compartments with different concentrations of H+ ions. This concentration difference, or H+ gradient, is used by the ATP Synthase complex to force a reaction between ADP and P, to form ATP. Most of the ATP produced in cellular respiration is made by the ATP Synthase complex. The resulting ATP molecules are then used to power many different types of biochemical and mechanical work in the cell.

a mitochondria. They are directed to click on this organelle, which transports them to a new scene within the mitochondria, where they are asked to arrange the constituents of the process (cytochrome b-c1 complex, cytochrome C, NADH dehydrogenase, etc.) in the proper order. They do this by inserting the constituent complexes into a virtual membrane and then "running" the simulated process to see that it is operating properly. Next, they are presented with a system that has a damaged constituent and directed to perform experiments to determine which one is faulty.

IMPLEMENTATION

The VCell consists of three software elements: (1) a collection of 3D worlds representing a virtual laboratory, the interior of the Virtual Cell, and the interior of cellular organelles; (2) a server and database that contain the textual material (help file and experimental output data) and control the single and multi-user interactivity; and (3) a client interface for students to interact with the system from school or home. The 3D worlds provide the visual context, while the server and database, along with the interface, control the interactions. The Virtual Cell simulation processes run in the background on a network server that permits multiple users to simultaneously connect to, and interact with, the 3D worlds and their associated data.

CELLS ON DEMAND

The design of the VCell has created several implementation challenges in addition to coordinating and synchronizing the 3D views, when multiple players share the same scene, using a low-bandwidth, text-based server. Those challenges are (1) avoiding overcrowding within the scenes, (2) collision detection, and (3) implementing virtual tools and instruments to support student experimentation, managing virtual tutors and guides, managing a system of goals and experimental results, and implementing a game-like scoring system.

   The strategy to avoid overcrowding involves a scheme whereby copies of the Virtual Cell are created on demand, to accommodate peak load. For example, the regimen currently calls for two students to occupy each cell. When a third player logs on, a second copy of the cell is created for that player. A fourth visitor joins the third, and yet another copy of the cell is created when a fifth visitor logs on. So it goes, two by two, as long as new players log on to the system. The other technical issues are discussed in detail elsewhere.

TUTORING

Tutors in the Virtual Cell are built on the Geology Explorer model (Slator, 1999), where student actions are tracked and tutors are invoked primarily in the event of student failure. Failures are detected and remediation is implemented based on the tutoring agent's knowledge of the students' goals. Tutoring takes the form of directing students toward the online material and/or experiments necessary to form a conclusion relating to students' goals.

For example, a student might be asked to identify the mitochondria in the Virtual Cell. In order to definitively identify the mitochondria, the marker assays for both DNA synthesis and succinate dehydrogenase must be performed. The tutor knows several things when students make an identification: (1) the correct identity of the organelle, (2) the experiments required to confirm this identification (in this example, the two assays just mentioned), and (3) which, if any, of these experiments the students actually have performed.

If students make an incorrect identification, or make a correct identification without performing the necessary experiments, then a tutor is activated. Currently, tutors take the approach of providing a hint in the first case, and refusing to accept an answer in the second case. Ultimately, tutors will guide students to the right experiments in the first case, and will query students for an explanation in the latter. In any event, it is important for the environment be an active one, where the players are stimulated by interactions occurring in the game. The tutors in the Virtual Cell are not merely passive and reactive; rather, VCell tutors seek opportunities to interact and tutor.

The virtual guide takes the form of a 3D laboratory assistant and is primarily responsible for tracking students' goals and their progress toward them. When players first visit the system, the lab assistant greets them and assigns a goal. Whenever students complete a goal, they report to the lab assistant, who congratulates them on their success, and then provides them with another goal. The current version of the Virtual Cell has an extensive help system to answer student questions, but the guide is also available to answer questions.

CONCLUSION

The overarching pedagogical goal of this project is to support role-based learning (Slator, Juell, et al., 1999), where students are presented with authentic problems that promote their learning to think and act like a biologist. This means developing a curriculum of authentic tasks and goals and providing an inventory of authentic tools and instruments to achieve these goals. In addition, the aim is to provide these experiences at a distance, which implies an Internet delivery mechanism. Further, to provide a self-paced element, there is a need for extensive online help and agent-based software tutors to supplement human intervention and remediation. Finally, it is extremely desirable in modern pedagogy to provide opportunities for group interaction and collaborative problem solving. In order to support these goals, it is necessary to develop a highly interactive and dynamic simulation of cellular processes, hosted on the Internet, and supporting multiple users.

Chapter 6

The ProgrammingLand
MOOseum

The ProgrammingLand MOOseum is a virtual world for computer science education. The environment is fashioned after an Exploratorium-style virtual museum filled with exhibits relating to computer programming and programming languages. The museum metaphor is used to structure the curriculum as a tour from room to room. Student visitors are invited to participate in a self-paced exploration of the exhibit space, where they are presented with introductory concepts in computer science. The exhibits provide interactive demonstrations of the concepts in action. The students are encouraged to manipulate the interactive exhibits as a way of "experiencing" the principles. The environment supports multiple users (so learners can interact with both the environment and one another), real-time simulations of various kinds, and interactive software agents, particularly tutors.

The ProgrammingLand MOOseum can be visited at http://euler.vcsu.edu/pland.html.

The ProgrammingLand MOOseum has been developed and is used in conjunction with traditional classroom instruction. However, the goal is for distance learning and nontraditional classes. It is intended to deliver content that normally would be obtained from a lecture or textbook, yet also to have many of the attractive qualities of games and other learner-centered activities.

ProgrammingLand is primarily a text-based game. The players experience the environment by reading, and issue commands by typing. It is called the MOOseum because it is built on a software platform called a MOO, which stands for MUD, Object Oriented. MUD stands for Multi-User Domain (in earlier days, the D usually was ascribed to Dungeon instead of Domain in tribute to the game "Dungeons and Dragons," popular in the 1970s). Technically speaking (Curtis, 1997), the MOO described in this chapter is identical to the server and database systems described in other chapters. The main difference here is the interface, which is primarily text-based instead of graphically based as in the other systems.

THE PROGRAMMINGLAND MOOSEUM

ProgrammingLand (PLand) is being developed on the Valley City State University campus in North Dakota as an adjunct to introductory programming language classes. The paradigm employed is that of a museum where students examine exhibits and read the explanatory text displayed on the walls of each room. In addition to the text there are a number of interactive demonstration objects in the museum that clarify or demonstrate the concepts. One such object is a code machine, which contains a short segment of programming language code and can display the code, display with line-by-line explanations, or display a line-by-line execution of the code. ProgrammingLand augments programming language courses, either locally or at a distance. The museum contains four wings (some currently under construction). One of these is an introduction to using a MOO; each of the other three deals with a popular programming language, in particular C++, Java, or BASIC, three of the most commonly taught languages in introductory programming courses.

Each wing of PLand is loosely structured into topics, lessons, and sublessons. A topic is composed of one or more lessons. A lesson is the amount of instruction that reasonably could be completed in one sitting, whereas a topic is usually several lessons and hence too large for a single session. Sublessons are convenient conceptual divisions within lessons. It should be noted that these distinctions are somewhat arbitrary terms without hard boundaries in PLand. If students want to learn one lesson in several sittings, they have the freedom to progress at their own pace in whatever way they choose.

A lesson does not have to be exhaustive on the topic, but it does need to be self-contained. Lessons in ProgrammingLand are usually hierarchical; that is, most lessons contain sublessons. A lesson is composed of the following parts: (1) an introduction that motivates the students or demonstrates the need for the topic, (2) the content material, (3) some kind of exercise that causes the students to use the new knowledge, and (4) some type of assessment of the students' grasp of the material. Although there is no real attempt at formal mapping, and while there are many exceptions, a lesson can be thought of as akin to a chapter in an imaginary textbook.

A lesson in ProgrammingLand usually consists of several exhibits as well as several specialized objects. Typically, there is an entryway that is the only way into or out of the lesson. The entryway is often a signpost/menu room, suggesting an order of perusing the material; but the students ultimately decide how to take the lesson. A signpost room often does not convey much technical information, but is usually the entrance to several other lessons and topics. The Compound Statement room in Figure 6.1 is an example of a signpost room.

The first line, "The Compound Statement," is both the name of the exhibit and the PLand room name. The next seven lines are the room description. The last six lines are a listing of the exits from this room. As a signpost, this description does not convey very much significant technical information, but it is intended to be "scene setting" and motivational, and to direct students to a series of lessons. This particular signpost is arrayed like a menu. For example, a student simply types "b" and goes to the exhibit about the "Scope of variables in a compound statement." The descrip-

Figure 6.1. The Compound Sentence Statement Signpost Room

THE COMPOUND STATEMENT

The compound statement is not a flow of control statement; however, it is used in most flow of control statements and is essential to the Structured Programming model.

In the Structured Programming model there is the notion of a block. The block in C++ is the compound statement. It is a wrapper that binds several statements into one. It is also the block that greatly affects the scope of variables.

You may choose any of the following exhibits to consider next:

a) The syntax of the compound statement
b) Scope of variables in compound statement
c) The compound statement and other statements

or

x) Return to the main exhibit on flow of control

---

tive text usually is thought of as "writing on the wall" in an exhibit room, and is the main means of conveying what information is contained in exhibits.

The most common type of exhibit is highly informational—a room where some specific course content is given. This can take any of the forms that a lecturer would use. For example, the introductory text in Figure 6.1 is mostly motivational—why this content is useful to students. In an actual lecture, this is needed to pique the curiosity or otherwise show the need of the concept about to be discussed. Adjacent rooms (Figure 6.2) will have the more technical content of other parts of the lesson: descriptions and examples.

PLand records which exhibits have been visited, and this is used as a measure of progress and as a diagnostic tool for assessing the students. For distance learners, this history forms a concrete record of activity for students, who may have no other communication with the instructor. Of course, this history is not evidence of comprehension, but it does demonstrate exposure. Using this history data, the system can invoke software tutoring agents to advise students having problems, by directing them to exhibits they may have missed.

This history of exhibits also has enabled an improvement to the structure of the museum. As PLand has grown, it has developed many more possible paths than would be ideal for a novice. This is mainly because designing a lesson requires a balance between the single linear path, which penalizes advanced or returning students, and the potential for too many choices, which invites novices to exhibits where they are more likely to be confused than educated. The "active exit" (described below) has been developed to assist with managing this complexity.

FUNDAMENTAL OBJECTS

ProgrammingLand is built on the enCore database (Haynes & Holmevik, 1997), which is one of the more popular MOO systems that are freely and publicly available. Because the motif of ProgrammingLand is that of an Exploratorium-style

Figure 6.2. The Exhibits in the Compound Statement Lesson

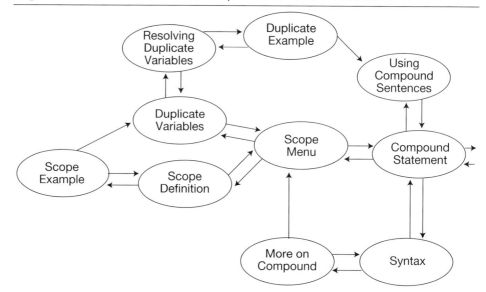

museum, the term *exhibit* often is used instead of *room*—but these can be used interchangeably.

As mentioned above, MOO stands for MUD, Object Oriented. The phrase *Object Oriented* refers to a technical branch of computer science called "Object Oriented Programming," where objects are complex structures containing both data and procedures. In the discussion that follows, objects should be thought of as unique, possibly complicated things. In other words, imagine, say, an automobile where there are places to store certain things (people can sit on the seats, groceries can be carried in the trunk) and the automobile also can do certain things (such as move, turn, and stop).

In a MOO, everything is an object. Rooms are objects, exits are objects, players are objects, and so on. These objects have properties that carry information, and procedures (sometimes called methods) that perform useful functions. However, the students are oblivious to most of this. They walk through the museum without much thought to the processing the server is doing.

PLAYING THE GAME

When students log into PLand, their characters are activated. These player characters are the objects they use to navigate within the world, and where their history is stored. Their history includes a list of every room they have visited, as well as activities they have completed and goals they have achieved. The students score points by visiting an exhibit, taking a quiz, working with an interactive object, like a code machine, and so forth. They also receive homework assignments that are to be completed outside the museum. Finally, as with all the systems described in this book, students always have a goal assigned to them, which also is stored on their player character.

LESSON STRUCTURE

While ProgrammingLand is designed to allow maximum flexibility to players, it is not a random collection of rooms containing instructional material any more than a textbook is a random collection of pages. There is an order imposed that organizes rooms into related clusters forming lessons and sublessons. There is often only one entrance into each group and usually just one or two exits out. The first exhibit in the group is usually a signpost room with a short introductory paragraph and a menu of available rooms. Often, one of the rooms has only text that attempts to motivate the students or explain how the topic fits in the overall scheme of things. There is often a workroom in a sublesson as the final example. A sublesson may be nested within a larger sublesson.

The following objects were created to support the lesson: a sublesson, a sublesson exit, a quiz room, a dispatcher, and a "roving goalie." These all work together.

The Active Exit

When an exhibit is added to PLand, part of that process is to define what prerequisites should exist for that exhibit. The active exit is like a gatekeeper that checks for these prerequisites when a student tries to enter a room. Students taking a path to an advanced topic have their history checked against the background exhibits and activities listed for the new room. If the students have visited the rooms that form the foundation for the room to be entered, they are allowed in, without knowing their prerequisites have been tested. If they have not visited the prerequisite rooms, the system suggests the room may be more confusing than helpful and asks the students if they really want to proceed. Students are not forbidden from entering a room, since an advanced student may have acquired the needed knowledge outside PLand and thus can go forward without undue concern. On the other hand, a merely curious novice at least has been warned, and so knows there is the potential for confusion ahead.

Sublessons

A sublesson contains a list of all the exhibits it includes. Students earn credit for the sublesson by visiting some required combination of rooms within the sublesson or by performing specific tasks, such as operating a code machine, or by a combination of both. To maximize the flexibility of the student experience, there is usually more than one combination satisfying the requirements. In some cases there is also a quiz option, described below. The order in which these requirements are satisfied is normally irrelevant. The only requirement is that the students do at least one set of required items.

The sublesson exit is an instance of the active exit described earlier. When students choose an exit that will leave the sublesson, their progress toward

satisfaction of the requirements is checked. If the students have met the requirements previously, the exit moves them to their intended destination with no
action out of the ordinary. If any of the requirements of the sublesson have been
met recently, students are told they have completed the sublesson, and this is
recorded in their history.

However, if they are leaving the area without completing the requirements
of the sublesson, students get a different set of messages. They are shown which
unmet activities remain, and they are asked if they want to continue to their destination and finish the sublesson later or if they want to prove their mastery with
a quiz. If they opt for a quiz, they are transported to a quiz room.

Quiz Rooms

When students elect to take a mastery quiz, they are transported to a quiz room.
A quiz room cannot be reached except by accepting the challenge of a quiz when
leaving a sublesson. There is one quiz room attached to each sublesson, and the
students take a multiple-choice quiz. If they pass, they are given full credit and
their history is updated to reflect their accomplishment.

The quiz room randomly generates multiple-choice questions, which cover
material the students missed. Attached to each exhibit room is a series of quiz
questions on the material covered. Each question consists of three parts: the question, one or more right answers, and one or more wrong answers. The quiz generator looks at the players and determines which rooms they did *not* visit. Then, it
gathers the questions from these rooms.

The quiz is reduced to five questions. If there are fewer than five questions
available, some general questions are taken from the lesson to bring the number up
to five. The students then attempt to answer the quiz questions. If they answer incorrectly, the correct answer is given. If they answer four of the five correctly, they
pass the quiz and receive credit for the sublesson. If they miss a second question, the
quiz is terminated and they are instructed to resume navigating the lesson in order
to receive credit. If they attempt a second quiz, they get different questions.

The quiz room is used to verify student mastery of material in the absence
of the usual evidence: completing the goals as assigned. It is also a way for experts
to short-circuit the lesson structure, if they choose.

Quiz questions are written and stored with multiple right and wrong answers. The quiz generator randomly selects one of the right answers and four of
the wrong answers for each question. This approach helps to prevent students from
communicating quiz questions to their peers. However, the randomization means
certain types of multiple-choice answers like "both (b) and (c)" and answers like
"all of these" and "none of these" cannot be used to form quizzes. When the students answer, they are given immediate feedback, either the correct answer or
confirmation that their answer was correct.

INTERACTIVE OBJECTS

PLand is populated with a variety of software agents. One such agent may appear
as a code machine that occupies a room and has various commands that operate

it. A code machine gives an explanation and trace of a piece of example code. Another is called a workbench, which allows students to construct a small piece of code and then evaluates it. Students are given credit for operating these machines. This credit is stored in their history and used to satisfy the requirements of relevant associated goals. In addition, there are tutor robots that approach students as they walk through the museum and that students may not be able to distinguish from other students.

Lastly, it is necessary for PLand to give homework assignments to be done outside of the museum. This is accomplished by an interaction among several objects, including a lesson dispatcher and a roving goalie agent.

Code Machines

A code machine is an interactive object placed in appropriate exhibits. The main job of the code machine is to demonstrate short pieces of programming language code. Code machines accept several commands.

- *Show* lists the lines of code.
- *Explain* gives an explanation of each line in succession.
- *Trace* shows the execution of each line in succession.
- *Next* advances an explanation or trace by one line.
- *Help* explains the possible commands of the machine.

Code machines are intended to raise the interaction level and engage the interest of students in an active way. Figure 6.3 shows an exhibit with a code machine named "simple." The exhibit gives instructions on how to operate the machine and suggestions on how best to use it.

The code machine contains a piece of programming code, which it will display, explain, or trace. The code machine may display the code with or without line numbers. The line numbers are important for the explanation and trace, but suppressing line numbers allows students to copy the code from PLand for their own use. Figure 6.4 demonstrates the results when students give the command

Figure 6.3. An Exhibit with a Code Machine

A short program with assignments

This code machine is named simple, with an alias of s. It demonstrates a short program with assignments and outputs. Use

help simple

to get help on using code machines.

It would be a good exercise to look at the code in simple and try to compute manually what values will be left in the variables a, b, and c. Then use the trace feature to determine how close you were.

You see simple here.

Obvious exits: [exit] to Practice with the assignment statement

Figure 6.4. Displaying Contents of a Code Machine

```
                    =>show simple


                    1: #include <iostream.h>
                    2: #include <iomanip.h>
                    3: int main () {
                    4: int a = 3, b = 5, c = -7;
                    5: a = b + c;
                    6: b = c + b * a;

                    . . .
```

"show simple"—six lines of program code, written in the C++ programming language, are displayed for the players to see.

The explanation of the code works on a line-by-line basis. The numbered line is displayed with the explanation of just that line. The students then request the next line. The trace of the code is a simulated execution. Figure 6.5 demonstrates the results when a student gives the command "explain simple"—the same six lines of computer code are displayed, but this time accompanied by an explanation of each line.

Workbenches

A workbench provides lines of programming language code that can be used to construct program fragments. Students' efforts are evaluated by the workbench,

Figure 6.5. Receiving the Explanation of a Code Machine

```
=>explain simple

1: #include <iostream.h>
     The first include obtains access to the I/O stream objects of cin and cout as well as the
put-to and get-from operators.
. . .
=>next simple

4: int a = 3, b = 5, c = -7;
     Declare and initialize the three integer variables. The initialization uses literals, rather
than computed expressions.

=>n s

5: a = b + c;
     Store the sum of b and c into a. Whatever value a had before is now lost. Thus the
initialization of a was not needed.
```

and the students receive credit when they are successful. This allows the students to test whether they know the correct syntax of a programming language construct. The students build a small program fragment from the pieces that are inserted into the workbench. When complete, the students can ask the workbench to determine whether the fragment is syntactically correct or not. In very simple instances the workbench also may interpret the code and run the program fragment. Like the code machine, the successful operation of a workbench results in credit toward achieving goals.

GOALS AND SCORING

The typical lesson has a single entrance and exit. However, that is not the only shape a lesson may take. A lesson may have several lesson exits that start within the lesson cluster and end outside the lesson cluster. There are also active exits that check the requirements and possibly may transport the students to a quiz room. Moreover, lessons may be hierarchical in two senses. First, a lesson may contain other lessons. Second, a lesson may have, as one of its requirements, the completion of another lesson. For example, if students have not visited certain required rooms, they may take a quiz instead. However, if the students have not interacted with a required machine or completed a prerequisite lesson, they may not satisfy these types of requirements with a quiz.

The lesson structure, lesson exit, quiz room, lesson dispatcher, and roving goalie work together to assign goals, provide content, and measure student progress. When students have earned enough credit, they are given a programming assignment by a roving goalie—these assignments are completed outside the MOOseum.

Lesson Dispatcher

Either a lesson exit or a quiz room may give credit for completing a lesson. These also notify the lesson dispatcher of the students' achievement. Certain lessons are allowed to change the goal of students, which causes the matching roving goalie to be activated, to inform them about their new goal.

Goalies

A roving goalie is used to give each student a separate, personalized assignment, usually a programming assignment. This is accomplished by maintaining a list of equivalent assignments and an index that records the next assignment to be given.

Some lessons easily lend themselves to creating multiple equivalent homework assignments. With other lessons, it is more difficult. When there are more assignments than students, each student will get a different one. If there are more students, then several may receive the same assignment.

The assignment message may be quite lengthy, not just a single sentence. If the students ever want to reread the assignment, the goal and roving goalie are noted in their history, making it easy for students to reread an assignment when necessary. Moreover, the roving goalie records what assignment each student received.

Tutor Robots

Synthetic environments, such as PLand, are dynamic and extensible spaces. This flexibility permits complementary approaches to student tracking and modeling, as well as mentor-style interactions, where an "over the shoulder" software tutor monitors student actions and visits participants with timely and felicitous help and advice. This tutoring strategy is essentially the same for all the systems described in this book.

Tutor Robots were implemented to make the exhibits in the MOOseum more active and engaging. They are created from a prototype Tutor Robot provided with the EnCore MOO (Haynes & Holmevik, 1997), based on the ELIZA model (Weizenbaum, 1966), which was inspired by Turing (1950/1963). The Tutor Robots are programmable and capable of matching key words and sentence patterns and can be implemented with random responses and question responses.

TOYS IN THE ATTIC

In the spirit of the Exploratorium, the ProgrammingLand MOOseum is populated with a range of demonstrations, toys, robots, and interactive exhibits. These artifacts are intended to engage visitors in the exploration of the content stored in the museum. They are designed foremost to be playful and entertaining, with a secondary goal of teaching.

Demonstration Machines and Checker Machines

Demonstration machines were built for Lisp functions. Lisp is an older programming language that is used mainly in specialized circumstances and sometimes as a teaching tool. The idea was to create a machine with a "demo" function that would illustrate the operation of a function. These machines are accessed in rooms made specially for them. The Lisp "cons function" room is one example (cons is an operation for adding a member to a list, among other things).

Students visiting the cons exhibit can ask for a demo of the function in action. They also can demonstrate their knowledge of the function by choosing from sample executions hanging on the wall and plugging correct ones into the cons checking machine. These checking machines act like a hands-on quiz system.

When the students plug a correct value into the machine, a congratulatory message is returned and an "award" is added to the players' history. When the players make a mistake, the feedback includes the correct answer.

The Recursive Leprechaun

Since recursion is one of the most difficult concepts for computer science students to master, it is considered important to expose students to recursion as early and as often as possible. In order to make this difficult concept entertaining, we implemented a "recursive leprechaun," which resides in an exhibit named the "Realm of Recursion." The recursion leprechaun demonstrates a recursive counting function in a visually descriptive manner.

The Ring Toss Game

The ring toss game is intended to provide an amusing challenge in associating programming languages with their historical antecedents.

The goal of the ring toss game is to associate languages with people and other concepts. More than one ring can be tossed on a single peg. So, for example, the student scores points by tossing the "John McCarthy" ring onto the Lisp peg (because he was the originator of the programming language).

The History Jukebox

The History Jukebox is a device for summarizing programming language history in an entertaining and on-demand fashion. For example, pressing the "1959" button on the jukebox causes it to "play" the associated material, as seen in Figure 6.6. In other words, the Jukebox plays historical "tunes."

CONCLUSION

A very important consideration for any educational tool is the interest level that the tool maintains in students. The Exploratorium model for museums originated with the desire to make modern museums more interesting than older museums, with their glassed-in exhibits and no interaction.

The ProgrammingLand approach implements an Exploratorium-style museum to create a hyper-course aimed at structuring the curriculum as a tour through a virtual museum. Student visitors to the museum are invited to participate in a self-paced exploration of the exhibit space, where they are introduced to the concepts of the particular domain, are given demonstrations of these concepts in action, and are encouraged to manipulate the interactive exhibits as a way of experiencing the principles being taught (Duffy & Jonassen, 1992; Duffy, Lowyck, & Jonassen, 1983).

Figure 6.6. Playing the History Jukebox

=>press 1959 on History Jukebox

Lisp: Lisp was designed at MIT by John McCarthy. Modeled after the Lambda Calculus, it was intended to process lists, rather than arrays, for symbolic computation, rather than numbers. Lisp has only two native data types: atoms and lists, and program control is via recursion and conditional statements. It pioneered functional programming and is still the dominant language for AI, although it has largely been replaced by Common Lisp and Scheme, the contemporary dialects (Sebesta, 1996).

Chapter 7

The Economic Environments

Dollar Bay is a multi-user retailing game where players are given a store to run. The goal of Dollar Bay is to teach a wide set of skills associated with running a retail business by allowing the microeconomics student to run a simulated store in a simulated world. The pedagogical domain is microeconomics, in particular, retailing. The teaching goals revolve around the strategic importance of targeting specific customer groups in order to gain competitive advantage in the retail marketplace. The game is designed to reward players who learn to think analytically about markets and customer demand.

The Blackwood Project is an attempt at the next generation of role-based virtual environments for education. In this case, the pedagogical simulation is designed to build on Dollar Bay by supporting cross-disciplinary content (embedding the economic simulation in an historical setting), and by offering a choice of roles in order to promote player interaction and potential collaborations.

Both environments aim to teach the principles of microeconomics, retailing, and targeting. Both are built on an agent-based economic simulation where "shoppers" visit stores to purchase items offered for sale, and "employees" conduct the transactions.

In order to play these games, the students must learn how to employ the tools of retailing, hiring, advertising, and inventory management, and to master a market research module. Software tutor agents assist with decision making.

Dollar Bay can be visited at http://dbay.ndsu.edu/, while the progress of Blackwood can be monitored by visiting http://wwwic.ndsu.edu/.

Dollar Bay is a multi-user, educational retailing game implemented with an agent-based economy (Slator & Chaput, 1996). The role of the players is to manage their store by hiring employees, ordering inventory, purchasing advertising, and so forth. The actual transactions, where products are sold to customers, are carried out by software agent shoppers being served by software agent employees.

Dollar Bay avails itself of the full range of software agents described earlier. Atmosphere agents, lending local color and a measure of authenticity to the environment, are designed largely for their entertainment value. In Dollar Bay these include a fire inspector, a juggler, a beat cop, and several others. Infrastructure agents, contributing in a meaningful way to the "play" of the game, are essential to the pedagogical goals of the educational environment. In Dollar Bay these include the customers who create economic demand by seeking products to buy, the employees who control the day-to-day workings of each synthetic retail establishment, and the agents who supply wholesale goods, advertising services, and banking. Intelligent tutoring agents that monitor, mentor, and remediate the human learners in the performance of their roles are like subtopic experts who have access to problem-solving experiences, context-sensitive help and advice, and stories of success and failure. In Dollar Bay, software agent tutors communicate with players by sending them email messages.

ECONOMIC MODELING

The single most important element in the success of the Dollar Bay game is that its economic simulation be plausible and consistent. The cues provided by the simulation must be sensible and authentic. For example, if shopper agents complain that prices are too high, it must be because they have seen a better price elsewhere in the game. If the market research module says certain shoppers will respond to certain types of advertising, that must, in fact, be true. If the game appears to act in a random or chaotic manner, the students will lose faith in the learning experience. The overarching goal of the Dollar Bay game is to construct a plausible economic simulation in order to create an authentic learn-by-doing environment for microeconomic education.

The Model of Consumer Decision Making

Realistic simulations are computationally complex and therefore computationally expensive. This complexity is desirable if players are to believe the simulation, but undesirable if the game is to be played in real time. A balance between complexity and efficiency must be found or the game will be either too simple or too slow. The Dollar Bay game comes close to this center point—the simulation is easy to maintain, easy to expand, and efficient, while still being sufficiently complex to hold the players' interest.

Rather than attempting to model economic behavior solely with complex mathematical formulae, Dollar Bay uses psychographic characterizations manipulated by simple arithmetic calculations combined with a detailed, although straightforward, representation of consumers and products. This simplicity facilitates the implementation of products and consumer groups and makes it fairly easy to add and modify products.

Assumptions

The Dollar Bay economic model assumes rational, cost-minimizing consumers (Hooker & Slator, 1996). Therefore, consumers consider travel costs, search costs, service benefits, and product quality as well as price when making buying decisions. This cost versus price distinction is important for students to grasp.

Dollar Bay models the entire consumer population by defining it in terms of consumer groups. The concept of consumer groups is similar to the idea of psychographic segmentation, employed by many advertisers and marketers. Psychographic segmentation is the classification of a population into groups that share similar values, attitudes, and life-styles (Piirto, 1990; Rice, 1988).

This is different from the somewhat simpler idea of demographic segmentation, where consumer groups are defined by census data. For example, consider the usual census category, 18–34-year-old males. This is an enormous group with a wide variety of interests and buying behaviors—some are wealthy, some are poor, some have children, some do not. The demographic model is a very poor predictor of economic activity because of this diversity. However, by modeling behavior in terms of life-style parameters, there is more hope of finding good norms. For example, in Dollar Bay, 18–34-year-olds with children have significantly different buying behaviors than 18–34-year-olds with no kids. The assumption is that persons with similar values and life-styles will have similar buying behavior. Psychographic segmentation is a well-established method in marketing, as it provides insight into the emotional and life-style factors that motivate consumer buying behavior.

Customer Agent (Shopper) Behavior

The Dollar Bay simulation concentrates on the role of the customer (or shopper) agents in implementing the economy, using product classes and models as the level of representation. A model represents a particular good for sale, like a CD player, and a product class is used to describe the market for an entire class of goods, like electronics.

Based on the information stored in the product class representation, the customer agents decide the amount of a particular product, at what price, and from which stores they will buy. The individual purchasing decisions of these agents implement the economic activity of Dollar Bay.

In other words, customer agents in the economic simulation are what drive the action. The simulation randomly chooses customer agents to go shopping, and the customer agents randomly choose one item from their shopping lists to look for. The product chosen from the shopping list becomes the object of their search. The customer agents first scan a list of stores in order of "attractiveness," looking for one that sells products of the type needed. Then the customer agents visit these candidate stores in turn, attempting to buy the item.

It is interesting to note that customer agents visit stores without knowing in advance that the stores actually carry the product they seek. This is because stores advertise and are cataloged according to their product lines, for example, hardware or pets, but customer agents are searching for specific products, such as table saws or fish. When customer agents visit a store, they know they want a product, a table saw, but not specifically which model of table saw, and they know the store carries that product line (hardware), but not which particular products, and not whether the store has the items on hand or is sold out.

This approach has two obvious benefits: (1) the simulation is plausible in that customer agents must search for products, operate without perfect knowledge, and can quite easily go home empty-handed, and (2) players are permitted to improvise and adapt, so that if a succession of customer agents visit in search of fish, and the player owns no fish, he or she can order some quickly to take advantage of the perceived demand. This maneuvering on the part of the player is imperceptible to the customer agents, who are merely searching for products; so when a player suddenly orders fish, the customer agents are perfectly willing to buy them, even though the player acquired them only moments before.

PLAYING THE DOLLAR BAY GAME

The players in the Dollar Bay game are assigned a location, and they must decide what to sell, how much to stock, where to get inventory, and what price to set. The players also decide, indirectly, the level of services they offer, by deciding how much to pay their employee software agent. They also must determine where and at what level they wish to advertise. In addition, they must decide whether or not to borrow money from the bank and, if so, how much.

The Dollar Bay game provides players the financial tools to monitor their inventory, assets, liability, expenditures, and profits. The players also are able to research their competitors' prices, inventories, and staffing decisions (but not profits or other presumably "secret" information). Further, each player has access to local newspapers, radio, competitors' advertisements, and a range of wholesale suppliers.

The Dollar Bay game consists of interface objects, including a map of Dollar Bay, a set of forms for managing inventory and other functions, and the ability to "talk" to software agents by clicking on them.

The Dollar Bay game divides a mythical region surrounding a mythical bay into small towns and models the entire population of consumers into a number of distinct psychographic groups based on age, income, life narrative, interests, values, and life-styles.

Customers

Players normally are visited by customers shortly after they enter the game for the first time. Each customer actually represents an entire consumer group from a particular neighborhood, and each has two defining data structures.

1. An "attractiveness" list, where vendors are ranked according to a complex formula determining the level at which they attract each shopper. The attractiveness formula takes several factors into account, including advertising as it relates to, and is targeted toward, specific consumer groups, the level of service as it relates to specific consumer groups, and a notion of "loyalty" that depends on whether a customer has succeeded in purchasing products from the player in the past.
2. A "maximum demand" list, where each of the product types is associated with a demand value; this list is copied into a "shopping list" at the beginning of each "virtual week," and customers attempt to exhaust their shopping lists by buying products from stores.

The players do not interact directly with the shoppers. Rather, the sales transactions are conducted between the shoppers and the employee software agents, while the player looks on. The player's role is to manage the store, setting prices, buying advertising, and so on. The sales are handled by employees.

Employees

Employee agents conduct the actual transactions with the customer agents. Hiring an employee is usually the first thing that players do, since sales to shoppers cannot be accomplished without an employee software agent. There is a range of employee proficiencies—at least three levels:

Novice—reports that inventory is gone after supplies have run out.
Intermediate—reports that inventory is low before it runs out.
Experienced—attempts to order more supplies when inventory is low.

Each level of employee costs progressively more in terms of wages and contributes more in terms of service—both to the customers and to the players. For example, more proficient employees can be asked to prepare reports that assist players with decision making.

Advertising

Dollar Bay assumes that advertising increases sales by reducing the search cost to consumers in finding information about desired products. In this way advertising helps consumers find the best value on goods they already want. Not all economists are so positive about advertising. Many assert that advertising increases companies' sales by misguiding consumers into paying more than they need to, or by instilling in consumers desires that they normally would not have (Galbraith, 1967; Thomas, 1981). Dollar Bay assumes that players do not have access to a budget sufficient to afford the kind of advertising that would be needed to change consumers' preferences or create artificial desires (i.e., no players can "create" desire because their means are too limited).

Players advertise by placing ads in the local newspaper or on the local radio. The goal of advertising, which can be expensive, is to target particular consumer groups with ads relevant to those groups, but spending as efficiently as possible to minimize the cost to the store.

Products, Ordering, Pricing

There is a range of products available for players to sell—hardware, pets, furniture, and so forth. There are two methods for procuring products to sell. The first method is to use the map interface to navigate the Dollar Bay region and visit wholesale warehouses. The warehouses sell specific product lines and offer volume discounts. Some products are available in multiple warehouses but at different prices, so carefully comparing prices can lead to savings.

The second is to employ the "order" button, which is equivalent to ordering inventory from a catalog. To do this, the player stays in his or her store and fills out an order form. However, this convenience comes in exchange for extra shipping costs, which the warehouse suppliers do not charge. Some products are available through both the warehouses and the catalog, but some products are available only through one or the other.

When products are delivered, they are priced according to the supplier's recommendation. However, players can change their prices either up or down, using the "stock" function.

The main window of the Dollar Bay game is the lower right panel of Figure 7.1, showing the game controls and a view into the world of Dollar Bay with the interior of a store and a shopper agent (far lower right) attempting to buy a sofa from the salesperson agent (lower right), while the store owner (player) asks, "How is the store doing?" The lower left shows the ordering interface, with a computer being purchased from a wholesaler. In the upper left is the map of the Dollar Bay region, used for navigation. The upper right shows a "sales details" report, which is part of the information players use to make decisions about their stores.

Software Tutor Agents in Dollar Bay

There are three kinds of software tutor agents in Dollar Bay. The first employs a fairly simple rule-based scheme, where players are monitored for exceeding predetermined parameters. For example, players may decide to try to maximize profits by pricing their products at ten times the wholesale price. This is a naive strategy that says, "I might not sell very many, but each sale will be very profitable." The simulation recognizes this as a losing strategy and knows the player is unlikely to sell anything at all.

Figure 7.1. The Dollar Bay Interface

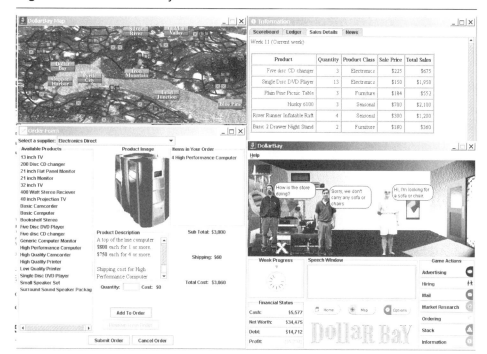

When the game detects a strategic mistake of this type, it sends a message to the player saying, "You may be setting your prices too high." The player can then decide to ignore the message or pursue it. This unintrusive method of tutoring is implemented to be consistent with the educational game principles of leaving the players in control and letting them make their own mistakes.

The second tutoring strategy is simply price-based. When players set prices that are well above the competition, they receive a message from a tutor noting that fact.

The third tutoring strategy is case-based (Regan & Slator, 2002) and relies on developing a "picture" of the players and comparing it with profiles that have been stored for previous players. In this scheme, the players are alerted to their similarity with other players, and cautioned to examine their strategy, since it has been observed to fail in the past.

Lessons Learned

Dollar Bay has been played by groups of high school students over the past few years. These students are high-achieving and highly motivated business students who participate in a number of school-related activities.

In general, players found the game-play realistic, and for a period of several weeks the game sustained a lively interest. Ultimately, a few players were able to dominate the simulated market, and it became nearly impossible to compete against them. It turned out these few players got an early advantage, due to either an optimal location or constant effort.

Over the weeks, this small group, which had accumulated vast capital compared with the other players, was able to undercut the competition and could afford to operate near margin, but made it up in volume. This outcome was quite realistic and plausible given that Dollar Bay simulates a completely unregulated business environment. In other words, Dollar Bay replicated the monopoly formation of the past century. Once these players were rich, they got richer.

The lesson learned is that Dollar Bay is both highly engaging and instructive, but also flawed in certain ways. The Blackwood Project is being developed to address some of these issues.

BLACKWOOD

The Blackwood Project attempts to recreate a virtual 19th-century western town intended to teach American history and microeconomics. The simulation begins in the spring of 1880 with the population of Blackwood at 2,500. The game lasts for 6 virtual years (312 virtual weeks), until the Great Flood destroys the town in the spring of 1886. This game is a part of the research effort of the NDSU World Wide Web Instructional Committee and is not available to play as of this writing. However, we discuss it here to illustrate certain points that likely will become part of future systems.

Like Dollar Bay, Blackwood aims to provide an engaging context for role-based, immersive, distance education and a platform to teach business-oriented problem solving in a learn-by-doing pedagogical style (Duffy et al., 1983; Norman,

1988; Slator, 2001). However, unlike Dollar Bay, the Blackwood virtual environment simulates a 19th-century western town. One significant difference is that Blackwood is populated with intelligent software agents that simulate an economic environment representative of the times. For example, rather than customer agents representing "blue collar workers with children," the categories are things like "ranchers from the western hills" and "silver miners from Fort Black." We have invented this virtual environment, but by borrowing freely from historical records and employing freely available digital images.

The Blackwood game is one where players join the simulation and accept a role in the virtual environment. Rather than everyone vying for a portion of the same economic market, roles are variable and specific. In the Dollar Bay game, for example, every player "inherits" a storefront and then competes for a share of the market, using whatever combination of products the player chooses. In the Blackwood simulation, players choose a "role" and can be purveyors of one thing: dry goods, blacksmithing services, leather goods, and so forth. Therefore, players directly compete only against other players with similar roles, or with software agents in the same profession.

The Next Generation

Blackwood differs from Dollar Bay in several ways. In addition to a more variable and comprehensive economic model, this project concentrates on implementing a more authentic cultural simulation. For example, the environment supports a period-authentic atmosphere in the form of entertainment: The circus might come to town, the weekly train will arrive from the east, a cattle drive will appear on the scene, preachers, circuit judges, and medicine shows will pass through the town.

By combining an economic simulation, where players are expected to compete for a slice of the retail pie, with an authentic historical simulation, we hope to engage learners in two aspects of role-based learning: microeconomic strategizing as before, but now focusing on a role, and combined with historical enculturation.

The Impact of History

One major challenge for this project is to find ways to make American (and world) history meaningful to the players of the game. In the inherently hands-on world of retailing, a learn-by-doing approach is a natural and plausible approach. Players will learn about microeconomics and related topics by actually running a store. However, there is no obvious way for players to "do" history, beyond whatever means can be developed to have them "experience the effects" of history firsthand. At this stage in the design of the Blackwood Project, we are considering the following mechanisms:

- Newspapers: The simulation will track events in the 1880–1886 time frame. As events happen in the nation and around the world, they will be reported in "Special Editions."
- Economic trends: The simulation will reflect the impact of western expansion, the advance of the railroads, and the discovery of silver deposits, in terms of fluctuations in population. This will have immediate and

discernible effects on players' businesses as demand (and prices) rise and fall.
- Climate: Weather records will be researched in order to be more authentic about farm yields and their effect on the economy.

Software Agents

The Blackwood environment will be populated by many of the same software agents as Dollar Bay. Customer agents will be defined on the Dollar Bay model. The preliminary list of consumer groups in Blackwood will be farmers, ranchers, railroad workers (by year 2), soldiers, lumbermen, transient settlers, riverboat workers, teamsters, miners (by year 3), and ultimately white collar townspeople. The merchant class and townspeople will be a special class of consumer group because they will represent the demand of agents who run businesses in competition with human players. The merchant agents in Blackwood are blacksmith, cartwright, wheelwright, dry goods store operator, tailor, and wood lot operator. Players will be able to choose from among this limited set of roles. The system will preserve plausible ratios to avoid having 100 blacksmiths and no tailors. This is done by offering new players a controlled set of choices. In any case, there is a small number of software agents operating in each of these roles so that the simulation can proceed in the absence of human players.

Employee agents also will be defined on the Dollar Bay model. Each will see to the daily operation of retailing outlets and will conduct the actual transactions with the customer agents. Conceptually, employees also do the actual producing of goods; for example, the employee agent in a blacksmith shop does the actual smithing. Employees also will "board" with players, and will complain if food supplies or fuel begins to run low. Therefore, players will be required to procure food and fuel in order to run their households and keep their employees warm and fed. This is expressly intended to promote player interaction. We are very interested to see whether collaborations arise from this.

Banker agents will be defined on the Dollar Bay model. Each will write loans depending on the player's ability to pay. Banks will target specific player groups, and there might be bank failures written into the simulation. Advertising will be defined on the Dollar Bay model but will take only two forms: newspapers and handbills. A town like Blackwood might support several newspapers, but each would tend to be small. Handbill advertising would be available, but also from the newspapers, which likely would have the only printing presses in town. Periodically, newspapers will publish "Special Editions" to broadcast important historical events.

Products also are defined on the Dollar Bay model, where the definition of products is what drives the economic simulation. Products are defined in terms of consumer groups, and the demand value they have for those consumer groups. The preliminary collection of product types is groceries and household goods, lumber, firewood and charcoal, cloth and garments, tools, supplies (salt, coffee, flour, sugar, saltpork), wagons and wagon wheels, horseshoes, nails, wheel rims, and metal strapping.

In Blackwood, wholesale suppliers of products are conceptually "back east," and players order goods through a catalog interface. An important part of the ordering decision will be shipment method, which will be one of three types.

- By wagon: The slow and cheap method; deliveries will take 6 (virtual) weeks, or approximately 2 full human days.
- By riverboat: The somewhat faster and more expensive method; deliveries will take 3 (virtual) weeks, or 1 full human day.
- By train (after the fall of 1881): The fast and expensive method; deliveries will take 1 virtual week (approximately 8 human hours).

Goods are delivered by teamsters who either haul them in from back east or pick them up at the riverside landing (or the railroad depot after 1881), and distribute them around town. The other source of supplies is other players in the game, who can sell goods to one another.

The Structure of Blackwood

The center of Blackwood is a town square, with a park in its center. The north/south roads are called "streets" and the major north/south street is "Center Street." The east/west roads are called "avenues" and the major east/west avenue is "Main Avenue." There are some angled streets, and these are called variously "road" or "boulevard" (but never street or avenue). Because of the local terrain, it is not always possible to travel the shortest distance between two points. For example, the only way to get to the railroad depot is to move east from the town square to the riverside neighborhood, and then northwest to the depot; there is no angled road directly from the town square to the depot (see the Town of Blackwood map: http://www.cs.ndsu.nodak.edu/~slator/html/blackwood/). Locations in the Blackwood region are defined in terms of consumer groups and their population. These population values will change over time to simulate the various ebbs and flows of the demographic landscape.

Stores are where business is transacted. Each store will be built the same: a front room where customers visit and transactions are accomplished, a back room for storage and/or production of goods, a basement for storage, and living quarters upstairs with a living/cooking/dining area and a sleeping area. Every store accommodates a live-in store employee who works for wages plus room and board.

Public places include the town square, the government/financial district, all the roads built into the simulation, and the wide-open spaces, which include ranchland, farmland, hill country, and forestland.

FUTURE PLANS FOR SOFTWARE AGENTS

Implementing more advanced agent functionality would introduce some interesting possibilities. For example, the customer agents in Dollar Bay and Blackwood are not aware of one another. Each virtual week, when the agent receives its shopping list, it blindly goes from store to store in the environment looking to make purchases. If these agents were able to view only a small part of their environment, the possibility arises for there to be a "rush" on a store, where suddenly customer after customer arrives as they can all sense a good deal—a plausible scenario.

Another possibility is that an agent observes many other agents frequenting a certain store and purchasing the same item. The observing agent originally may not want the item that the other agents are purchasing (not on its shopping list), but the agent buys the product anyway, figuring it must be desirable.

Finally, an agent representing an elite class (wealthy or retired person) may purchase an expensive item near an agent of a less elite class (blue collar worker or college student). Then, for example, the college student agent may observe this and decide, against its usual judgment, to purchase the more expensive item, since it now carries the weight of being purchased by someone who is wealthier. By giving the agents in Dollar Bay and Blackwood the ability to dynamically change their shopping lists, new and interesting aspects could be added to the games, giving participants a more realistic simulation.

CONCLUSION

Dollar Bay has been under development in various forms for several years. It is descended from a rich heritage of business simulations dating back to the 1950s and is still being improved today. The game has been used by a number of student groups over the years and has provided good results. However, it has shortcomings, as outlined above. First, the players have no incentive to interact, which reduces the value of the multi-user aspects of the game. Second, after 2 or 3 weeks, the simulation tends to "settle" so that certain players come to dominate sales. Third, Dollar Bay provides a weak role model and allows players to do everything and anything they want. This is not how stores operate at the "mom and pop" level, where specialization and niche finding are how to succeed.

Blackwood is designed to address some of the weaknesses of Dollar Bay, by creating a more structured environment to promote the role-based elements of the game. Players are given a choice of roles and then provided the tools necessary to succeed in the roles. The notion of time in Blackwood is more explicit, as opposed to in Dollar Bay, where each virtual week is much like the rest. In Blackwood, things change with time, and the economy grows and shrinks because of those changes. Lastly, Blackwood is an attempt at introducing students to American history by having them experience it, in a manner of speaking. The external events, and the stories in the newspaper, are taken from the historical record. In some small way, it is hoped, the idea of westward expansion will come through because of the Blackwood game.

Chapter 8

The Virtual Archaeologist

The Virtual Archaeologist uses an immersive virtual environment to present, in an intellectually engaging and stimulating way, the science of archaeology. Our goal is to develop an authentic simulation of an archaeological site within which the students face the problems archaeologists strive to solve while conducting field research. The site of concern here is Like-A-Fishhook, a village occupied in the 1800s by a combined population of Native Americans living in earthen lodges along the banks of the Missouri River in central North Dakota. Through the Virtual Archaeologist, the students shift from the world of the archaeological excavation to the past, when the site actually was occupied. By way of this virtual time travel, students learn how to use the faint traces and shattered remnants left in the ground to interpret what they represent.

The Virtual Archaeologist can be visited at http://fishhook .ndsu.edu/.

Archaeology is a discipline based on fieldwork. Normally, students learn about the conduct of archaeological research by taking a field school course, but there are severe limitations to such courses: Cost can be high, remote locations and conditions create various difficulties, only a limited number of students can participate at a time, and more. The conduct of a field project is also costly to the institution, as there are needs for supplies and equipment, radiocarbon or other dating methods, shipping of materials recovered from excavations, laboratory processing, curation facilities, and so on. Yet another issue is ethical in nature. Archaeological excavation is, by its very nature, a destructive process. Once an area is dug, there is no replacing it, and no going back to correct mistakes. As a result, there is a long-standing debate within archaeology about the ethics of using field schools for training students in archaeology. Many argue that nonrenewable, irreplaceable, archaeological sites should not be used as training grounds for novices prone to making mistakes.

There is, then, a very real need for a method of training that can eliminate the logistic, financial, and ethical problems entailed in teaching new generations of students about how archaeologists come to know about the past. We maintain that an acceptable alternative to fieldwork is authentic learning through an immersive virtual environment (IVE). The learner is placed in the environment of an archaeological site and faced with the challenges of interpreting the traces of past human behaviors revealed in the soil. The intent, here, is to teach not the

71

facts of the past, although some facts will be revealed through the process, but the practice of the science that is used to reveal the facts and to understand what they may tell us.

VIRTUAL ARCHAEOLOGIST

The goal of the Virtual Archaeologist (Slator, Clark et al., 2001) is to engage the players in how to think like an archaeologist: how and when to use techniques available to researchers, how to reason as an archaeologist, how to test ideas, and how to arrive at well-supported interpretations. To achieve that goal, we are constructing a highly interactive virtual archaeology simulation. The archaeological site selected for the simulation is Like-A-Fishhook Village in central North Dakota and dating to the mid-19th century. The simulation will consist of dual environments, or worlds, representing two different time periods at the same location. One world will represent the location as a modern archaeological excavation. This will be the primary world in which the students operate. The second world will mirror the first spatially, but will represent the Like-A-Fishhook/Fort Berthold site as it was—at least as can be reasonably modeled from all available evidence—in 1858. This mirroring will support "time travel" that will enable students to visit both times and to visualize the relationships between a dig and the life that produced the site and remains being dug.

We are basing the immersive environment on an actual site rather than an invented one because we are striving to make the immersive experience as authentic as possible. The choice of a site to model was difficult, as there are strengths and weaknesses for any selection. We needed a site at which extensive excavations had taken place and for which we would have ready access to excavation documentation and the artifacts recovered. We opted for a site that provided us with historic documents and visual guides in order to enhance our ability to produce an authentic representation. We also sought a site in which students will virtually experience a significant period of American history, as that will expand the ultimate usability of the simulation. Even though we are designing the game explicitly to teach students how to "think like an archaeologist," there are other domains of learning that will be incorporated through the use of an actual place and time. The Virtual Archaeologist can provide a learning environment for cultural anthropology, as students come to understand, for example, how a tobacco pipe or house altar fits into and informs us about the belief system of a group of people. Students also will be exposed to information and techniques in history and ethnohistory, Native American studies, and culture change.

The Like-A-Fishhook site matched all of those conditions. But it has a major drawback: The excavations were carried out half a century ago, so the methods used and analytical tools available were far from today's standards. We are, then, in a bind. To be completely faithful to the actual site and excavations, we would be forced to use outdated practices. We decided to avoid the messiness of having students deal with in three time periods—2004, 1954, and 1858—by taking artistic/creative license. We used the 1954 excavation data but dressed it up in modern methodology. Also, we soon realized that while the artifact collection from the site was extremely rich and varied, it lacked many objects that might have been recoverable; some of those objects will be added based on ethnographic collections. In all instances, though, we will be absolutely faithful to the realities of the time, place, and culture depicted.

CONTENT OF THE PROJECT:
THE LIKE-A-FISHHOOK STORY

In the years prior to and after the coming of White European-Americans (or from the late prehistoric into the early historic eras), the northern Great Plains of North America were occupied by multiple communities of Native Americans. Organized into tribal units, these groups practiced different adaptations to the plains environments. Some, such as the Mandan, Hidatsa, and Arikara, lived in sedentary villages along the Middle Missouri River, with earth-lodge houses built of timber and soil. They lived by farming small gardens, fishing in the rivers, and hunting on the plains. Others, like the Lakota, or Sioux, adopted the horse soon after it appeared on the plains and were nomads, moving with the bison upon which they relied for life. At the beginning of the 19th century, Americans of the fledgling nation began to explore the continent. As more European-Americans began trickling in, they brought various trade goods (e.g., guns, metal objects of all sorts, cloth, bottles, and so on), new ways of life, and new diseases.

Soon after White contact, bouts of smallpox began sweeping through the Middle Missouri villages. In the aftermath of the disease, and in the face of continuing attacks by Lakota (Sioux) tribes in the area, the Hidatsa tribe consolidated at a new village in about 1845, where they were joined almost immediately by the remnants of the Mandan tribe, all finding safety in numbers (Smith, 1972). This village was located just north of the confluence of the Missouri and Knife Rivers in central North Dakota, at a place where the Missouri had a sharp curve, making it reminiscent of a fishhook and giving the village its name, Like-A-Fishhook.

European-Americans were part of the community almost from the beginning. P. Chouteau, Jr. and Company, an offshoot of the American Fur Company, established a trading post on the northern periphery of the village. With a stockade and log buildings, this post became known as Fort Berthold. A wooden palisade was built around the village on three sides (the fourth being protected by the river) in 1850 to protect the inhabitants from Sioux raiding parties (Woolworth, 1969). In 1858, a competing fur trading company began construction on another fort, named Fort Atkinson (or Fort Berthold II). A few years later the first Fort Berthold burned to the ground in an attack by a Sioux war party (Woolworth, 1969). Although a few Arikara families had moved to the site earlier, in 1862, the Arikara arrived en masse for protection from the Sioux and established themselves in a new section of the village.

As the last earth-lodge settlement of the northern Great Plains, the site documents an extraordinary episode of cultural transformation (Smith, 1972). The fur traders were followed by missionaries, U.S. government representatives, and soldiers (Gilman & Schneider, 1987). As European-Americans moved into the region and the area surrounding Like-A-Fishhook Village, life changed significantly. By the 1860s the site was a mixed community of Native Americans, European-Americans, and mixed bloods, and it had become a base for U.S. military units campaigning against the Sioux and other militant Indians in the Dakota Territory. In the late 1880s, the U.S. government forced the village inhabitants to abandon Like-A-Fishhook and move to reservation land distributed to individuals.

The old village lay silent for decades, visited occasionally by its old residents, until the late 1940s when a dam was built on the Missouri River downstream from the village site. Archaeological salvage excavations were carried out at the site in 1950–1952 and 1954 by the State Historical Society of North Dakota and the National Park Service. Rising waters from the Garrison Dam and Reservoir ultimately inundated the site, which now rests about a mile offshore under the waters of Lake Sakakawea. The final report on that work was written by G. Hubert Smith (1972), who noted that "the abandonment of Like-a-Fishhook Village marked the close of a decisive era of Indian history in the Northern Plains" (p. v). All that remains of the Like-A-Fishhook site are the excavation records and the artifacts collected during excavations that occurred over half a century ago. Those materials, together with a rich ethnohistorical record, provide testimony to a significant period in American history. Through a virtual simulation, we will bring that important site back to light and use it as an educational tool.

THE VIRTUAL ENVIRONMENT

For the excavation world, the Like-A-Fishhook site is being treated as if it were not yet flooded, but the dam and flood are imminent. Thus, it is again, as is so often the case, a matter of salvaging invaluable information before it is lost forever. The layout of the simulation will be based largely on the records from the actual excavations in the 1950s. From those records we will reconstruct the landscape (as best as we can in the absence of precise information), establish the locations of the excavation units, and determine the distribution of archaeological features and floor plans (or bird's-eye views) of those features. These archaeological features include such things as linear trenches with wooden post remnants, low circular rises where earth lodges stood (20 were excavated) with a series of stains from structural posts, and a variety of soil discolorations from pits, fireplaces, and other features.

The historical world of the village will be recreated for the year 1858, a time when all three tribes were present, although the Arikara were there only in small numbers. The village had not yet become as crowded as it would just a few years later. Fort Berthold I was still standing, and construction of Fort Berthold II was beginning. We are basing the reconstructions of the site features on a variety of materials: excavation notes and maps (Smith, 1972; documents archived at the State Historical Society); photographs, paintings, and drawings (e.g., by Bodmer, Catlin, and de Trobriand) depicting the village or other villages and/or forts in the Middle Missouri region from the mid- and late 19th century, and numerous textual descriptions. Archaeological, ethnographical, and ethnohistorical publications on the site as well as the three tribes are extensive, with over 400 items identified and listed in our bibliography thus far. This bibliography will be accessible through the game (and posted elsewhere online; http://fishhook.ndsu.edu/biblio/), as will a compiled list of textual observations relevant to the reconstruction, organized and searchable by topic (e.g., "earth lodge" for information on what they looked like and how they were constructed). Digital copies of all the photographs and paintings for which we can secure releases will be made available to players through the site documentation portion of the game. In addition, we have the prior research of other scholars, which was used in the actual physical reconstructions of comparable earth lodges at two other sites, On-a-Slant and Knife River Indian Villages. What they learned in making their reconstructions aids us in our virtual reconstructions.

The earth lodges are reconstructed within the site based on their locations as depicted on the site maps. From a sketch map made in the 1800s, we can associate some of these lodges with actual named owners. The archaeological floor plans map out where the major posts and internal features (e.g., fireplaces and cache pits) were located. Approximate heights of the posts and construction techniques are gleaned from ethnohistorical accounts. One can then extrude the posts from the post molds, as shown in Figure 8.1.

The way to look at this graphic is counterclockwise from the upper left. There, the floor plan is encoded, using data from archaeological records, giving the dimensions from above (the "plan" view). Then 3D structures are created by extruding posts from the excavation floor plan (lower left). These structures are then "filled in" (lower right), and finally "textures" and other elements are added (upper right; also shown in Figure 8.2).

After experimenting with a few software packages, we selected Maya Unlimited, by Alias, as the primary tool for creating the virtual environment. Maya is arguably the premier 3D authoring software package available due to its capabilities and usability. Photoshop is used to create textures, which are 2D images that are then mapped onto the geometry created in Maya. Eventually, character

Figure 8.1. JPEG Image of the Infrastructure of a Lodge Created by Extruding Posts from the Excavation Floor Plan

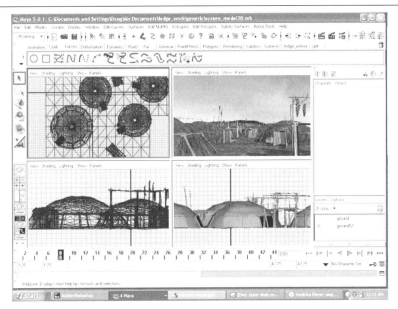

animations of people and animals (e.g., dogs and horses) will be added to the environment.

We will embed three-dimensional models of actual artifacts recovered from the site excavations, an innovation not found in other IVEs, throughout both of the virtual worlds. We are creating these models, or artifact surrogates, by scanning them with noncontact laser digitizers. The models can be fully manipulated to be viewed from all angles, and they are sufficiently precise to allow for a wide range of detailed measurements and analyses.

The Archaeology Technology Lab at North Dakota State University has been creating an inventory of 3D models of artifacts recovered from Like-A-Fishhook, and neighboring Mandan and Hidatsa sites, for inclusion in the Digital Archive Network for Anthropology and World Heritage (Clark et al., 2001; http://DANA-WH.net). In the virtual worlds, artifacts for which a 3D model is available are indicated by a clickable symbol that opens a new window within which the 3D surrogate appears. Artifacts in the excavation world will appear as they are now, which is typically broken. For the virtual village world, though, they will appear reconstructed, as they were when they were used. When those artifacts are presented to students for examination in the lab area of the environment, the students will be able to apply virtual calipers to take a variety of measurements and then record those measurements for subsequent analyses.

TEACHING WITH VIRTUAL ARCHAEOLOGY GAME PLAY

A critical feature of the game is that student users will be able to do what every archaeologist probably has dreamed of—to travel back in time and see how artifacts were really used, what soil features really represent, what activities really took place at some location, and much more. We are still in the development phase of this game and are operating on the basis of a game plan that undoubtedly will change as its implementation unfolds. With that in mind, what follows is an outline of the game plan as it currently is being developed.

The game premise is that a hydroelectric dam has been constructed on the Missouri River, and a Native American site is about to be inundated by the rising floodwaters. This site is a potential source of invaluable archaeological, anthropological, and historical knowledge, and so an emergency team has been dispatched to conduct a salvage excavation. Work has proceeded at a furious pace, and much of the excavation is underway, although some areas are yet to be opened (they will open as part of the game-play). More important, the documentation, analysis, and interpretation of the site and the materials it is producing have lagged far behind. Students have come to the site to aid in those processes.

When student players log in and arrive at the site, they are greeted by a software agent or tutor in the form of a seasoned, grizzled archaeologist who tells them what is going on at the site. He tells them that as archaeological field assistants, they will be given a series of assignments that they must carry out to aid in the excavation and interpretation of the site. The archaeologist points out which sources of help and information are available in the system, and describes the virtual tools and instruments the students have at their disposal. For instance, the tutor instructs the students on how to use the "utterance constructor" to form sentences from a list of word choices and phrases that can be stored in their electronic logbook, which is the portfolio they accumulate as they progress through the simulation. The students also are advised that software tutors will visit them if they are stuck or need help. Another important tool they are given is a "time arcing device" that will allow them to see into the past. They can use it, however, only after they have completed a specific assignment, and even then they are shown only glimpses of the past that relate to that assignment.

With this background, the students are given their first assignment: "Go north and west from here until you find the XU5 excavation area. It is clearly marked on your map." Once there, the students are given an assignment, which involves some analytical and interpretive task. In some instances, students also will be provided with interpretations of similar features or artifacts published by an eccentric archaeologist many years previously. The students will be asked to assess the validity of those interpretations against their observations and interpretation of the archaeological data. When that assignment is completed, the students will be allowed to use the arcing device to get a view of the past that will confirm or invalidate their interpretation. Then another assignment is issued, and so on, until the game has been completed. The interpretive goals will increase in complexity as the game progresses, eventually leading to interpretations of more abstract sociocultural phenomena (e.g., region). Because this is a multi-user environment, students may meet and converse with other students who are at the site.

In general, students earn points as they work their way through each assignment. In most cases, student actions are driven by a set of drop-down menus of "actions" that are short lists of choices. The choices are differentially valued, with points based on the level of acceptability of the action, although the point values are not displayed until an action is selected. Once the points are displayed, students are guided as to which of the actions to implement with the next click. These menus and points lead students to employ the proper method for the specific case, to record their findings, to analyze the data collected, and to arrive at a conclusion relevant to the assignment. Their initial selection at each set of actions, however, is what generates the points.

To illustrate, we provide a condensed summary of an assignment scenario. The students are directed to an excavation area in which they see a dark, grayish stain in the soil, about a meter in diameter. The assignment is to determine what the stain represents. From the drop-down menu they see multiple options from which to select: "To proceed, you should: a) continue digging the entire unit; b) map and photograph the stain before proceeding to dig out the discolored soil [the correct procedure]; c) dig out the stain area separate from the rest of the layer." After the students click on a response, the points for each action are revealed: a = 0, b = 10, c = 5.

Based on the revealed points, the students select again, this time to initiate the action: generate a map and a digital image of the stain, which are stored in the field logbook.

The students then select from the next set of options for excavating the stain area: "a) bisect the stain and dig out only half at a time, saving the soil for subsequent water separation at the lab (10); b) bisect the stain and dig out only half at a time, screening the extracted soil and picking out and saving materials left in the screen for the lab [as all of the other soil in the unit has been handled] (5); c) dig out the entire unit as a whole, discarding the soil but saving any artifact or bone discovered while digging (0)."

The students are given this information: "While digging, you observe the following conditions: the soil is gray to white at times but it is not uniform in color, having darker and lighter bands. You rub it between your fingers and find that it is soft, almost silty. You also observe, scattered through it, bits of hard material that vary in color from white to gray to black, sometimes with an almost spongy character on one side of a piece. There are also bits of black material that crush easily between your fingers and smudge black. Record these observations in your field logbook and hypothesize what each represents."

The student then selects from the next set of options: "In digging, you quickly discover stone slabs that seem to be standing on edge, and they form a circle surrounding the stained soil. You then: a) remove the stones as you encounter them (0); b) map each one and then remove it (5); c) leave them in place and revealed as you continue to dig out the stain (10)."

The student is then presented with this question: "While digging, occasional large pieces of what appears to be carbonized wood are revealed: a) save each, wrapping it in clean foil, and labeling them for radiocarbon or wood analysis (10); dig them out with the rest of the soil (5); c) discard them (0)."

The student is asked to decide: "You completely remove the discolored soil to reveal the semicircle of stones and underlying soil that is similar to the surrounding soil. Next you: a) photograph and map the area excavated, and draw a cross-section view at the line of bisection (10); dig out the other half of the stain following the same procedure (5); c) dig out the other half of the stain but discard the soil because you already have a sample (0)."

After photographing and drawing the feature, the students are directed to excavate the second half and again photograph and map it.

They are then instructed, "Record in your logbook what you think the feature represents. Is it cultural or natural? What do you think it is? How would you test that interpretation?"

The recorded conclusion should be that they have excavated a fireplace (10 points, 0 for any other response). From there, the students are directed to the field lab to test their hypothesis. Using the soil collected from the feature, they are guided—earning points as they go—to test the soil and its contents. In doing so, they discover that the soil has significant ash content. They are guided to do water separation of a large sample to recover organic matter. They recover carbonized seeds, which they later will identify as to species for information on ecological surroundings. They will find that the dark smudgy bits are charcoal, and that the hard white and black pieces are burned bone, which again will be identified later as to the animals represented. Finally, they are asked if their original hypothesis is supported (10 points), not supported (5 points), or refuted (0 points). If it is not supported, how do they now interpret the feature?

At this point, the players are told they can use the time arcing device. By pressing the "mini-arc" button, they get a glimpse of the past, as a new window pops up with the feature "restored" as it was when it was used. They see a large, stone-lined circle with burning wood, a low flame and some smoke, perhaps a rabbit cooking on a spit. Then, the image disappears and a new assignment pops up on the screen. And so it goes. They excavate and interpret a sweat lodge, a cache pit for storing corn, the area of the horse coral, the posts of the lodge structure, and so on. Ultimately, they come to realize that these features are all are part of a single social and structural entity—that they are all constituent parts of an earth lodge. Beyond the lodge, they find the remains of scaffolding where food was dried and kept away from animals, an area where men flaked stone to make tools, an area where women made and fired pottery, the village palisade, the trading post, and much more. At one point, they will explore an area where they recover extensive charcoal, large pieces of burned logs, lots of ash, pink to orange oxidized soil, and other evidence of burned domestic tools. From this evidence they will come to conclude that an earth lodge burned down at that location.

As with any game, there should be rewards and a goal. First, as noted, student players will earn points for their efforts. They can compare their assignment scores with a list of possible points for that exercise, or their total points with the number possible for the game. The larger goal is to see the village simulation in its entirety. Once students have completed all of the assignments, the time arcing device can be used to its full effect, which is to virtually transport the students back in time to the full site. Once there, they can wander through the village as they please, in and out of earth lodges, down to the river, to the gardens, and so on. All of the past images of the site that the students saw after each assignment now fit into the larger picture. The features, artifacts, charcoal, bones, and so on, are now revealed in their full context, and the students can explore the world at their leisure.

The village is visualized with earth lodges, as seen in Figure 8.2, with various authentic elements, including a drying rack, on the far right, where foodstuffs were raised off the ground to keep them away from children and dogs.

Figure 8.2. Screen Capture of the Exterior of the Village (Still in Development)

IMPLEMENTATION DETAIL

The Virtual Archaeologist will be designed on the client–server model, with the server processes hosted on LambdaMOO and the client software implemented in Java. The client software will be accessible via the Internet and standard browser software and the use of a registered password. Along with hosting the virtual worlds, the server database will manage all associated records (e.g., student logins and all aspects of play history) and synchronize the interactions between multiple users. For the simulated worlds, the server will store the descriptions and orientations of the landscape, site structures, and embedded artifacts. In short, the server will enable the client to know which VRML elements to load for the players' current state and what information students are requesting or storing.

The 3D structure developed from the engineering software (Figure 8.1) produces a 3D lodge, which is placed in the reconstructed village (Figure 8.2). Then, the interiors of selected lodges are constructed with features taken from the archaeological record. Figure 8.3 shows a fire pit with a pot hanging from a chain in the foreground, with sleeping chambers against the back wall, and light flowing in from the smoke hole in the roof.

An innovative feature, not found in other WWWIC IVEs, is being developed for the Virtual Archaeologist. For the client side interaction, we plan to create an utterance constructor to allow students to make statements in their logbooks about their findings. These statements need to be coherent and interpretable by the system so they can be evaluated automatically for accuracy. We have developed a prototype of such an interface, which is mainly a set of sequential menus of word choices, allowing students to select vocabulary from lists and compose sentences using the words. This has the advantage of requiring the students to generate their statements rather than selecting from predetermined choices (note also that a large number of choices are available to students at any point, as they select from a sequence of lists of nouns, then verbs, then prepositions, and so forth; the "space" of possible statements can be quite large, which is good, and not limiting). Similar interfaces have been implemented elsewhere (e.g., Saunders, Sierant,

Figure 8.3. Screen Capture of the Inside of an Earth Lodge (Still in Development)

Downey, & Blevis, 1994), although ours will differ somewhat in being contextual and server-loaded to support multiple users.

As with other WWWIC systems, the Virtual Archaeologist will employ intelligent software agents to provide guidance to the players. These agents will provide domain-based expertise and, as such, will constitute automatically generated surrogates for the instructor. The agents are triggered by user actions. Since all of the information for the simulation is readily available from the server, tutors can be generated immediately in response to player actions in order to provide explanations, give warnings, or make suggestions. The utterance constructor will play an important role in this regard.

This project will follow the procedures already established by Virtual Cell and Geology Explorer in conducting both formative and summative evaluations. The formative evaluation will provide us with information necessary to continue to improve both the conceptual learning and virtual components of the game. The summative evaluation will provide an overall indication of project success. The summative evaluation, to be completed at the end of the initial development and implementation period, will be especially useful for dissemination of project results to other institutions.

We plan to develop an Instructor's Manual for the Virtual Archaeologist that will be refined with use and made available to new adopters. We also will prepare a Student Users' Manual that can be consulted before the game or between sessions. This tutorial will contain specific instructions and an FAQ section with answers to questions about logging in, getting goals, obtaining background information, performing experiments, drop-down menu descriptions, and user-to-user communications.

CONCLUSION

While this project presents some interesting challenges in terms of software innovation (e.g., the contextual utterance constructor, synchronizing 3D visualizations of different time periods, and developing software guides and tutors relevant to the subject matter), the principal innovation lies in educational materials development. Since the 1980s, a small number of archaeologists, both anthropological and classical, have experimented with 3D graphics and virtual reality modeling for archaeology (see Barcelo et al., 2000; Forte & Siliotti, 1997; Higgins et al., 1996; Lockyear & Rahtz, 1991; Stancic & Veljanovski, 2001). Those applications have aimed predominantly at creating limited virtual reality environments. Those efforts have increased in sophistication and number, especially in the past few years, but they are still comparatively uncommon. Moreover, they have been used primarily as "display pieces" and not as exploratory, goal-driven, role-based simulations for student learning. Further, we are not aware of any such reconstructions that facilitate "time travel" between different models of the same place or of the effective embedding of 3D artifact surrogates within a virtual world. What we are creating with the Virtual Archaeologist is a new, innovative immersive virtual environment enabling students to virtually experience archaeology firsthand.

PART III

OTHER STUFF ABOUT OUR WORLDS

This part explores the other stuff that goes into constructing our worlds. Each chapter concentrates on something that adds to the overall group effort. The similarities of the projects are intentional, in an effort to maximize sharing and software reuse, among other things. The games are designed to resemble one another, and this signature is designed to assist with perceiving these projects as part of a single piece—a coherent set of related efforts.

There are many similarities among the games, and assessment and evaluation procedures are similarly conjoined. The assessments and evaluations are all built on the same model. This is so the projects can be compared both longitudinally and latitudinally. In other words, there is a master plan, and this becomes nowhere more obvious than when general concerns like assessment and evaluation are considered.

This part begins with a description of the range of procedures used for the assessment of student learning and the evaluation of instructional systems that permeate the many ongoing efforts described in earlier chapters.

Following that is a chapter describing work by others related to what has been done here. Next is a chapter filled with technical details for those seeking a nuts-and-bolts explanation of how these systems are built. Finally, there is a chapter devoted to speculation about the future.

This is the other stuff about our worlds.

Chapter 9

Assessment and Evaluation

The terms *assessment* and *evaluation* sometimes are used interchangeably. However, it is more common for assessment to refer to assessment of student learning, and evaluation to refer to evaluation of instructional programs—and this is how we use them here.

Assessment of student learning most often is attempted through the use of standardized tests, which is the most convenient and economical approach. However, this method is sometimes criticized for being superficial and inauthentic. In keeping with the theme of this book, this chapter describes a more authentic method called scenario-based assessment. In addition, results are reported from some studies using our virtual worlds.

Evaluation of instructional programs usually refers to the feedback gathered from students (and teachers), probing for perceived value. There are a number of methods for doing this: surveys and questionnaires, post hoc interviews, focus groups, and so on. The evaluation of virtual worlds poses a problem that is somewhat different from the norm, and this chapter describes the approach and instruments we have developed to address the issue.

We have developed software systems to streamline the assessment and evaluation processes. This includes systems for gathering data, managing student records, scoring assessments, and even training graders.

Lastly, we report on a small study conducted using transcript data that attempted, using simple data-mining techniques, to discover meaningful patterns of student behaviors in virtual worlds. We believe these preliminary results may lead to future research questions in the educational uses of virtual worlds.

The process of learning has been the subject of countless experimental studies in the past century. Indeed, the history of modern education is a circular tale of innovation, first theorized, then introduced, studied and debated, and finally rejected or incorporated, followed by a short spell of quiescence, which ends with a new theory being introduced, to start the cycle over again.

Quantitative measures are extremely important in any discipline where research and innovation lay claim to improvement. Empirical studies in education have become increasingly emphasized in recent years, and standardized tests have gained enormous currency at state and national levels. Meanwhile, the results of international competitions between the grade school children of various nations has fueled national pride and education funding initiatives around the world. Thus, assessment and evaluation are very important topics in education. The results of controlled studies are used to make decisions that can have far-reaching effects.

ASSESSMENT METHODS AND MEASURES

The study of learning attempts to show how different tools and pedagogical techniques affect student ability to acquire and retain knowledge. Quantification of this acquisition and retention is approached empirically, using a variety of methods and measures. In these experiments, typically students first are tested and rated along some objective scale, then are subjected to some form of "treatment," and finally are tested again. These pre- and posttreatment data are analyzed for signs of improved student performance, and the effects are causally attributed to the treatment. Objective methods for the assessment of learning generally rely on measuring student recall of factual material. They seldom attempt to measure higher order thinking or problem-solving skills.

Over the years, the nature of these treatments has varied considerably: from the ambient light in a classroom, to the number of students in a class, to the kinds of technology available for student use. From these studies has come much of what we know and believe about effective education: Small class size and individualized instruction are helpful, adequate lighting is important, and technology through the ages has made little real difference (Gormly, 1996).

Indeed, experiments to measure improvements in student learning as a consequence of new pedagogy, or new technology, are typically inconclusive from a statistical standpoint. Historically, large student groups are remarkably resistant, overall, to the influences of alternative methods of instruction, changes in pedagogy, or new technology, and few studies show statistically significant improvement in learning when compared with control groups. This is probably due to a combination of factors, but the case remains that no treatments have been found that result in a statistically significant difference in student performance as measured by changes in the usual objective instruments (i.e., standardized tests or final grades).

SCENARIO-BASED ASSESSMENT

One proven method of learner assessment is pre- and posttest interviews. In Bell, Bareiss, and Beckwith (1994), an innovative approach is employed. A pretest interview is conducted in which the interviewer recounts a problem-solving scenario to the individual subjects. These narratives take the form of stories about facing problems in the domain of interest. The subjects are then encouraged to pose possible solutions and are allowed to ask any questions that come to mind. The interviewer is armed with a small set of additional facts with which to answer questions, and makes note of whatever issues the subject attended to in the course of the interview. Subsequent protocol analysis shows whether this method was effective at uncovering the variables deemed important to the subject in terms of solving the problem. For example, in a story about finding a rock with a brilliant metallic yellow streak, do they ask about the hardness of the streak (hypothesizing it might be soft and malleable like gold)?

Subjects then are exposed to the particular teaching or training system being tested. Afterwards, subjects are engaged in a similar posttest interview session. Advances in student learning are recorded and evaluated in terms of the students' recall of important problem-solving variables. Notice that students are not given recognition tasks (i.e., a multiple-choice exam). This method of learner assessment has been shown to be effective, and is particularly attractive in requiring generative behavior from learners. Unlike objective tests that present alternative answers for learners to recognize and choose from, this method gauges recall rather than recognition.

Scenario-Based Assessment Protocol

The problem with scenario-based assessment, as just described, is its labor-intensive nature. First, interviewers must be trained, and each interview takes a certain amount of time to complete. Then, transcripts must be analyzed and results coded for statistical analysis. Therefore, the expense in both time and money is considerable, and the result is a relatively small data set (a few dozen student interviews being the most that could reasonably be expected).

Because of access to fairly large student groups (discussed below), it was feasible to take another approach—a strategy that traded the detailed results of interview-based methods for the reliability that comes along with large numbers. This was accomplished by implementing an online software system designed to capture equivalent data but at much less expense.

The first step in this process is to create an experimental design. Figure 9.1 shows one particular example. In this case, an entire class of more than 400 students is given a pretreatment assessment instrument (see Figure 9.2) that tells the story of finding a rock with a brilliant metallic yellow streak while on a fishing trip. The students (in this case, taking a first-year college course in physical geology) each read the story and answer the questions at the bottom of the form.

Note that the questions are open-ended. There is no "right answer" and students are not asked to provide one. Rather, students are asked to list the questions they would ask and the factors they would consider in making a decision.

The pretreatment data are put aside for later analysis. Next, the students are asked to volunteer to test educational software (in exchange for extra credit points). Those that do not volunteer form a control group of sorts—although later they are excluded from the study data set due to unequal participation.

Meanwhile, the volunteers are given a computer literacy survey with about 40 questions designed to determine how experienced and proficient each is with computers. The survey also asks for gender and whether they have had a related laboratory course in the past. These three factors, computer literacy, gender, and lab experience, are used to create two random but balanced groups. In other words, both groups have the same range of computer experience, the same number of men and women, and the same number of people with and without lab experience. In this way we ensure the two groups are equivalent and that comparisons between them are fair.

At this point, the study is ready, and the students are given a period of time (usually a week to 10 days) to complete the assignment at their own pace. One of

Figure 9.1. Scenario-Based Assessment Protocol Flowchart

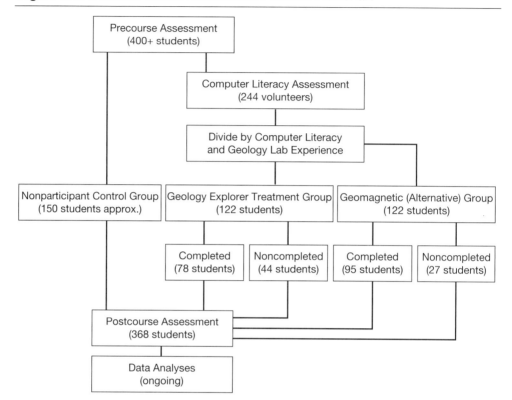

the groups explores a virtual world, while the other group does some sort of alternative exercise—usually a web-based reading and quiz assignment, or something else where the content is relevant to the course, and the time-on-task is approximately the same. This last point is quite important, as time-on-task is an important variable in learning and so must be accounted for in the experimental design; otherwise, the results can be confounded—that is, the study will be judged as flawed.

At the end of the treatment period, the students are asked to fill out a second scenario-based assessment, usually a slightly different story, but on the same theme; further, they are required to fill out an evaluation form about how they perceived the game, its strengths, and its weaknesses. Trained experts then evaluate student responses for both content knowledge and correctness of scientific reasoning, using a structured rubric (see Figure 9.3).

The figure shows the form used by graders, sometimes referred to as "coders," to evaluate student responses to the scenario-based assessment questions (Figure 9.2). A different rubric is developed for each scenario, but they all follow the same general pattern. Up to 60 points are assigned for problem-solving responses, broken down into three subcategories: hypothesis formation, experimentation, and drawing conclusions. Another 25–30 points are available containing specific information, such as the relative hardness of different substances.

Figure 9.2. A Sample Scenario—Manitoba Fishing

> You are in northern Manitoba on a fishing trip. Fishing has been good. At dawn on the day of your departure, you cut across country to a remote bay and have more good luck: You catch your limit of walleye.
>
> On the way back to the lodge, you stumble across a heavy, moss-covered rock on the shoreline, flipping it over. Looking down, you see the underside of the rock shining with a brilliant metallic yellow. You pick up the rock and lug it back to the lodge.
>
> At the airport luggage check-in, the baggage agent notes that you are 20 kg overweight . . . exactly the weight of the rock that you found. He says, "It's okay to ship rocks back to the States, eh, but at $15 per kilogram, eh, you're going to owe $300!"
>
> As a geologist, what do you do? Please respond to the following:
>
> 1. List the questions you would ask yourself, giving reasons behind asking those particular questions:
>
>
> 2. List the factors that you would consider in making your final decision:

Lastly, an additional 5–10 points for expert knowledge can be earned by giving relevant specialized information relating to the problem, such as that gold is indeed found in Manitoba.

These rubrics are used to guide the graders as they evaluate the student answers. The scores are recorded and then the difference between pre- and post-treatment answers is calculated for both groups. Finally statistical analysis is conducted to determine whether one group has performed better than another. The results of some of these experiments are detailed below.

Two additional points should be noted concerning the scoring rubrics. First, they are designed to assist the graders with a view toward maintaining consistency between them. In the experiments described here, it is typical for the scenario answers to be graded by two or more experts. Statistical measures are applied to their grading, and correlation is measured between them to ensure that consistency is maintained.

Second, as might be guessed, it is quite difficult to record the maximum score under these rubrics. Indeed, the rubrics are designed so that a very knowledgeable and mature answer is required to score all the points. This is intentional, as the rubrics were designed to account for a very wide range of skills. As a consequence, the scores are often quite low, especially in the pretreatment case, where zeroes are not uncommon.

It should be noted, too, that scenario scores are kept confidential and are not even shared with the students. These data are used to measure the relative success of the treatments, typically are not shared with the course instructor, and do not affect students' grades. Rather, students get course credit through the use of "embedded assessments."

Figure 9.3. Scoring Rubric for the Manitoba Fishing Scenario

Scoring is divided into three categories weighted from highest to lowest as follows:

1) General Problem Solving: 60 points
2) Specific Information: 25–30 points
3) Expert Knowledge: 5–10 points

General Problem Solving
   Scoring consists of three sections worth 20 points each. With 60 points possible, this category is weighted highest because it deals with students' ability to scientifically approach, manipulate, and make conclusions on a problem. The three sections include:

1) Hypothesis Formation: 0–20 points based on the strength of questions and strategies for solving the scenario. Hypotheses are judged on how well they fit the problem and their testability
2) Experimentation: points awarded for listing diagnostic tests on the following scale. Points are compounded with a maximum of 20:
   • 8 points for first correct test
   • 7 points for second correct test
   • 5 points for third correct test
   • 3 points for naming a test unsuitable for the situation
3) Drawing conclusions based on evidence/theory: 0–20 points based on the strength and reasoning of conclusions

Specific Information
   Divided into several elements each worth 5 or 10 (most important to solving problem) points. Naming a test is given 2/5 credit, while giving actual mineral properties is given full credit for the element (such as "quartz should scratch glass, but not diamond"). Examples of elements are: hardness, cleavage, taste, soluability.

Expert Knowledge
   Points awarded in this category are for other expert geologic or specific knowledge. Points are based on the usefulness of the information in helping to resolve the problem. Examples of useful knowledge receiving points in this category are:

   • the value of gold per ounce
   • locations where diamonds are found
   • presence of artifacts in specific regions

Embedded Assessment

When learners join the synthetic environment, they are assigned goals, selected by content matter experts to be appropriate to their experience. Goals are assigned point values, and learners accumulate objectively measured scores as they achieve their goals. The goals are taken from a principled set, where easier goals are followed by more advanced ones. Similarly, some virtual worlds divide the goals further. For example, in the Geology Explorer, certain goals in a set are required, while others are optional. In this way, designers can ensure that highly important concepts are thoroughly covered, while allowing learners the maximum flexibility.

   Subject matter experts identify the objectives in more-or-less traditional ways based on their experience with teaching the subject, while learner outcomes are assessed in terms of the performance of specific and authentic tasks. This is the particular strength of learn-by-doing immersive environments—that the learners' success in achieving their goals provides an automatic assessment of their progress.

ASSESSMENT EXPERIMENT RESULTS

A number of studies have been conducted using the experimental design described above. Two of these are described below. A warning to the uninitiated—the next several sections include technical details concerning statistical analysis.

A Geology Explorer Experiment

The following Geology Explorer experiment was conducted in a first-year college course, Physical Geology 105, affectionately known as "Rocks for Jocks," which traditionally is conducted in a large lecture hall seating more than 400 students in the fall semester every year. The details of the experiment are as follows.

1. On the first day of the semester, all 425 students enrolled in NDSU's Physical Geology course completed a pretreatment assessment scenario (Figure 9.2).
2. At mid-semester, all students still enrolled were invited to participate in an evaluation of web-based geologic software in exchange for a small amount of extra credit. Of the approximately 400 students, 244 volunteered. This cadre of volunteers was then divided into two evaluation groups, split equally relative to computer literacy, gender (evaluated by survey), and geologic laboratory experience.
    a) One evaluation group was assigned to the Geology Explorer, where they were required to complete 500 points worth of goals on the virtual Planet Oit. Each student was given a two-page description of the task and a list of URLs providing background information, a graphical map of the planet, and an online user card. Of the 122 students assigned to the Geology Explorer exercise, 78 completed the requirements of the project.
    b) The second evaluation group was assigned to complete a geomagnetic/map analysis project of similar rigor to that of the Geology Explorer. This group was required to obtain basic map and elevation data and then interact with those data through the National Geophysical Data Center web site. Each student was given a two-page description of the task and a list of URLs providing supporting information resources. Of the 122 students assigned to the geomagnetic exercise, 95 completed the requirements of the project.
3. On the last day of the semester, all 368 students still enrolled in Physical Geology completed an assessment scenario similar to that given on the first day. Thus, students who participated in the Geology Explorer exercise could be assessed for learning performance versus two control groups: (1) those who participated in the web-based geologic software exercise of similar rigor, and (2) those who did not participate in any additional exercise at all.

In addition to this formatted assessment, every student involved in the Geology Explorer exercise was automatically tracked through the program's software relative to such factors as

1. time-on-task,
2. completion of assigned (100-point) goals,
3. completion of unassigned (25-point) goals,
4. experiments (field tests) conducted,
5. movements through the virtual environment, and
6. requests to the online help system and visits from tutoring agents.

Geology Explorer Experimental Results

Analysis of covariance (ANCOVA) models was conducted for each of the three graders: Brian, Ned, and Jane (not their real names). ANCOVA models were analyzed using PROC GLM in SAS. The ANCOVA model predicts the graders' postscore (after treatment) using the group variable (Oit, Alternative, Control) and the graders' prescores (before treatment) as the continuous covariate.

Since the scenarios differed (some were easier than others), the postscenario number was also an important variable in predicting postscenario scores. Gender and prescenario number also were included in the initial models.

We examined the ANCOVA model using all the above variables, including interactions. In all but one instance, no interactions were significant, and all interactions were excluded from the models. Main effect models using the above variables were examined, and no gender or prescenario number effects were found to be significant.

The final model included postscenario number (Brian $p = 0.0001$, Ned $p = 0.0001$, Jane $p = 0.0001$), group (Brian $p = 0.0003$, Ned $p = 0.0339$, Jane $p = 0.0116$), and prescenario score (Brian $p = 0.0001$, Ned $p = 0.0004$, Jane $p = 0.0004$) as the continuous covariate.

The results for all three graders paralleled one another. Brian's scores showed the clearest performance gain for Planet Oit. Duncan's multiple range test (Duncan, 1955) was used to investigate the main postscenario effects; results are presented in Table 9.1. Duncan's multiple range test forms clusters with similar means. The Planet Oit group had higher scores than the other two groups, which were the same.

The way to read the table is to look at the row headings, which are A, B, and B. These are key indicators in statistical analysis, denoting groups. In this table, the first row, A, is statistically different from the second and third rows, labeled B. For example, the first column shows that Brian graded the Planet Oit group, and the group average was 40.5 out of 100. The "no activity" group averaged 29.3 and the "alternative exercise" group averaged 25.1. The difference between 29.3 and 25.1 is not statistically significant, so these are both labeled B. However, the difference between these two and 40.5 is statistically significant, and this demonstrates that the Planet Oit group did significantly better than the other two groups. The other implication of Table 9.1 is that this result held true for three different graders, not just one. Ned and Jane also came to the same conclusion. And, all three graded all of the posttreatment scenario answers independently, which strengthens the result.

Now we describe a similar study, with similar results, for the Virtual Cell.

Table 9.1. Duncan's Multiple Range Test on Planet Oit Group Means

Duncan grouping	Brian mean	Ned mean	Jane mean	Group
A	40.5	35.4	53.4	Planet Oit group
B	29.3	27.0	42.6	Control (no activity) group
B	25.1	25.5	42.6	Alternative exercise group

A Virtual Cell Experiment

The long-term project goals of the Virtual Cell are to: (1) develop an innovative, role-based environment for teaching cell biology; (2) investigate and measure the efficacy of this approach for science learning; and (3) partner with educators at other institutions in order to implement this approach as an alternative to existing strategies.

The experiment described below used a working prototype that consisted of two modules: Organelle Identification and Cellular Respiration. The results of this experiment, with a large first-year college course, General Biology 150, demonstrated that users of the Virtual Cell perform significantly better on tests that gauge the ability of students to act as a cell biologist.

To test whether users of the Virtual Cell have an increased ability over other students to solve cell biology problems in a manner reminiscent of a professional in the field of cell biology, we collaborated with instructors teaching the large-enrollment General Biology course. General Biology is an introductory course for science majors that concentrates on cellular and molecular biology, genetics, and evolution. The course is geared toward serious science students, such as those in the pre-med program, and has a reputation for being a hard course. Students were recruited to the experiment by being offered the opportunity to earn extra credit points. Participants completed a self-evaluation in which they rated their abilities and experience working with computers and computer software—the same computer literacy survey described above, which also determines gender and previous laboratory experience.

The volunteers were assigned to the Virtual Cell and alternative experimental groups in a manner such that the distribution of computer skills, gender, and lab experience was equal for both groups. Those students who did not volunteer formed the control group. This group did not participate in any educational activities beyond the usual lectures and laboratories.

Members of the Virtual Cell experimental group completed two Virtual Cell modules. The first module, Organelle Identification, was completed at the beginning of the semester. The second module, Cellular Respiration, was completed 6 weeks later. Students were given 10 days to complete each module. Student progress through the modules was followed by a game-like point scoring system and by analyzing Virtual Cell progress data stored on the Virtual Cell server.

The alternative group was included to serve as a computer-based, time-on-task control because it is important to determine whether any improvement is related to the Virtual Cell or the additional time students spent with the course materials. Students assigned to the alternative group were sent to a series of web sites that contained content material similar to that offered in the Virtual Cell modules. Participation was monitored by completion of an online quiz. Each quiz was evaluated to determine whether the students made an honest effort to study the web sites. Specific questions were included that could be answered only if they visited the site.

All students, whether in control or test groups, were asked to complete two scenario-based questions at the beginning of the semester before the Virtual Cell or alternative assignments were given to the participants. One question asked them to act as a cell biologist and design experimental approaches to solving a problem in which they must distinguish between cellular organelles (see Figure 9.4). The second question tested the students' ability to determine experimentally why reactions related to mitochondrial electron transport were not functioning properly. Similar scenario questions were given to all students at the end of the semester. A total of 332 students answered both the pre- and posttreatment questions.

Two M.S. students in biology independently graded each of the 1,328 answers (332 students, 4 questions each, two pre and two post). Prior to grading, the students were trained according to standard evaluation rubrics. The standardized rubrics developed to guide the VCell graders were virtually identical to those used in the Geology Explorer study described above.

The grading scale for each question ranged from 0 to 100. A score of 100 reflected the type of answer a Ph.D. practicing in the field of cell biology might provide. Like the Geology Explorer assessment described above, it is extremely difficult to get a perfect score on this assessment. This scale was chosen because in the future we intend to expand testing of Virtual Cell modules on high school, advanced undergraduate, and graduate students. This indicated the need for a grading scale that would apply to students of any educational level.

Meanwhile, the grader training appeared to be effective because the correlation between the 1,328 scores assigned by each of the two graders was significantly different from zero ($r = 0.75$). On this basis, the average of the two grader scores was used as the experimental observation in this study.

Figure 9.4. A Sample Scenario Used for VCell Assessment

You are on a foreign fellowship to work with Dr. Larsson in Sweden. Dr. Larsson is a cell biologist who specializes in human diseases. A new group of patients arrived recently exhibiting myopathy, a severe muscle weakness. The most prominent symptom is the severe muscular weakness that occurs after a short period of exercise. Using his vast experience with cellular diseases, Dr. Larsson immediately suggests the Golgi apparatus is not functioning properly. This strikes you as not quite right. You suspect another organelle is not functioning correctly. You quickly volunteer to test Dr. Larsson's hypothesis.

1. While thinking as a biologist, list the things you will consider when designing your experiments.
2. Briefly describe the experimental results that will allow you to define which organelle is not functioning properly.

Virtual Cell Experimental Results

One-way analysis of variances was performed to compare the mean scores for the pre- and posttreatment scenarios for the combined data of the two graders. From the group means, it can be concluded that students who completed the Virtual Cell modules performed significantly higher on the postscenario tests than either the control or alternative group. This result was observed for questions relating to both the Organelle Identification and Cellular Respiration modules. In contrast, the pretreatment test scores among the three groups were not significantly different for the Cellular Respiration module.

This large experiment clearly demonstrates that the Virtual Cell experience has a significantly positive effect on the ability of students to solve problems in the role of a cell biologist. The fact that the mean value for the Virtual Cell group is significantly higher than for the alternative group strongly suggests the improved ability is not simply the result of computer-based time-on-task, but rather is directly related to the Virtual Cell experience.

This analysis, shown in Table 9.2, is slightly more complex because the Virtual Cell results are broken down by module. The way to read the table is to look at the lower case letters next to the numbers. For example, in the cellular respiration columns, the average score for the control group before the experiment was 7.6, and the alternative exercise and Virtual Cell groups scored 8.8 and 8.0, respectively. All three of these numbers have a lower case "a" next to them, meaning they are essentially the same, statistically speaking. In other words, 7.6, 8.8, and 8.0 are effectively tied—there is no real statistical difference between them.

The next column, however, shows us that the control group scored 10.6 and the alternative exercise group scored 13.7. These two groups were statistically tied, and they both have a lower case "a" assigned to them. By contrast, the Virtual Cell group scored 17.3, which has a lower case "b" assigned to it. In other words, the VCell group did significantly better than the other two. The organelle identification columns are less clear because 11.5 and 13.5 are tied, and 13.5 and 15.5 are also tied—but 11.5 and 15.5 are not, thus 13.5 has a lower case "ab."

These results are more than just encouraging. The experimental effect is similar to that observed with the Geology Explorer, which used the same type of control and alternative groups as in this Virtual Cell experiment. In both of these

Table 9.2. Mean and F-probability for the Virtual Cell Experiment

	Organelle Identification		Cellular Respiration	
	Pretest Scenario	Posttest Scenario	Pretest Scenario	Posttest Scenario
Control Mean*	11.5a	17.4a	7.6a	10.6a
Alternate Mean	13.5ab	19.7a	8.8a	13.7a
Virtual Cell Mean	15.5b	22.7b	8.0a	17.3b
F-probability	0.005	0.001	0.431	0.001

* Population sizes are: control = 145; alternative = 94; and Virtual Cell = 93.

experiments, the test scores of the students who used the virtual world were significantly higher than those of either the control or alternative group. Combined, these large-scale experiments provide solid evidence of the worth of virtual worlds in science education.

SUPPORT SYSTEMS

It turns out that developing virtual worlds for education entails a lot more software development than it would seem at first. Assessment and evaluation data must be collected, and scenarios must be graded. User accounts must be created and managed. Student progress must be tracked and recorded. Teachers need to set up and schedule activities. None of this is automatic—it all needs to be implemented and tested.

To meet all these needs, we had to develop innovative methods for managing research studies by building web-based educational research management tools. These tools were used to develop, coordinate, and manage the studies described above. One of the more recent Virtual Cell studies, for example, included four institutions of higher education and was conducted with more than 1,000 introductory biology students.

Web-based education research management systems (WERMS; Opgrande et al., 2002) consist of web-based interfaces that manage and coordinate the assessment-based research from the initial registrations through scoring of the assessments. The interfaces also manage all the user and administrative interactions during the study—in this case from four institutions: North Dakota State University, a research-intensive Ph.D. granting university; Minnesota State University–Moorhead, a comprehensive 4-year university; Concordia College, Moorhead, a 4-year liberal arts college; and the North Dakota State College of Science, a 2-year technical school. Five introductory biology classes were involved, with each enrolled student required to participate.

The Student Experience: Virtual Cell Example

To begin, the students registered and completed both a computer literacy survey and a pretreatment scenario-based assessment (see Figure 9.4) during the first 4 weeks of the semester. After 4 weeks, the students were sorted and placed into one of the three treatment groups: a Virtual Cell assignment group, a web-based assignment group, and a textbook assignment group. This was based on the computer literacy scores, gender, and previous biology experience, as described above. After the initial registration phase, the students participated in their assigned activities during the 5th and 6th weeks of the semester.

The students assigned to the Virtual Cell group were required to play the Virtual Cell game; the web-based group was required to visit and review related web sites; and the textbook group was required to read additional material from a textbook. Both the web-based group and the textbook group were given a quiz by the system at the end of their respective assignment.

Immediately following the assignment, the students provided feedback using online forms provided by the system. In the 7th week of the semester, the students completed a follow-up computer literacy survey and the posttreatment assessment.

The student sites are a unified area where students are provided with a listing of activities they are required to complete during the course of the study. It is important to note that a key requirement for the development of the student sites was to make the technology transparent to the students in the study.

The WERMS provides the foundation for the Virtual Cell study, which consists of six ordered activities that students are required to complete in order and at their own pace. The lone exception is at the end, when the posttreatment assessment and the study assignment are available to students only during specific periods in the semester, coinciding with when the related topics are being taught in the classroom. If the students fail to finish a posttreatment or study assignment during the allotted time period, they are promoted to the next activity. The activities are completed in this order:

1. Pretreatment computer literacy survey,
2. Pretreatment content assessment,
3. One of three treatment assignments (Virtual Cell experience, web-based browsing and quiz, or textbook reading and quiz),
4. Posttreatment user feedback survey,
5. Posttreatment computer literacy survey and posttreatment content assessment.

Students enter the study by visiting the Virtual Cell site and registering. The registration process consists of three steps. In the first step, the students are presented with a list of the institutions currently participating in the study. They choose their institution and then proceed to the next page of the registration process. There, they enter their name and email address, then select and confirm a password, then provide their student ID number and choose their specific class from a list provided by the system. The students finish the registration process by submitting their data, after which they are presented with a response detailing their account information. After these three steps, they are asked to begin the first activity of the study.

The first activity is a 24-question computer literacy survey, which is used to divide the students evenly among the three treatment groups. The first 20 questions are used to determine their comfort level with various computer-related technologies, such as the World Wide Web, chat rooms, and playing games. The last four questions ask for age, gender, college class, and previous biology lab experience. Two examples of the first 20 questions are:

Question 1: I have used a computer to (mark all that apply): A) Play games, B) Browser or "surf" the WWW, C) Download files or graphics images, and/or D) Access online syllabus, class notes, homework, or other school assignments.
Question 11: How comfortable are you with using computers for doing homework or other school assignments? A) Not at all, B) Moderately, c) Very.

Based on this information, the students are distributed into different experimental groups where there is an equal distribution of:

- Student skill and comfort with hardware and software;
- Male and female participants; and
- Students with prior biology lab experience.

Once the students complete and submit the pretreatment computer literacy survey, they are forwarded to their personalized activities page. The activities page provides them with a list of all the activities in the study and shows the status of each. Activities they have completed appear grayed out with a checkmark next to the activity name. The current activity is active and clickable and, if it is a time-sensitive activity, shows the end date. All uncompleted time-sensitive activities have either a start date or an end date. Similarly, once students have been assigned to their treatment group, their activities page provides them with a list of assets specific to each assignment. For example, the textbook assignment provides a list of pages from the class text that the students need to review as part of the assignment. The web assignment provides links to the additional web sites they are required to review. And the Virtual Cell assignment provides a tutorial demonstrating how to move around in a virtual world, a link to an FAQ section, and a link to the help message board.

Another important feature of the activities page is that instructors and study administrators can include messages for the students. The messages may be specific to the treatment group or relevant to the whole study.

Whenever students who have not completed the pretreatment computer literacy survey or pretreatment assessment visit the activities page, they are presented with a pop-up alert message that states: "Please complete the survey and pretest scenario as soon as possible. See the instructions for more information." This was introduced after it was found that many students were not completing the pretreatment survey and the pretreatment assessment in a timely manner, that is, until after the assignment was scheduled to begin. This caused problems since these students could not be divided into study groups (VCell, web, or text) with the other students, which necessitated their being placed in the default group and marked as not grouped. In addition, students not completing the assessments in a timely manner were farther along in the class lectures when they completed the assessment activity, resulting in their removal from the study analysis to prevent the skewing of data.

After the students finish their assignment, they are asked to complete an evaluation feedback form with questions specific to their assignment. This includes several multiple-choice questions asking them to rate the usability and effectiveness of the system. In addition, the students are provided with an open-ended question where they can address any additional issues they wish.

The Virtual Cell evaluation feedback form is composed of 30 questions, while the text assignment and web assignment forms have 15 and 16 questions, respectively. Each question on the text and web assignment feedback forms corresponds to one of the questions on the Virtual Cell feedback form. This provides a means to correlate the feedback across the different delivery methods.

The Administrator Experience

An administrator who logs in to the site is provided with a summary of all classes that are participating currently, along with the start and stop dates for each study activity and the number of students enrolled. Using this information, an administrator can perform several administrative tasks, including creating a study; adding, updating, or deleting an institution or class; adding or updating a faculty member or student account; and distributing a set of students into assignment groups.

Setting up a pilot study is accomplished in one of two ways. The first occurs when a new faculty member visits the site and requests that a study be set up. When a faculty member submits such a request, an email notification is sent to the administrator. In the email, the administrator is provided with a direct URL link, corresponding with the class request. When the administrator clicks on the link, the new class request form is displayed in the browser. From there, the administrator can either accept the request and create the class or deny the request and delete the data.

When administrators add a new class, they have the opportunity to fine-tune the details of the request. Administrators who choose to do this use a class modification form, where they are able to define, for example, the start and stop dates of each aspect of the class, and add any important announcements.

All data pertaining to institutions and classes can be edited at this point also. From the class details page, the administrator can view a list of all the students belonging to that class. Each student is selectable, and the administrator can access all student account details, such as ID, login, password, and email address. This allows the administrator to update a forgotten password, change an email address, or update other account information.

One of the most important tasks in administering a study is evenly distributing the students into treatment groups. The distribution of students is done by first selecting all the students from the class, along with their pretreatment computer literacy data. The students are divided into four groups based on their gender, and then on whether or not they have had prior biology lab experience.

The Grading Experience

The WERMS manages scenario-based assessments to study the effectiveness of the treatments on student learning. The pretreatment assessment scores are compared with the posttreatment assessment scores to determine a given treatment's effectiveness. The WERMS grading suite provides the means to develop, update, and score assessments; train graders; and export the data for further analysis.

To create a new grading form, the administrator selects a class, and then is given a default rubric template for the new grading form, which consists of three sections, with three criteria, two criteria, and one criterion, respectively. Each criterion consists of four options. The administrator then is able to add or remove criteria and options as required. Each criterion can be of one of three types. The first type is "choose the best answer," which allows the grader to choose one of the possible answers. The second type is "choose all that apply," which permits the grader to choose all the answers that fit the grading criterion. The last type is "choose a point value on the scale," which allows the grader to determine how many points to assign each answer.

Next to each criterion option is a place to type the option name and give the option a score or a range of scores. Each criterion is given a maximum score, which is useful for the "choose all that apply" type. In the end, all the criteria maximum scores are tallied to create a maximum total for the entire grading form. The Virtual Cell assessments typically are scored on a scale of 0 to 100 (see Figure 9.3 for an example).

Grader Training

Administrators create a training assessment rubric by choosing a class assessment. They then are presented with an assessment grading template that allows them to create a grading form, a special form used for grader training on that assessment.

After the creation of the training form, administrators are asked to enter sample grading assessments that will be used to train the graders. When entering sample assessments, the administrators use the newly created form to establish the correct values for each training assessment, along with an explanation of the grading.

Before graders are allowed to grade actual student assessments, they are required to complete a training session of 25 samples with a .75 correlation between the standard and trainer, which is calculated against the total scores. The purpose of this training is to ensure statistically similar grading results between graders. The reliability and validity of the results depend on this. The correlation is calculated by the formula shown in Figure 9.5.

Graders begin training by creating a new training session. Once a grading session begins, a list of samples, both graded and ungraded, is presented to the graders. The graders select an ungraded sample to begin the process. The training for the grading process is identical to the grading process of the actual student samples, except that when the grading rubric is submitted, the graders are provided with a critique of their grading. This critique provides an explanation of the correct grading criterion, as entered during the sample grading by the administrators, explaining what the correct answer or answers are and a description of why the answers were chosen. Each grading is saved for future reference and is used to determine the correlations. Once the graders complete their session, the statistical correlation of that session is calculated according to the formula in Figure 9.5. If the session has a correlation higher than 0.75, the graders are permitted to begin grading. If unsuccessful, they undergo the training again. At any time after grading a training sample, the graders can return and review the critiques of that sample from the most recent training session.

Figure 9.5. The Correlation Formula Used to Rate Graders

$$r = \frac{\sum_{i=1}^{n} X_n * \sum_{i=1}^{n} Y_n}{\sqrt{\sum_{i=1}^{n} X_{n^2} * \sum_{i=1}^{n} Y_{n^2}}} \quad \text{where} \ X_n = x_n - \overline{x} \ \text{and} \ Y_n = y_n - \overline{y}$$

Assessment Grading

The graders begin by choosing a class; a list of all available assessments belonging to that class then is presented. Scenarios where the graders have completed a training session successfully are available for grading, whereas scenarios where the graders either have not completed a training session or have not achieved a sufficient correlation value are noted as such. Upon choosing an active grading assessment, the graders are presented with a randomly ordered list of ungraded students.

When the graders choose a student to grade, they are presented with a review of the assessment and the student's response along the left side of the grading form. The graders are able to see both the assessment question and the student's response, and complete the grading by answering each criterion in the rubric.

When the graders choose a score for each element of the rubric, that value is added to the running total. They are required to score each element before submitting the grading form. If they attempt to submit a form without scoring each element, messages alert them to the unscored portions. Upon submission, a review sheet is presented to the graders showing that the grade has been successfully entered. At this point, they may either correct submitted scores or move on to grade other scenarios. This pattern continues until all scenarios have been graded.

The last option available in the grading system is the ability to view graded scenario assessments. Each of the graders is provided with the ability to view any assessment he or she has graded, whereas the site administrators are allowed to view all the graded assessments. The assessment scoring can be set to download into a spreadsheet program, such as Microsoft Excel.

The Faculty Experience

All faculty members have access to a secured area that provides them with a list of the classes currently participating in a study, along with a detailed summary for each student involved. These summaries provide the teacher with a list of the students registered for a given study, along with the status of each activity and the assignment score for each student.

Discussion

Systems that enable teachers and researchers to conduct studies over the Internet have become an interesting area of research. By implementing these systems, WWWIC has grown from conducting paper-based studies at a single institution to successfully conducting studies at four institutions with over 1,000 students a semester, while achieving the goal of minimizing the impact these studies have on the classroom.

In some respects, the system described here resembles Internet-based course management software. However, it is different in many aspects. First, the students are required to complete a computer literacy survey, which is used to create balanced distributions of students among the study groups. This is a fundamental requirement of any scientific study. Second, the students complete pretreatment and posttreatment assessments that are used to study the effect of the treatment on their understanding of the content. This collection of assessments itself is not unique; however, the methods by which the assessment data are scored by trained graders are. The assessments are graded against a standardized set of criteria, which, when tallied, is used to correlate the pretreatment and posttreatment assessments. In addition, trained graders, who have established a correlation of greater than 0.75 between the standard scoring and their assessment grading scores on a sample set of scenario training data, grade the assessments. This is important, as the 0.75 correlation shows that the graders have been trained to the point where their scores and the standard scoring can be viewed as statistically equivalent.

LEARNING STYLES

Through the course of the Geology Explorer experiments, and by interacting with students both off- and online, we came to believe that identifiable learning and problem-solving styles were being employed by students. Some students appeared to take an analytical approach: frequently referencing the online help, conducting sequences of experiments, and making diagnoses leading to points in a deliberate fashion. Other students seemed to take a pattern-matching approach: exploring far and wide in search of outcrops that seemed to match the description of what they were looking for, and then scoring points with relatively few experiments. There was also a small but noticeable group taking a straight brute force approach, simply visiting location after location and identifying everything there, one after another, as their goal, and eventually succeeding after many tries. One monument to this approach was the student in 1998 who made 1,244 guesses on the way toward obtaining five correct answers.

To investigate the nature of the trends we believed we were seeing, we conducted an analysis using logging data to count the number of "reports" (i.e., guesses), the number of locations visited, and the number of experiments conducted (e.g., hit, scratch, streak, etc.) for students who had completed the game and the evaluation survey (all student actions are recorded in a history file so this kind of analysis can be conducted, and for other reasons).

Using these values for average and standard deviation, we developed a classification of behaviors by looking for combinations of either much higher, or much lower, than average activity in terms of reports, moves, or experiments, or combinations of these. As shown in Table 9.3, there are a total of 24 clusters, each marked with a code, which represent the three significant categories.

The way to read the table is to look at the codes and their values in each of the three positions. A total of 81 students participated in this particular study (40 + 24 + 17), and each was scored according to their activities in reporting, moving, and experimenting. For example, the code RME (three students in the middle column) indicates an above-average number of reports, movements, and experiments. These are presumably the students who spent the most time playing the game. On the other hand, the code rme (10 students at the top of the first column) indicates below average in all three dimensions—paragons of efficiency. Meanwhile, the code--- (two students in the righthand column) were within one-half standard deviation on all three variables: reports, movement, and experiments. It is interesting to note that out of 81 students, only two were statistically "average" on all three dimensions. This is a testament to the variance in student performance

Table 9.3. Student Game-Play Activity on Planet Oit

Consistently normal or below-normal activity		Consistently normal or above-normal activity		Mixed problem-solving activity	
rme	10	-ME	5	-Me	4
r-e	8	--E	4	rM-	2
r--	5	R-E	4	r-E	2
-m-	5	R--	3	RmE	2
-me	4	RME	3	---	2
--e	4	RM-	3	Rm-	1
rm-	4	-M-	2	-mE	1
				rmE	1
				R-e	1
				Rme	1
Total 40 (49.4%)		*Total 24 (29.6%)*		*Total 17 (21.0%)*	

Key:	R = many reports	r = few reports
	M = many moves	m = few moves
	E = many experiments	e = few experiments

Example: -M- means normal reporting, many moves, normal experiments (where normal is within one-half standard deviation from the mean).

data mentioned earlier. There is a large group of students who perform to average levels, but there is a great deal of variability among this group. This indicates that a wide range of approaches are supported by the Geology Explorer, a testament to the user-centered and user-controlled nature of the simulation.

Almost half of the students (49.4%) can be classified as consistently efficient, economizing their problem-solving efforts along one or more dimensions.

Meanwhile, over half were above normal in one or more dimension, with 18 making excessive reports (code R, the brute force approach); 19 making excessive movements around the planet (code M, the pattern-matching approach), and 22 making more than the normal number of experiments (code E). Note that only three students were excessive on all three dimensions (code RME, middle column), and only two students were within one-half standard deviation on all three (code---, righthand column).

EVALUATION OF INSTRUCTIONAL PROGRAMS

In this chapter, *evaluation* refers to the evaluation of instructional programs. This usually is accomplished with survey instruments that seek to gauge the level of satisfaction that students had with their experience in the treatment, which in this case is their satisfaction with their experience in virtual worlds.

When the Geology Explorer was incorporated into the physical geology curriculum, data were gathered, using an online evaluation questionnaire (see Figure 9.6), with a view toward answering several questions about student use

Figure 9.6. Sample Evaluation Questions

1. The game was complex to learn	1	2	3	4	5	The game was simple to learn
4. Purchasing an instrument was easy	1	2	3	4	5	Purchasing an instrument was complicated
8. Getting information on the planet was easy	1	2	3	4	5	Getting information on the planet was complicated
10. I was able to keep track of my goals	1	2	3	4	5	I was unable to keep track of my goals
18. The game was too simple	1	2	3	4	5	The game was too complex
32. I liked the concept of the game	1	2	3	4	5	I disliked the concept of the game
33. I learned something from the game	1	2	3	4	5	I did not learn anything from the game

of technology and student perceptions of, and satisfaction with, the Planet Oit simulation.

The primary goal of the study was to investigate the effect on the student experience with physical geology as consequence of introducing the Geology Explorer prototype as a supplementary resource to classroom instruction for a nonmajor introductory course. To do this, we implemented tracking routines on Planet Oit in order to get statistics for time-on-task, correlations for computer literacy and attitudes toward technology, effect on final grade, and classification by learning style.

Evaluative Categories

Since 1998 the protocol has been the same—students complete the Geology Explorer assignment, scoring the required 500 points, and then complete an online follow-up evaluation form. This form is web-based and requires identification information (e.g., name, student ID number, and email address), and is composed of 35 questions about the Planet Oit experience (see Figure 9.6 for examples). The questions are answered on a 5-point scale, where ideal answers are usually either a 1 (e.g., questions 4, 8, 10, 32, 33), or a 5 (e.g., question 1), but sometimes a 3 (e.g., question 18). In addition, the form contains a field for students to estimate their time-on-task, and a few other implementation-dependent questions, as well as fields for listing likes, dislikes, and suggestions.

There are four main categories of information sought by the evaluative survey, with questions of each type scattered throughout.

1. game playability and user control in terms of the operation of the software interface (e.g., Q4 and Q18 in Figure 9.6);
2. game playability and user control in terms of access to information about the software (Q1 and Q8);

3. task and goal transparency in terms of operating within the simulation (Q32);
4. task and goal transparency in terms of access to information about the simulation (Q10 and Q33).

Average student agreement or disagreement with evaluative questions can be calculated using an approval-rating metric, based on ideal scores. For example, in Q1 of Figure 9.6, "The game was complex/simple to learn," a 1 indicates a perception of complexity and a 5 indicates a perception of simplicity. To calculate group attitudes, the average of all responses is expressed as a percent that captures group agreement with the statement.

Student Perceptions

In the posttest evaluation, 82.8% of the students said they somewhat agreed or strongly agreed they had learned something from the game, and only five students (5.4%) disagreed or strongly disagreed that they had learned something. At the same time, only 9.7% somewhat or strongly disliked the concept of game, and 62.4% thought they might like to play the game again. Meanwhile, the students perceived the game to be at an appropriate level of difficulty, with only 8.6% describing the game as much too complex, and no students believing it was much too simple.

Discussion

We continue to collect and analyze data, with a view to future longitudinal studies that compare student behavior across years. Meanwhile, the survey data reported here strongly indicate that the game is implemented at a manageable level for first-year college students, with 88% group agreement that the game was neither too fast nor too slow, and 88% agreement that the game was neither too difficult nor too easy.

However, results also indicate that students found it relatively difficult to access the online information needed to play the game and achieve their goals, which indicates that further work is necessary to make the knowledge encoded in the simulation more easily available to the students. On the other hand, information about current score, current goal, and current progress was readily available, with a high degree of group agreement.

CONCLUSION

This chapter surveys the range of quantitative activities we have engaged in while developing our worlds. The idea of measurement has become increasingly important over recent years. More attention than ever is being paid to experimental design and statistical analysis. By and large, this should be viewed as a positive change within the discipline.

Chapter 10

Related Work

The idea of using technology in education has found a wide range of applications. This chapter surveys many of them but concentrates on comparisons to systems that employ the interesting elements we care about: meaning that they are multi-user, exploratory, and game-like—and the many worthy efforts of others working toward what we are working toward.

Multi-user virtual environments for education are a relatively recent development. These systems are the evolutionary consequence of the confluence of a number of other innovations. This history draws on everything from the early computer "console" games, to the role-playing games (RPGs) most famously exemplified by "Dungeons and Dragons," to the "electronic communities" that arose in Multi-User Dungeons (MUDs) and MOOs, which are MUDs that are Object Oriented, on the Internet—finally culminating in the systems that are the subject of this book.

This chapter surveys some of that historical development and discusses some of the research involving the assessment and evaluation of educational software. Following that are some short essays on a range of related topics, including other uses of MUDs in education, and other systems that are similar in some ways to our virtual worlds.

This chapter is research oriented and somewhat technical.

Educational computer games have a history dating back to the 1950s when business colleges began requiring their students to compete in simulated business environments—by feeding punch cards into the campus mainframe computer. These efforts have persisted and evolved to the present, and have been supplemented with a vast array of implementations ranging from math drill-and-practice, such as MathBlaster, to keyboarding skills, such as Mavis Bacon Teaches Typing, to research-driven, problem-solving adventures like Oregon Trail. Many of these have worked their way into the schools and form a productive niche.

MUDs, or Multi-User Dungeons, are an outgrowth of computer chat lines and bulletin boards plus the popularity of adventure role playing as exemplified by Dungeons and Dragons. They are environments that one can log in to from a computer connected to the Internet, and then interact in text with objects, places, and other players within a game-like setting (Carlstrom, 1992). This technology has been a major part of the current online community that subsequently has morphed into a number of areas: message boards, file-sharing sites, and, most recently, blogs. History has shown that one thing leads to another, and where we are now is an amalgam of what has gone before. The MUD community started a lot of what we have today.

Far and away the most common approach to implementing synthetic multi-user environments is the text-based MUD: the multi-user, text-based, networked computing environments that are mostly for "gaming." According to Tamosaitis (1995), the two most common varieties are adventure MUDs and social MUDs. The adventure-oriented MUD originated in Essex University in the United Kingdom. In the spring of 1979, Roy Trubshaw and Richard Bartle wrote the first MUD-like program in MACRO-10 (a computer programming language mostly used in Europe in the 1970s and 1980s). This program had a series of locations where people could move around and chat. Bartle wrote in his article, "How It Really Happened," that this actually was not called a MUD. However, the very next version, also written in MACRO-10, was a little more sophisticated and actually was a MUD. It had a database with commands, rooms, and objects that were kept in separate files (Bartle, 1999).

As the program became impossible to manage, Trubshaw rewrote everything in BCPL (a programming language, precursor to the popular C programming language), and it became the core of the current MUD. After Trubshaw left Essex University, Bartle started to add game features into the program, such as a point-scoring system, more advanced communication commands among players, and privileged characters like wizards (Bartle, 1999). In the spring of 1980, Essex University and the Arpanet were linked, and the MUD actually was played by external players. Eventually, the copy was sold to CompuServe and was played by many RPG fans throughout the United States.

The other type of MUD is more socially oriented. Jim Aspnes, a graduate student at Carnegie Mellon University, first created this type of MUD, calling it TinyMUD. This was in August 1989, almost 10 years after the Essex MUD was introduced. It was called a socially oriented MUD because of the unique game objectives. Instead of the customary game-play of MUDs (killing other players and gaining points), TinyMUD adopted a monetary system. Players needed Pennies to build rooms and objects. Pennies were earned by visiting other players' rooms and finding treasure items. Therefore, TinyMUD encouraged players to communicate with one another and create an environment. TinyMUD soon became very popular because of its simple usage and the low cost of the license—it was free to everyone.

CONTEXT: OTHER MUDS AND MOOS

There are literally thousands of MUDs and MOOs operating on the Internet. This section surveys just a few of the most relevant to the work described in this book.

The Social Virtual Reality project at Xerox PARC extended MUD technology for use in nonrecreational settings. The goal of the project was to keep the strength of MUDs—shared computing with a powerful real-world metaphor—while correcting their shortcomings by adding audio, video, and interactive windows. The project built two specific prototypes: Astro-VR, for use by the professional astronomy community, and Jupiter, for use by researchers within Xerox (Curtis & Nichols, 1993).

MOOs for different ability levels are becoming common. Amy Bruckman (1993) has built a programming language to make it simpler for children to construct objects and participate in MOOs. She has combined construction and community in the hope of creating a constructionist learning culture in her MOOse-Crossing MOO.

The Donut MOO in Stark County, Ohio, addresses the needs of K–12 students. Students build the MOO by creating "textually anchored virtual reality spaces." Although the site is open to all students, many are older (Suzie, 1995).

MOOs have shown their importance in elementary schools. Two in particular, MariMuse and MicroMUSE, have been geared so that elementary school students can participate. One notable success has been with underachieving students who had left school. These students reportedly became involved, started to form friendships, and began to take a greater interest in returning to school (Poirer, 1995).

Other examples of virtual reality MOOs, sometimes called "multi-user computer simulations," are being implemented in a virtual physics classroom being developed at NASA, and in interactive programs run at the Loma Linda Medical Center in southern California. McLellan (1994) cites some early conclusions about the VR MOO experience in connection with other entertainment games such as "Battletech."

CONTEXT: LANGUAGE LEARNING IN VIRTUAL ENVIRONMENTS (MAX POOL)

There are many virtual environments that focus on foreign languages. These provide an excellent opportunity for students anywhere to "step out" of their current surroundings and immerse themselves in an environment where only a particular foreign language is spoken (Virtual Writing Center web page).

MundoHispano is a MOO-based environment that was founded and developed by Lonnie Turbee and Mike Mudge at the University of Missouri–St. Louis in 1994. MundoHispano is a community of native speakers of Spanish from around the world, teachers and learners of Spanish, and computer programmers, all of whom volunteer their time and talent to make this a dynamic virtual world (MundoHispano web page).

Containing thousands of rooms representing over a dozen countries, all are written by native speakers from those countries. MundoHispano provides nearly limitless contexts in which language learners can communicate for authentic purposes, learn about the many Spanish cultures, and create a home of their own in cyberspace's oldest Spanish MOO (MundoHispano web page).

In the same style and also hosted by the University of Missouri–St. Louis, MOOFrançais is a French-based virtual environment. Over 100 rooms have been built to represent different areas of Paris. As users walk down famous streets and explores famous sites, MOOFrançais allows them to meet other French speakers, exchange ideas, and improve their language skills.

schMOOze University was originally built as the first text-based virtual environment of nonnative speakers of the English language. Created by Julie Fallseti of Hunter College in 1994, schMOOze University is a place where people studying English as a second or foreign language can practice their skills while sharing ideas and experiences with other learners and practitioners of English. Students have opportunities for one-on-one and group conversations as well as access to language games, an online dictionary, and USENET feeds (schMOOze web page).

CONTEXT: CLASSROOM-ORIENTED VIRTUAL ENVIRONMENTS (MAX POOL)

Virtual campuses are emerging. For example, the CollegeTown MOO at Buena Vista University (CollegeTown web page) holds classes, seminars, and other academic events in a MOO. Another example is MOOville, a text-based virtual environment hosted by the University of Florida. MOOville models the topographical layout of the campus. The players include students enrolled in classes that employ the Networked Writing Environment IBM Writing Lab, teaching assistants in those labs, graduate students and faculty from the English department, and instructors from other institutions. Players are allowed to create their own offices in certain halls, participate in virtual lectures and seminars, and engage in writing assignments that involve unique opportunities for research in humanities computing. Additionally, instructors have a place to provide an electronic forum for in-class discussions, a space for instructors to develop experiments in hypertextual instruction, and a space in which instructors are able to hold "virtual office hours" (MOOVille web page).

In the same vein, PennMOO is a virtual environment hosted by the University of Pennsylvania and based loosely on the geographies of the Penn campus and the city of Philadelphia. PennMOO provides a virtual space, where the faculty hold classes and office hours, students gather for group projects, and real-time events bring users from Penn and around the world together in cyberspace (PennMOO web page). A particular application of PennMOO provides a unique environment for the English 88 course. Online assignments, virtual seminars and speeches, and the annual MOO Poetry Slam provide students with an introduction to English with a technological emphasis (PennMOO English 88 web page).

CafeMOO is a virtual environment developed by the University of California, Berkeley, to provide a virtual place to conduct class business. Classes such as Statistics 21 and German 101 have virtual office hours and provide virtual supplemental class material; however, a more interesting application of CafeMOO is in the humanities area of the English 108 course. English 108 uses the MOO to do course business, just as the other courses do; however, this course's core emphasis is composition about technology and its effects on society. Writing assignments that deal with the ethical issues of a digital world, and required texts such as WIRED magazine and Microserfs, by Douglas Coupland, are supplemented by the virtual environment that enhances the experience of writing. This is a very different, yet effective, approach to immersion (CafeMOO web page).

Diversity University is a MOO-based project of DUETS, Inc., a nonprofit educational organization dedicated to meeting the online distance learning needs of individuals and institutions. Hosted by Marshall University and the University of Wisconsin, Parkside, Diversity University Main Campus is an immersive virtual campus where thousands of students, teachers, and administrators worldwide use the Diversity University's classes, literature, and consulting services. The Diversity

University campus has rooms for almost every high-level discipline, including a K–12 area and a library for resource hunting (Diversity University web page).

CONTEXT: COMMUNITIES OF LEARNING (MAX POOL)

One of the better-organized educational resource environments (or communities) is TAPPED IN. TAPPED IN is an online workplace of an international community of education professionals, where K–12 teachers and librarians, professional development staff, teacher education faculty and students, and education researchers engage in professional development programs and informal collaborative activities with colleagues (TAPPED IN web page).

Within this virtual environment, educators can plan and conduct projects with colleagues and students; participate in (or lead) topical discussions; conduct and attend courses; find resources, experts, and new colleagues; serve as resources for other educators; or try out new ideas in a safe, supportive environment (TAPPED IN web page).

The Virtual Writing Center (VWC) is a MOO-based environment hosted by Salt Lake Community College. The VWC is a place where writers can get together and learn about their writing. It presents college-level writers the opportunity to chat with other writers, share their writing, take college-level writing courses, get help from writing tutors, and partake in the building of the VWC virtual reality. The Virtual Writing Center MOO is also a real-time communications environment. It gives writers a synchronous forum to discuss issues in writing, composition, rhetoric, and related pedagogy (Virtual Writing Center web page).

MediaMOO is a research project of Amy Bruckman started at the Epistemology and Learning Group at the MIT Media Lab and now hosted at the College of Computing at Georgia Tech. MediaMOO is a professional online community for media researchers. It is a place to meet colleagues in media studies and related fields and brainstorm, hold colloquia and conferences, and explore the serious side of this new medium (MediaMOO web page).

Membership in MediaMOO is selective, and it is necessary to submit a membership application from inside MediaMOO. To become a member, one must be involved in some form of media research. The requirement that new members be actively involved in research is more rigorously enforced, as this is a professional community. Graduate students in media-related fields are especially welcome. MediaMOO was founded by graduate students and continues to be grounded in an academic environment. This is a place to come and make professional contacts in a media-centric field. It is also an excellent place to meet other graduate students, learn what they are doing, and be inspired (MediaMOO web page).

BACKGROUND: ROLE-PLAYING GAMES (MICHAEL LEE)

Role-playing games vary from pencil-and-paper-based games like Dungeons and Dragons to text-based computer games like Multi-User Dungeons and graphical console-based games such as Final Fantasy. The basic idea of all these RPGs is for the user to play a role that creates or follows a certain story line. In the early years,

RPGs were mostly limited to MUD users, until the concept and technology of console systems were introduced.

Console systems such as Atari and NES were very popular among certain age groups and started many series of popular console RPG games. The very first console RPG, Dragon Stomper, was introduced on the Atari 2600 system in 1982. It represented the player as a small white dot. Players could explore three different levels of the game. In the first level, players walked around, fought against monsters, and gathered treasure items. When players encountered monsters, they could decide whether to run, fight, or use items such as potions or spells. All these commands could be executed by navigating through a text-based menu system. In the second level, players could purchase items and recruit help for defeating the dragon in the last level, where the players were put into a dungeon and fought against the ultimate dragon (Vestal, 2002).

Ten years after the introduction of the Atari system in 1975, a Japanese console system, NES, was introduced in the United States and became very popular. Soon, a console RPG was developed for NES and three major console RPGs were introduced in the United States: Dragon Warrior, Final Fantasy, and Zelda. These are still well-known titles and have very unique systems that influenced future RPG (Vestal, 2002).

In 1986, Zelda was introduced. This was the first action-adventure RPG and sold over 1 million copies in the United States. The director of Zelda, Miyamoto, wanted to "reproduce the feeling he had as a child exploring the fields just outside his home in Japan," which was implemented throughout all eight dungeons of the game (Vestal, 2002).

The next significant title was Dragon Warrior. It was first introduced in Japan in 1986 and came over to the United States in 1989. This game had many of the features still in use today: upgradable weapons, hit points and magic points, and turn-based battle. It also served to introduce three soon-to-be-famous game creators: Akira Toriyama (the author of Dragon Ball), Koichi Sugiyama, and Yuji Hori. The popularity of Dragon Warrior was so profound that, in Japan, the government passed a law requiring the Dragon Warrior series to be released on Sundays or holidays, to prevent children from skipping school. Dragon Warrior generally is credited with being the first product to popularize Japanese culture in the United States (Vestal, 2002).

The last significant title, and until recently the largest selling video game series in the world, is Final Fantasy. The first version was introduced in the United States in 1990, and its descendants are still beloved by RPG fans all over the world. When the first version came out, it introduced two important features: parting and transportation. Transportation allowed players to explore larger areas in less time. This resulted in bigger and more detailed environments for the game. The concept of parting made it possible for a player to use up to four characters at once in a battle and created the idea of character classes (Vestal, 2002).

RELATED WORK: ASSESSMENT (LURA JOSEPH)

Over the past 2 decades, there have been a number of meta-analyses of the literature pertaining to the effectiveness of technology on learning. According to Phipps

and Merisotis (1999), one study recently concluded that most of the research indicates no significant difference in effectiveness of learning when comparing the
use of technology at a distance with conventional classroom instruction. According to Gormly (1996), in spite of great expectations, the overall impact of technology on education has been very small.

Some meta-analyses have reported favorable results from the use of technology in learning (Kulik & Kulik, 1991; Moore & Thompson, 1990; Roblyer, 1989;
Snowman, 1995). However, a number of authors have cautioned that much of
the research is flawed and that results should be questioned (Lookatch, 1996; Moore
& Thompson, 1990; Phipps & Merisotis, 1999; Regian & Shute, 1994). Kulik (1994)
points out that meta-analyses usually ignore factors such as experimental design,
which may affect the evaluation results of the meta-analyses.

Current criticism of past research includes the lack of control for extrane-
ous variables by random assignment of subjects to experimental and control groups
and the use of measurement instruments with questionable validity and reliability (Phipps & Merisotis, 1999). Other problems include lack of research with regard to critical thinking skills (Coley, Cradler, & Engel, 1997; Dunlap & Grabinger,
1996; Kearsley, 1998; Phipps & Merisotis, 1999; Trotter, 1998), the lack of consideration of differences such as preferred learning styles and gender, small sample
size (Phipps & Merisotis, 1999; Trotter, 1998), failure to control for external effects, and the need for longitudinal studies (Trotter, 1998). Very few studies have
been found that randomly assigned subjects to groups.

Several studies have been reported as exemplary in the literature (Coley
et al., 1997; Huppert, Yaakobi, & Lazarowitz, 1998; Phipps & Merisotis, 1999; Regian
& Shute, 1994; U.S. House of Representatives, 1997; Viadero, 1997). One, the Adventures of Jasper Woodbury, is a set of 12 video-based adventures designed by
researchers at Vanderbilt University's Learning and Technology Center to improve
the complex mathematical thinking ability of students. A number of studies with
different experimental designs have been conducted to test the effectiveness of Jasper (Goldman, Pellegrino, & Bransford, 1994; The Cognition and Technology Group
at Vanderbilt, 1997; Van Haneghan et al., 1992; Viadero, 1997; Vye, Goldman, Voss,
Hmelo, & Williams, 1997; Young, Nastasi, & Braunhardt, 1996). Jasper classrooms
perform as well as traditional classrooms at solving standard, one-step word problems, but they are significantly better than traditional classroom control groups at
solving multistep word problems that require complex reasoning. Random assignment to groups was used in some of the studies.

In a study of a computer-based treatment (HAT) to enhance higher order
thinking skills in physics (Mestre, Dufresne, Gerace, Hardiman, & Tougher, 1992),
college students (n = 42) were randomly assigned to three groups: experimental group,
control for novelty, and traditional group. The experimental group was the only group
to show a statistically significant improvement in the number of deep structure
matches. Although HAT does not present or teach content, it allows the user to practice a principle-based, problem-solving procedure in a menu-driven environment.

Keegan (1995) reports the results of several studies of the effectiveness of
scenario educational software. Apparently none of the reported studies randomly
assigned individuals to groups, and the results were mixed. Keegan concludes,
"Overall, students learn subject matter as well and sometimes better with scenario
software than with traditional, more didactic classroom instruction" (p. 58).

Viadero (1997) reports another effective technology-based program, National Geographic Society's Kids Network, where classes collaborate on research projects via the Internet. He reports, "An independent study of the project involving 36 California schools found that students who participated in the network outscored students in traditional classrooms on their grasp of some scientific concepts" (p. 13). Details of the experimental design were not given.

SimCalc (U.S. House of Representatives, 1997; Viadero, 1997), another computer-based program, has been tested in inner-city middle schools. Middle school students trained with SimCalc were able to perform as well as, or better than, typical high school or college age students on problems using graphical representation and other calculus skills. Details of the experimental design were not given.

Huppert and colleagues (1998) studied the effectiveness of computer software that simulated the growth curve of microorganisms. Classes were randomly assigned, rather than individuals. The experimental group achieved significantly higher mean scores than the control group; however, the significant differences were attributed mainly to the girls in the experimental group. The tests consisted of a combination of multiple-choice and open-ended questions.

Sherlock (Gott, Lesgold, & Kane, 1996; Lesgold, 1994) technology was developed for the U.S. Air Force and is intended to train personnel in complex, transferable, problem-solving abilities. According to Lesgold (1994), airmen in the experimental Sherlock group significantly outperformed the control group on the posttest. The gain in terms of experience was about 4 years from pretest to posttest for the experimental Sherlock group. A follow-up test at 6 months showed retention of over 90% of the gains. Subjects were given a problem statement and then answered the questions, "What would you do next?" and "Why would you do that?" They were told the result of their action, and then the questioning cycle would continue until a solution was achieved or an impasse was reached. The total number of subjects was 32. It is not clear whether random assignment to groups was used.

Dede and Loftin (Dede, 1996; Dede, Salzman, & Loftin, 1996, Nadis, 1999) have been working on Science Space, a series of artificial realities created to explore the effectiveness of using physical immersion to teach science.

A U.S. House of Representatives report (1997) mentions several other exemplary programs (ICONS, Global Lab, Virtual Canyon), but no details of any of the studies are given. Regian and Shute (1994) mention several successful studies of LISP.

There are also a number of simulation tools that have been developed for job-related training, including VRML tutors for training power transformer operators, and CAD-based tutors for machine tool operators (Tam, Badra, & Marceau, 1999; Venner, 1999). Other science learning projects include NICE, an immersive environment that allows children to construct and maintain a simple virtual ecosystems, collaborate virtually with children at remote sites, and form stories based on their interactions (Mahoney, 1998).

RELATED WORK: GEOLOGY EXPLORER (OTTO BORCHERT)

Most often, geology is taught via a combination of three things: lectures, field experience, and laboratory experience. In lectures, students are given the necessary background in the facts of geology. During field trips, students apply that knowledge to real-world scenarios by traveling to specific locations and performing geologic tasks. Finally, laboratory experience allows for more controlled applications of lecture material without having to leave the physical campus. There are numerous Internet resources available that enhance all of these approaches to geology education.

For example, lectures can be extended to include animations of earthquakes and volcanic eruptions, photos of realistic locations, or other techniques for enhancing the lecture content. One site with material of this type is Earth System Science Online, which is a joint effort of NASA, the Universities Space Research Association, and several universities across the United States to create a repository of resources for professors teaching earth sciences in a cross-disciplinary fashion (Johnson, Ruzek, & Kalb, 2000; Universities Space Research Association, 2002). This site indexes a variety of other web sites related to geology, including government agencies, sites giving information about environmental issues for study in class, and sites that contain data, images, maps, and other useful tools that professional geologists would use. These resources can be used to supplement a geology curriculum, but none of the resources involve all of the design strategies of immersive virtual worlds.

Just as lectures can be expanded with web-based content, field trips can be enhanced by virtual field trips. Virtual field trips provide a less expensive experience, and a variety of these are available on the web. Students virtually travel to a place on the Earth and perform different geologic tasks, including observation, mapping, and learning about various processes.

One specific example is the Virtual Geology Project at California State University at Long Beach (Morris, 2000). This project has a list of virtual field trips to various different locations in southern California. Students on the field trips view a series of pictures with related text describing various features of a particular location.

The virtual field tour of Nova Scotia, written by Ralph Stea (2001) for the Nova Scotia Department of Natural Resources, has more multimedia content. This field trip includes movies and air and ground photos. These field trips, however, lack much of the interactivity intrinsic in the Geology Explorer—the web simply does not provide the same level of interactivity and lacks a multiplayer option, where students would be able to cooperate or compete with one another in some fashion.

The third component of geology education is the use of laboratory sessions, where students apply lecture knowledge, but do not leave the campus. In the Virtual Geology Labs exercises at California State University at Los Angeles, students use a learn-by-doing approach similar to the Geology Explorer (Novak, 2000). On the opening page, students choose which lab they wish to explore: currently, Virtual Rock Dating, Virtual River, and Virtual Earthquake. To enhance a laboratory experience, students enter the Virtual River, for example, and go through a series of web pages where they measure the depth, width, and velocity of a river to discover the water discharge. This exercise is similar to the Geology Explorer in that students perform measurements and calculations like a scientist, but it is very linear and does not allow for any collaboration as the virtual labs are mainly static web pages.

An interactive game was developed at Tufts University for teaching historical geology. Over a 10-week period, a room-sized board game was created that teaches students various historical geology and paleontology concepts, including fossil identification, classification, and morphology, and shows the importance of different events over time (Reuss & Gardulski, 2001). This differs from the Geology Explorer in the obvious aspect that it is not computer based. However, it does have game-like aspects and is suitable for competitive/cooperative play.

There are also a myriad of educational CD-ROMs for students and teachers to use in geology classes. One example is the Understanding Earth CD-ROM by Video Discovery (2002), which includes video, pictures, glossary, and documentaries on various geology topics, including earthquakes, oceans, and environmental change. Another example is the common inclusion of a CD-ROM in geology textbooks. These CDs contain everything from visualizations to multimedia-laden interactive demos, to the full text of the book they accompany.

Another product similar to the Geology Explorer is a commercial software package by Eighteen Software (1999) called Mineral Venture. This product is designed to run in a workshop fashion, where a leader sits at one computer, which contains the main program, while students sit at other computers exploring a simulated environment and searching for specific types of valuable minerals. The students prepare an expedition using their computers, store it to disk, and then give it to the leader, who then processes the expedition on the main computer. This resembles the Geology Explorer in that players have a goal to find valuable minerals and are immersed in a game-like format. However, it is not Internet accessible, has no software tutoring support since tutoring is provided only by the leader, and is not explicitly multiplayer. Students are normally in teams at a particular computer but do not interact with one another.

Eighteen Software (1999) also makes a similar product called Deep Earth, which teaches students topographic and geologic mapping, and allows them to interact with a geologic environment. This is a slightly newer software product that does allow interaction over a network, but the software is not globally accessible through the Internet and, like Mineral Venture, lacks software tutor support.

There are a number of software packages that are not educational in nature but possess one or two features in common with the Geology Explorer. For example, software like ESRI's Arcview helps with GPS and mapping (Environmental System Research Institute, 2002). Other simulation software like SIS's Inside Reality provides a virtual reality interface for well planning and earthquake analysis (Schlumberger Information Solutions, 2002). Mapping is an important portion of current work in the Geology Explorer, and both Arcview and Inside Reality provide an immersive environment for geology work.

There are numerous projects with traits in common with the Geology Explorer. Ultimately, however, the Geology Explorer is unique in that it contains all of the design aspects of immersive virtual environments in a geology setting, unlike the other educational software, professional software, web-based tools, and multimedia sites discussed above.

RELATED WORK: VCELL (MEI LI)

Conceptually speaking, there are many abstract and microcosmic concepts and processes in biological science that cause students to have difficulty. The structure of a cell is not visible to the naked eye, for example, and it is not easy for a beginner to differentiate components, even under a microscope. Innovations in multimedia and computer-related technology can help biology education through simulation, and many of these have emerged in recent years. These are usually either on web sites or on CD-ROMs accompanying textbooks. These presentations are a great help to teachers looking for different methods to assist students with visualizing this complex and abstract science—from macroscopic biology, such as plants, animals, and ecology, to microcosmic biology, such as cells and genes.

SimLife

SimLife is a highly sophisticated and educational simulation of life, evolution, environments, and complete ecosystems. John Arle, a professor at Rio Salado Community College, said: "The program provides an opportunity to see the scientific method in ecological experimentation which is otherwise impossible" (MCLI SimLife web site). The idea is to build an ecosystem by designing animals and plants to put into it and then letting them live to reproduce, die, and so on, with evolutionary influences controlled by users. The users can experiment with scenarios and factors in order to observe the evolving responses to the environmental changes. Windows, graphics, and status reports provide an ongoing view of the complex simulations (MCLI SimLife web site). SimLife is a commercial game with good graphics and animation, sound effects, full-color maps of the game world, and a well-written manual (Meir web site).

The Virtual Frog Dissection Kit

The Virtual Frog Dissection Kit was designed for use in high school biology classrooms. It is an interactive, step-by-step frog dissection simulation. On this site, students can skin a frog to show 10 of its organ systems and the skeleton, learn dissection procedures, watch movie segments of a frog being dissected, and check what they have learned (Johnston; Learning In Motion). The Virtual Frog Dissection Kit has a simple and easy-to-use interface. The pages download quickly after each operation.

The Other Virtual Cells

There are several different systems and sites that go by some variation of the name "Virtual Cell."

The Virtual Cell Web Page originating at Brown University provides a site where students can take an interactive, 3D, animated tour through the internal components of a living cell or look through the virtual textbook chapters on cell biology and organic chemistry. It has a well-organized virtual textbook. There is not a lot of text, but between the text and the pictures, it is very effective. The interface is colorful and very attractive (http://www.ibiblio.org/virtualcell/index.htm).

The Virtual Cell at the University of Illinois provides a site where students can cut into a "virtual plant cell" in real time. Students can view the cell and organelles at different angles, view electron micrographs of the cell and organelles, and view animated movies demonstrating the function of the cell or organelle. Students can interactively manipulate the illustrations and accompanying text, which gives students the opportunity to discover on their own what they otherwise may have difficulty understanding (Learning In Motion). The interface of the Virtual Cell is simple, and it is easy for students to manipulate (http://www.life .uiuc.edu/plantbio/cell/).

The Cell, by ThinkQuest, is an interactive site that provides a series of lessons: cell basics, the parts of a cell, cells in our bodies, cell profiles, and implications. Each lesson has a quiz where students must submit answers in electronic form, which are then "marked" and returned. The Cell also provides plug-in programs, including a virtual cell animation, DNA sequencer, and chat line (La Velle, 2000). The content of this site is very rich and includes many aspects of cell biology (http://library.thinkquest.org/3564/).

Cell Biology at the University of Arizona is an interactive resource for learning biology. Students study cells, mitosis, meiosis, the cell cycle, prokaryotes, eukaryotes, and viruses. This site also provides an historical overview, an excellent section on the scientific method, and some useful bits about scaling. There are self-assessment questions with answers, clues, and encouraging remarks (La Velle, 2000). This site has rich content and thorough coverage (http://www.biology .arizona.edu/cell_bio/cell_bio.html).

RELATED WORK: PROGRAMMINGLAND (CURT HILL)

Doube (1998) describes a distance education system delivered, not on the Internet, but on CD-ROM. She argues that converting a course from a classroom form to a multimedia form should be based on a suitable learning theory and not the sequencing of lecture notes into a multimedia presentation. Although this is neither an Internet nor a collaborative system, the advice in course organization is well taken.

Hitz and Kögelar (1997) describe a C++ course and system that use a conventional web server in an attempt to get the content fully online. The content is organized in three layers of web pages in order to make the navigation of the pages easy and standardized. The first layer provides content in a sequential set of lessons on the language topics and resembles either a textbook or a presentation. The second layer is a reference layer where more detail on the syntactic and semantic issues may be considered. This layer allows the students to dig deeper into the material. The third layer is the pragmatics layer, and it considers some background information and some of the practicalities of using the particular feature of C++. Each of the layers has a different look to make navigation easier. ProgrammingLand offers much better interactive activities, tracking of students, and collection of data, among other things.

Carrasquel (1999) claims some success using an ordinary textbook and few class meetings. The Internet was used for the delivery of quizzes, assignments, and tests. He cites the advantage of a self-paced course for novices, who may work as long as needed on topics and thus not fall behind as is common with classes that operate on a normal academic schedule.

The British Open University, which is a leading source of distance education using the mail, also has pursued similar communications to enhance courses that deliver most of their subject content with printed matter and found these as

effective as traditional mail communications (Carswell, 1997). All of these techniques could be handled using a course management system. The Open University also has enhanced its print distance courses with online tutorials, including
things like Internet conferencing (Petre, 1997), which is not often a part of course
management software.

Wade and Power (1998) suggest nine requirements that an online course
should satisfy. Among them are some that web servers and course management
systems typically lack: student ability to experiment with newly acquired knowledge, substantial interactivity, and mechanisms to evaluate student progress and
retention. Such features have been discussed earlier concerning ProgrammingLand.
These web-based systems may include Java applets to support a greater degree of
interactivity and simulation. Incidentally, Street and Goodman (1998) contest the
positive effect of Java applet interactivity in learning, although they concede that
this interactivity makes the experience more enjoyable.

There are several projects that might be considered alternatives to either
the commercial course delivery systems or ProgrammingLand. A system described
by Shi, Shang, and Chen (2000) enhances web-based subject material with several types of software agents. A personal agent records and uses information concerning students' courses, preferences, and even learning styles. It attempts to
customize the interaction of the system with the individual student. A course agent
manages the techniques and materials of a particular course. A teaching agent is
a course tutor and functions as the intermediary between the course and the personal agent. Like ProgrammingLand, this system keeps much better track of its
students, includes interactive exercises, and uses software agents. At last report, it
was under development with only a prototype implemented.

Another proposal is described by Anido-Rifón, Llamas-Nistal, and Fernández-
Iglesias (2001). The goal is to enable standardized delivery of an interactive and
collaborative environment. The typical educational Java applet is an interactive
program that delivers an educational experience to users. However, making this
experience collaborative is quite cumbersome. This proposal is for a layered system with ordinary HTTP and FTP servers at the bottom. On top of this layer is a
component layer that enables the relatively easy collaboration by the client-side
applets. Web servers are not easily made collaborative; hence, the extra layer or
the need for a special chat room within commercial course delivery systems. In
contrast to this are MOOs, where interpersonal interactivity was part of the design goal.

ProgrammingLand gathers data by recording for each student the rooms
visited, the lessons completed, the quizzes taken, as well as other events. Some of
this information is used within the MOO. For example, the completion of a lesson
may require the visiting of certain rooms. Thomas and Logan (2001) developed
AESOP (An Electronic Student Observatory Project) to monitor students in the
Learning Works Environment. This system records student actions for replay and
analysis, which is done by hand.

Finally, the ProgrammingLand code machine is an interactive object that
describes a piece of code and simulates its execution. This is similar to, although
not as elaborate as, the ANNET system (Liffick & Aiken, 1996). ANNET uses a cognitive model, with five levels: lexical, syntactic, semantic, schematic, and conceptual. Any program may be examined and should be understood at any of these

levels. An instructor uses ANNET to annotate sample code from the lowest to the highest levels. The lower levels are more automated, while the upper levels require more instructor input.

RELATED WORK: ECONOMIC ENVIRONMENTS (CHIN LUA)

The first business-related educational games were implemented in the 1950s and have persisted to this day. Faria (1998) dates modern business simulation back to 1955 when the RAND Corporation developed an inventory simulation for the U.S. Air Force logistics system. The participants assumed the role of inventory managers in the Air Force supply system. In 1956, the first widely known business game, the Top Management Decision Simulation, developed by the American Management Association, was used in management seminars. In 1957, the Top Management Decision Game by Schreiber was the first business game introduced in a university class, at the University of Washington. Nonetheless, while the literature on agent-based games has been increasing very rapidly in the past few years, there are still a very limited number of studies to consider in this particular arena.

Swarm

Tesfatsion (1997) describes two case studies of agent-based economic models implemented using Swarm. Swarm is a collection of software libraries written in Objective-C (a programming language that preceded C++). Swarm assumes an oligopolistic competition with differentiated products; the consumers have a preferred product, and each firm produces and sells only one product. The economic model implemented in Swarm assumes that the firm chooses to produce a product at a particular location but may choose to change to a different location.

Earlier, Tesfatsion (1996) developed an evolutionary Trade Network Game (TNG) that combined evolutionary game-play with endogenous partner selection. This TNG is implemented in C++. Similarly, Vidal and Durfee (1996) built an economic society of agents in which buyers and sellers compete with one another and try to increase their total values and total profits.

Other Economic Games

There are four computer games, M.U.L.E., MUDBank, SimCity, and Smithtown, that simulate economic environments that are close to Dollar Bay/Blackwood.

M.U.L.E.

The M.U.L.E. (Multiple Use Labor Element) computer game was coded by Dan Bunten, Bill Bunten, Alan Watson, and Jim Rushing. It was published by Electronic Arts in 1983. The game is about supply and demand economic environments that are set on the planet Irata (Atari if read backwards) in some faraway space. One to four players compete among themselves in an effort to become the most successful businessperson.

The one who makes the most profit wins the game. To make money, the players have to own land and labor to produce food, energy, Smithore (material used to manufacture M.U.L.E.), and Crystite (a valuable underground mineral), and sell them via auction or collusion. The game employs the principles of supply and demand, economies of scale, the learning curve theory of production (where if the players specialize in one product on three plots of land, they increase the average yield due to efficiency gained regardless of land location), and diminishing returns. The Prisoner's Dilemma (a classical case of game theory)—the players are worse off if the colony does not survive, auctions, and collusion. Computer Gaming World's Hall of Fame (2001) inducted M.U.L.E. and one of its creators, Dan Bunten (or Dani Bunten Berry), into its Hall of Fame.

MUDBank

MUDBank was developed by C. J. Holmes in 1995 at Sonoma State University. The game is an international financial simulation. Players run a central bank or participate as commercial bankers, competing with one another for customers, deposits, and loans. The goal is to increase net worth. MUDBank was developed to teach economic concepts taught in first-year money and banking classes such as monetary base, reserve requirements, fractional reserve system, money supply, interest rate parity, and so forth. In MUDBank, three countries at a time can be set up so that some of the interactions in foreign currency markets can be observed. The game is networked over the Internet, so players from all over the world can participate in a single simulation.

There are a number of similarities between MUDBank and Dollar Bay/Blackwood (the economic virtual environments described in Chapter 7). They are all hosted on MUDs accessible through the Internet, and they all allow students to assume roles in learning economic principles. However, unlike Dollar Bay/Blackwood, MUDBank does not support online interactions among students, teachers, and agents (Holmes, 1995).

SimCity

SimCity was developed by Maxis and released in 1989 as console-based and player-vs.-computer video game. It became an instant success and was ranked one of the best computer games in 1989 by MacUser (Norr, 1989). With millions of units sold worldwide (Williamson, 2001), it became a model for other educational games.

In SimCity, the player takes the role of the Mayor, who is responsible for the economic growth and quality of life of the city. The Mayor must manipulate economic markets, zone lands, and balance budgets; build utilities and city infrastructure; control crime, traffic, and pollution; and handle natural disasters. The city is populated by simulated citizens. Like humans, these software agents build houses, churches, stores, and factories, and they complain about taxes and about the Mayor.

The citizens want more housing, better transportation, airports, or sport stadiums, and if they are not happy, they move out. Meanwhile, if the player collects excessive taxes, the city deteriorates. Thus, to win the game, the player must keep the city growing and the citizens happy (User Guide—SimCity, 1999). The main economic activities in SimCity are budgeting, zoning, and construction.

SimCity is a single-player game with many fine qualities. The main difference between SimCity and our virtual worlds for education is the point of view. In SimCity, the player is a sort of puppet master who controls vast resources and exerts more power and control than any real mayor on earth. This detracts from the authenticity of the role-based elements of the game.

Smithtown

Smithtown initially was developed at the University of Pittsburgh Learning Research and Development Center by Valerie Shute, Robert Glaser, and Kalyani Raghavan to teach microeconomics. The programs of Smithtown employ artificial intelligence methods to monitor student reasoning, track errors, and offer problem-solving advice.

Smithtown was used to evaluate student learning of microeconomic principles, including students' ability to observe consequences by varying one economic variable while keeping others constant to collect baseline data and observe changes, and to form hypotheses based on the collected data (Raghavan & Katz, 1989).

The heart of Smithtown is an exercise that asks students to predict the consequences of supply and demand shifts by constructing statements of the form, "If X increases (or decreases), then Y increases (or decreases)." The X and Y represent variables such as income, population, demand, supply, equilibrium price, equilibrium quantity, and so on. The if–then statements are an alternative to the usual textbook market equilibrium concept, forcing students to translate what they have learned from Smithtown into a format that is different from traditional approaches (Katz, 1999).

Evaluations indicated that students using this interactive program improved their examination scores by 15% (Raghavan & Katz, 1989). Shute and Psotka (1994) also found similar positive results for other systems. Smithtown (Shute & Glaser, 1990) was invented more as an experimental tool to measure economic learning skills than as a game for the public.

Chapter 11

Technical Details

This is a very technical chapter describing in some detail how the virtual worlds are implemented. This includes low-level information on how objects are defined and how servers and clients communicate with one another.

The virtual worlds are all implemented using MUDs or MOOs. It is technically true that most of these systems are implemented using LambdaMOO (a MOO, not a MUD), but MUD is a more general and accepted term, and for the purposes of this book, these terms are used interchangeably.

This chapter describes how MUDs are used to implement the simulations that host the virtual worlds, and how client programs then are developed to communicate with those simulations. These are all in the software family known as the client–server architecture. Specific technical details are discussed regarding the implementation of three of the virtual world projects to illustrate the similarities and differences that have emerged among them.

This chapter is not for the faint of heart and should be ventured into only by the technically minded.

The virtual worlds described in this book are quite different in some respects. These differences are most obvious in their user interfaces. The ProgrammingLand MOOseum is text-based, the Geology Explorer and the economic environments are "2½ D" (pronounced two-and-a-half-D, or 2.5D), and the Virtual Cell and the Virtual Archaeologist are 3D. Meanwhile, at other levels of description, the virtual worlds are quite similar. For example, although the Geology Explorer and the Virtual Cell might appear to be quite different, they are much the same at certain levels of implementation. Indeed, all these systems are pieces of a coordinated effort.

As an aside, the Geology Explorer approach to interface design, with graphically rendered backgrounds (i.e., an authentic-looking drawing of a desert scene) behind photographic foreground elements, is called 2.5D in some circles because it is intended to look like something in between 2D and 3D. This approach has the advantage of separating foreground from background, which assists players in determining where to direct their attention. Without this separation, there is a danger of the important foreground elements, like outcrops, being lost against the photographic background details.

The virtual worlds are just as different as they need to be to succeed in teaching what they have to teach. They all look and feel unique and distinct, but they all rely on a client–server approach, with a common strategy for controlling the interaction, and a number of other common elements. As we say in the midwest, they are all different, but it's the same difference.

IMPLEMENTATIONS OF SIMULATIONS

The World Wide Web Instructional Committee has developed the immersive virtual environments described in this book according to a general plan. This plan includes incorporating the key elements of the role-based learning strategy: that it is immersive, goal-oriented, exploratory, and so forth. The virtual worlds are all simulated on a MOO. These concepts and their implications have all been discussed and explained in earlier chapters.

MUDs are text-based electronic meeting places where players build societies and fantasy environments and interact with one another (Curtis, 1992, 1997; Curtis & Nichols, 1993). Technically speaking, a MUD is a multi-user server with a database and an embedded programming language. The basic components are "rooms" with "exits" connecting them, and objects for "containers" and "players." The MUD supports the object management and interplayer messaging that is required for multiplayer games, and at the same time provides a means for writing the simulation programming code and customizing the MUD.

The usual platform for operating a MUD or MOO is a machine running a UNIX-based operating system, although there have always been alternatives, such as a Macintosh server or a PC since Windows 98. Players typically connect to the server by using Telnet or some other, more specialized client program, which establishes a text-based session on the MOO. The simulations described in this book are implemented using freely available MOO environments, usually either the Xerox PARC LambdaMOO (Curtis, 1992) or the High Wired Encore MOO (Haynes & Holmevik, 1997).

Because WWIC projects are intended to be platform-independent distance education systems, client software is always built on a text-based connection using a Telnet client developed in Java. The graphical clients operate by having this embedded within—they are "wrappers" on the basic Telnet client. This enables connections from Macintosh, Microsoft Windows, or Linux X-Windows machines, using commonly available browsers.

IMPLEMENTATIONS OF GRAPHICAL CLIENTS

A key element of the exploratory game idea is the notion of a spatially oriented synthetic environment where learners explore and discover. The spatial metaphor maps a domain (and, consequently, its interface) onto the basic spatial elements of the simulation. The virtual worlds accomplish this by using client software written in Java that provides a visualizable window into the MOO running the game server—the interface to the MOO gives the user a "picture" of the state of the simulation.

This device, called a MOOPort, displays objects as they are represented by the graphical elements of the interface in such a manner that they can be manipulated in a way that makes sense to the domain. The MOOPort is the user's window into the virtual world.

One of the major shortcomings of MUDs is their low-tech communication system: text. What is needed, in many cases, is a graphical user interface layered on top of the networked multi-user database and messaging system that MUDs provide. While MUDs support the object management and interplayer messaging that are required for multiplayer games, and at the same time provide a programming language for writing the simulation and customization of the MUD, the text-based interface is problematic. This has led to the development of a number of MUD clients employing a graphical user interface (the MOOPort).

The MOOPort interface is intended to be customizable, along with the simulation itself, leading to the design of simulations and their user interface together. Once a game has been designed, the information for it is stored at the server site— both the simulation information and the user interface protocols are retained on the server, using the "directive" regimen, described below. This permits the potential for one client to be used with all simulations. It also allows for clients to be written on other platforms with minimal extra effort.

To accomplish this, a Java client and communication protocol has been developed. This supports the MOOPort, which is an accurate and consistent representation of the data on the game server. Changes in the server are reflected in the MOOPort, and manipulations of the MOOPort change the state of the server. The MOOPort on the client machines is a view in a window, which displays pictures that represent MOO objects such as exits, objects, and other players.

The MOOPort is responsible for

• Storing the current room information (identification).
• Storing a list of objects in that room.
• Notifying those objects when their state changes.
• Notifying the server when the user manipulates objects.

The MOOPort is used mostly for protocol between the server and the objects in the context, and also between the objects and the platform's user interface routines. Objects in the room are stored as MOOLogos. MOOLogos are responsible for

• Storing the object name and id.
• Storing the object's position.
• Retrieving and displaying the object's image.
• Responding to clicks, double-clicks, dragging, and drop requests.
• Responding to state changes by updating the object's image.
• Support for animation.

There are different subclasses of MOOLogos for different classes of objects in the MOO. The three main subclasses are object, exit, and player, where players are able to

- Navigate via maps.
- See authentic scenes.
- See and manipulate tools and instruments.
- See themselves and one another.

THE CLIENT–SERVER PROTOCOL

The main components of the virtual worlds, and the communication paths between them, are illustrated in Figure 11.1. The process begins with users sitting down at a desktop computer and launching a client browser such as Internet Explorer (top center of Figure 11.1). The users point their browser to a web site such as http://oit.ndsu.edu/ and request a web page from the www server (lower left of Figure 11.1). The web site returns a Java applet, which is a computer program that runs within the virtual machine (sometimes referred to as the "sand box") of the client browser. The Java applet is the client program that is used to play the game and is the interface to the virtual world. The Java applet then makes further requests to

Figure 11.1. Graphical MUDs, a System Overview

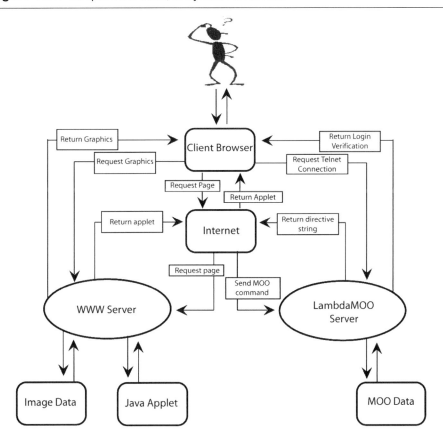

the www server, usually for "image data" to display in the MOOPort of the client program.

Next, the Java applet running in the client browser requests a Telnet connection from the LambdaMOO server, and the users log on to the game as a character in the simulation. After that, the users' actions (moving around the space, button presses, clicking on objects, and so forth) are translated to MOO commands by the client program (the Java applet running on the client browser) and sent to the LambdaMOO server. The server interprets the MOO commands (which cause the state of the server to change in some way) and responds with "directive strings" that tell the client how to reflect these changes in state. Often, this entails requesting graphics from the www server in order to change what the users are seeing in their MOOPort.

GEOLOGY EXPLORER IMPLEMENTATION STRATEGY

The Geology Explorer uses LambdaMOO to simulate Planet Oit. Students, armed with tools and instruments created as LambdaMOO objects, visit the planet to undertake a geologic exploration exercise. The Geology Explorer project has gone through two phases: a text-based phase, during which Planet Oit was defined in terms of its geoscience structure, and a graphical phase, where the existing functionality has been visually enhanced with landscapes and other images.

The purpose of this phased implementation is to capitalize on the relative simplicity of text-based development. Using text, a complex visual scene can be described in just a few sentences. To develop the graphically equivalent scene takes anywhere from hours to days. Therefore, as a development strategy, first implementing in text minimizes the cost of design missteps. If a portion of the simulation needs to be redone, it is much less expensive (and less painful) to revise or even throw away text descriptions. The analogous exercise, revising or scrapping a graphical user interface, is considerably more costly. In this way we guard against the common problem of making early decisions and then being stuck with them.

Similarly, the purpose of multimodal development, beginning with text and migrating to graphics, is to retain consistency across versions. In what has been described, both the textual and the graphical versions of Planet Oit are implemented with different client software *connecting to the same server*. By layering the simulations in this manner, we gain considerable leverage in terms of shared development and staged implementation. The model we follow, then, is one where innovations are developed in the text-based world, and the graphical world always follows behind, implementing only those elements that have been tested to some extent in the text-based environment.

GEOLOGY EXPLORER IMPLEMENTATION DETAIL

The Geology Explorer Planet Oit is composed of LambdaMOO objects. These include primarily the following:

- Room objects representing geologic spaces—mountains, caves, buttes, and the like—which are implemented as instances of the LambdaMOO "$room" object.
- Thing objects representing geologic entities—outcrops, minerals, streams, and so forth—which are implemented as instances of the LambdaMOO "$thing" object.

Objects and Actions

Rocks and minerals have behaviors that must be programmed—they must react to the geologist's instruments. For example, hitting (with a hammer or rock pick) might produce just a sound if, say, a tree is hit, or it will produce a sample if a rock outcrop is hit. Or, pouring a 10% solution of hydrochloric acid from an acid bottle will produce fizzing if there is calcite present in the rock.

In particular, rocks and minerals on Planet Oit are implemented as clickable objects. Each is further imbued with the properties of the kind of rock it is (igneous, sedimentary, or metamorphic). Those properties include whether it will produce samples capable of spawning children; whether it is movable; values for odor, flavor, and texture; and properties and values appropriate to a specific rock or mineral: density, height, weight, and depth in inches; color; luster; magnetic or not; hardness (a value in the range 0.0 to 10.0); and component minerals (a list of minerals and their proportion in the object).

Like the other objects on the planet, instruments and tools also must be programmed with "behaviors" appropriate to their use. These include both field instruments like a compass, a rock pick, and an acid bottle, and laboratory instruments, such as a spectrometer, used to perform complex analyses. To create instruments it was necessary to do the following: find out what kind of instrument each is, a laboratory instrument or a field instrument; make field instruments "fertile" because everyone who plays will need one; locate laboratory instruments in the Laboratory, where they should be made "immovable"; and assign values to identifying properties, such as odor, flavor, texture, height, width, and depth (integers representing inches), and to the weight property (a list of two integers for pounds and ounces, i.e., {5, 0}).

Then behaviors are defined by writing verbs on the instruments, with appropriate error checks, to describe behavior when reacting with rocks, minerals, or other elements of the environment. These verbs are mostly short and consist of two things: messages describing the actions of an instrument in terms of sight and sound, and a message sent to, or a verb invoked on, the object of the instrument's action.

Directives

The Geology Explorer server is an essentially text-based simulation environment (although it supports HTTP and thus is also capable of delivering web pages that might include graphics). In order to create a graphical interface to the text-based server, a system of directives has been developed. Directives are responses to the MOO commands that are implemented as LambdaMOO verbs. These verbs, which are (usually small) pieces of computer code, perform state changes in the simulation running on the LambdaMOO server. These state changes are returned to the client in the form of directives, which are text strings of a particular form that control the look of the graphical MOOPort.

The top line of Figure 11.2 shows the general syntax of the directives. Each directive is composed of fields, separated by vertical bars that specify the action, the name and number of the object the action is taken on, and so forth. As described above, directives are sent from the server to the client, the client parses them, and they are interpreted in order to control the visual display.

Figure 11.3 shows an inventory of the values that are legal in the action field of the directive. These include instructions like "cache an object," "cache a room," "connect a player," and so forth.

For example, if a player leaves a room, using an exit to travel to another room, and if that player's object number is 234, then the server will send a directive to the client of the form: #L|234|. If another player, #333, were to say, "What a beautiful day on Planet Oit," the server would send a directive to the client of the form: #S|333|What a beautiful day on Planet Oit!|

VIRTUAL CELL IMPLEMENTATION

In contrast to the Geology Explorer, the Virtual Cell has been implemented using the Virtual Reality Modeling Language (VRML; Hartman & Wernecke, 1996) and is a fully 3D game. Players "fly around" the Virtual Cell in a manner similar to the many arcade and computer games available to the public.

Figure 11.2. The General Directive Format for VCell

#ACTION|DOBJECT_NUM|NAME|FILE|DESCRIPTION|ADDITIONAL|OWNER|UNIQ_FILE|

ACTION: The ACTION is to be one of a set of DIRECTIVES

DOBJECT_NUM: The object the ACTION is intended for.

NAME: Name of DOBJECT.

FILE: The file can be of any type. The FILE path is assumed to be SERVER_PATH unless the
     absolute path of the file is specified, i.e.: http://hostname/file.ext.

Rooms are located in SERVER_PATH/rooms

Players are located in SERVER_PATH/players

Objects are located in SERVER_PATH/objects

SERVER_PATH: SERVER_PATH is set by the client parameters.

DESCRIPTION: Description of the DOBJECT.

ADDITIONAL: Additional parameters for unique cases.

OWNER: Who owns this object

UNIQ_FILE: This can be considered a detailed image of an object.

FILE type is assumed to be an image unless otherwise specified.

Figure 11.3. The Directive Protocol for Actions, with Examples

C - Cache DOBJECT and the FILE associated with it.

#C|109|player|playerimage|A wizard in the gamma quadrant|

CR - Cache Room, the unknown is the objects in the room,

#CR|118|BigRoom|roomimage|description|unknown|exit list|

CP - Connect player, (cache player) player is cached.

#CP|123|player|defaultplayer|The description|player|player.jpg|

DP - Player has disconnected, player is still cached.

#DP|123|

R - Room, when a player enters a room, the room specific info is sent.

#R|118|BigRoom|defaultroom|room description|234,345,456,678,897|

E/EP - DOBJECT has entered current room. If the E directive has a P, it's a player, add to list
    of players that are in the current room.

#EP|109|player|defaultplayer|text string|10,10,10|

#E|333|name|defaultmineral|An object|10,10,10|

L/LP - Leave, DOBJECT is no longer in the scope of the current scene.

#L|234| or #LP|109|

M - DOBJECT is moved to the coordinates

#M|109|imagename|10,10,10|

J - Execute java class specified by FILE.

#J|333|javafile

U - Update game data,

#U|INFO|INFO|INFO|MORE_INFO|

S - Say, text is displayed near the DOBJECT in a rectangular bubble.

#S|333|What a beautiful day on Planet Oit!|

NW - Spawn a new window with the given file type. If FILE is set to SERVER, Text is
    taken from ADDITIONAL.

#NW|333|IMAGE.JPG|TEXT|

P - Play sound file specified by FILE.-- .au is the assumed extension

#P|333|soundfile|

X - An exit, object, name, image, description

#X|118|North|imagename| description |screen coordinates|

However, there are only a few systems that attempt to provide multi-user 3D, and a very few that implement these worlds in biology education. The primary difference in the approach between this system and others is that the VCell system does not attempt to provide distributed VRML worlds. Rather, the VCell system attempts to provide a multi-user educational environment, which happens to be rendered as VRML.

In order to implement the VCell simulation, it is necessary to construct a multi-user environment that can use a portable rendering engine and operate efficiently over limited bandwidth. The environment must support user interaction with the environment and provide for implementation of complex agent behaviors. The practical design constraint was that freely available software components be used to construct the system. This led to the early decision to integrate three elements: (1) VRML (http://www.vrml.org/), (2) Java (http://java.sun.com/), and (3) LambdaMOO (Curtis, 1992, 1997).

The approach taken was to build a distributed programming environment, where VRML is used for rendering and user interface computation, but where more traditional programming models can be used to perform actual behaviors. Objects on the client side, implemented in Java, are reconstructed using a VRML object, which configures itself based on parameters stored on one or more servers.

In reverse order, the LambdaMOO server was chosen because it provides a persistent object-oriented database that supports multiple simultaneous users, dynamic creation and destruction of objects, and modification of object code without restarting the server. While intended primarily for text-based interaction, the LambdaMOO server has been modified to support out-of-band communications and can support various connection-oriented protocols.

In order to host the VCell simulation on the Internet, Java was chosen because it provides portable networking and user interface classes. Java also allows for the user interface elements to be extended as necessary for a particular application.

VRML was chosen because it represents a very capable rendering engine and provides the basic user navigation and interaction features needed for an immersive experience. The user interface is supplemented by Java-based windows and dialogs as necessary for a particular application.

The system is designed to provide multiple environments and allow for the user to move between these environments as necessary. For this reason, the environments are organized into distinct scenes rather than separate worlds. Thus, the client is primarily responsible for constructing and maintaining the user's current context in response to changes in the state of the simulation.

A distributed object model is used to describe the entities in each environment contained in the system. Each entity in the system is composed of two primary fragments: a server fragment and a client fragment. The server fragment is responsible for maintaining the persistent state of the entity and providing the data necessary to reconstruct the client-side portions. The client fragment is responsible for the visual appearance and local user interactions and is necessarily transient in nature. Both fragments of the entity are capable of data processing, although for the sake of consistency, most independent behaviors are performed by the server fragment. Naturally, the complexity of each fragment depends largely on whether the entity described is a static piece of 3D geometry, such as a wall, or something more complex, like an animated organelle.

The VCell Communication Protocol

The phases of communication between the client and server are as follows:

- Connection phase: The client attempts to connect to the server and identifies which entity the user has selected as a representation. Upon successful identification, the server transmits the identification number of the entity to the user's client.
- Maintenance phase: The client attempts to get representations for all referenced entities, apply updates to current fragments, and inform the server of any changes that occur.
- Disconnect phase: The user's client relinquishes all resources claimed, and the user's entity deactivates.

The VRML representations for objects are retrieved outside of the client–server communication protocol using direct HTTP requests. In a networked environment, the time required to download the representation of an object typically dominates the time required to request representations for an entire scene.

The Connection Phase

A web page launches a Java applet that spawns a Telnet thread. The Telnet process establishes a connection through a Unix port where the MOO is listening for login requests. The MOO executes its normal login sequence, password verification or character creation, and so forth. Then control is passed to special code that moves the player's avatar to the appropriate room in the MOO (either the Virtual Laboratory or the Virtual Cell, depending on the player's state). Once the MOO signals a successful connection, the client applet commences to create the interface regions for: (1) interactive help; (2) goal and status information; (3) VRML browsing; and (4) text-based MOO interactions.

The Maintenance Phase

The communication protocol between the client and the server involves the following basic transactions:

- Server tells the client which entity represents the user.
- Client requests representation for a given entity and implicitly expresses interest in that entity. When an entity's parameters (e.g., location or appearance) change, all interested entities are notified of the change.
- Server tells client the representation for a given entity. In response, the client creates the appropriate local fragment for that entity. At this point, the user's client becomes responsible for any processing necessary for maintaining the local fragment's integrity.

- Server tells client that an entity's parameter value has changed. In response, the appropriate fragment alters its behavior or appearance as needed.
- Client tells the server that an entity's parameter value has changed. In response, the server initiates the appropriate behaviors and broadcasts the necessary notifications to interested entities.
- Client terminates interest in an object.

Server-Side Implementation

The Virtual Cell is implemented on a LambdaMOO server running a modified version of the standard core database. Like the case of object hierarchies in Smalltalk, the LambdaMOO server supports only single inheritance, so it is quite common for the object hierarchy to bend during development. In the VCell object hierarchy, code and data are all inherited from the generic thing ($thing, see above).

Much of this functionality exists to support possible future research. For example, an editing client providing a Smalltalk-like browser would require a different representation format than the current VRML client. Likewise, multiple servers could be networked together for the purposes of distributing a complex simulation. If the need arises, the event listener model could be modified to support automatically ignoring unimportant events, although this has not been the case so far. One of the benefits of the listener model is that intelligent (or at least interesting) responsive behaviors are easier to implement. More important, objects that have no interesting behavior do not add overhead when placed in the vicinity of useful objects.

In LambdaMOO, the generic thing has two main children: the generic server and the VRML thing. The generic server is implemented to support distributed processing. Due to the nature of the LambdaMOO server, each active network connection eventually associates with an object in the database in a one-to-one manner. Most of the functionality in this object assists a foreign server in carrying out its tasks. Similarly, the VRML thing is parent to the generic player, which, like the generic server, assists foreign servers.

While players are conceptually a type of server, the fact that players normally are tied into an interactive object makes them a type of generic thing. Most of the functionality built into the generic player class is aimed at implementing tasks such as getting an object's local representation and expressing interest in order to receive updates. For example, the client calls get_representation on the player's object, and the server's implementation of this function automatically adds the player to the update lists for the appropriate object.

Since the primary concern for the server is communication with a client displaying VRML representations of an interactive world, certain functionality is required specifically to support tracking of location, position, orientation, and scale.

Location: On the LambdaMOO server, two properties, location and contents, are maintained for each object. Naturally, if object A contains object B, A's location is object B, and A is in the list of B's contents. Because of this duality, objects are moved by setting their location, and the contents field is updated as a side effect. Since sending updates on the entire contents list can be expensive, updates are sent instead on two special properties as needed: add_contents and remove_contents.

Position, Orientation, and Scale: To maintain correct client-side representation, the numeric values for each of these properties are converted to floating point numbers. This is largely for the sanity of programmers, since the LambdaMOO server refuses to automatically convert between the two.

VCell Client-Side Implementation

The chief technical difficulties involved in constructing the VCell client concern constructing a VRML world (a 3D visualization) that conforms to a simulated world maintained on a centrally located server.

VCell Scene Graph Maintenance

In VRML terminology, the objects in a scene are organized into a data structure commonly referred to as a scene graph. Since the scene displayed to the user is supposed to change in response to changes in the overall environment, updating the scene is one of the primary responsibilities of the client.

The algorithm used during connection is this:

- At connection, a reference to a player object is received. This becomes the first unresolved object reference.
- Whenever an unresolved object is encountered, the client issues a command to the server for that object's representation. A side effect of this request is that the client is listed as *interested* in updates on that object.
- When an object representation arrives, the client attempts to make that portion of the scene graph correct. This effort is largely devoted to ensuring that the location/contents relationship from the server holds for that object. A side effect is that the scene graph is reconstructed in a breadth first manner from the user's object.
- After the scene graph is partially constructed, it is possible that updates on location or contents may introduce new unresolved objects into the list or indicate that the current scene graph is incorrect. If this occurs, then parts of the current scene graph are recursively discarded and the process of constructing the scene graph continues in the same manner as if the user had connected recently.

Animation

The glue that binds the scene graph on the client side is a prototype called the RotationSocket. Currently the individual components of this prototype include a Transform node, a Group node, a TimeSensor, a PositionInterpolator, an Orientation-Interpolator, a Script node, and routing information sufficient to provide smooth gliding and rotation for all 3D objects.

Other forms of animation are possible as supported by VRML for the various geometries, but care must be taken that different users viewing the same 3D world receive appropriate versions of the animation.

The VCell Directive Protocol

The LambdaMOO server uses the TCP/IP Telnet protocol for communication with client applications. Because Telnet has very little support for binary mode communications, information is transmitted to the client in the form of directive strings. The basic format for these directives is #Directive|ValueList.

The general syntax of VCell directives is shown in Figure 11.4. Like the Geology Explorer directive set (see Figures 11.2 and 11.3), the idea is to form a string that informs the client about the new state of the simulation.

At present, the directive system is used for displaying regions for dynamically generated text and for displaying regions containing commands. The directive system also is used for communicating the player's identity, object representations, and value updates to the client. In order to simplify the coding of the server, the convention of "give the client only the updates it has asked for" is used. Rather than the server attempting to guess or assume what the client is interested in, the client is required to request state updates for any object for which it maintains a representation.

One benefit of the LambdaMOO server is that a text-based implementation of remote procedure calls is fairly simple. At present, the mechanism is quite

Figure 11.4. The VCell Directive Format

```
<Directive String> => #<Directive>|<ValueList>|
<Directive> =>
  A sequence of characters not including a | character
<ValueList> =>
  One of
    Nothing
    A sequence of the following separated by | characters.
    A terminating | character is required.
      A string surrounded by " characters.
      An integer in text format, e.g. 3.
      A floating point number including the
        decimal point. E.g. 3.0 or 3e-10.
      An object reference. The text
        representation is a # character
        followed by an integer in text form.
        E.g. #303.
      A list. The format has a beginning
        { followed by comma separated elements
        terminated by a }.
        E.g. {"url", "http://www.w3.org/"}.
```

basic, and support for synchronous procedure calls has not been necessary. The design details for synchronous procedure calls have been worked out, however, so they will be available if the need arises.

DISCRETE SIMULATION

Knowledge representation is a combination of data structures and interpretive procedures. In the Virtual Cell, the simulation environment is object-oriented, and objects are used to represent the conceptual knowledge of things, descriptions of things, and categories of things. Concepts in the Virtual Cell are modeled in a straightforward manner by mapping them onto the LambdaMOO object hierarchy.

In like manner, the simulation of events provides procedural knowledge of action, time sequences, and cause-and-effect. Process in VCell is implemented by discrete, outcome-based simulation where, for example, values returned by an instrument or assay simply are retrieved, whenever possible, from the object under inspection.

This approach to simulation is an implementation decision based primarily on efficiency considerations. In the most simplistic case, simulations of this sort are effected by a table that coordinates an entity's state with its measurable values. Therefore, VCell processes are rarely the product of continuous or numeric simulations, but the consequence of simple, discrete state changes within the biological constituents.

MUDS AND WEB SITES

It is tempting to argue on technical grounds that these virtual environments could be implemented using standard web-browsing technology. This, so the argument goes, would serve to make the technology more accessible and more mainstream, which would assist with a number of things, such as maintaining software coding standards, simplifying system portability issues, increasing the base of pre-existing "widgets" and thus streamlining development, and so forth. These are, indeed, tempting technical arguments. However, we have resisted them for a number of reasons.

Exploring a MOO is quite different from browsing a series of web pages. MOOs are much more interactive. A MOO allows interaction among students, between a student and the environment, and between a student and software agents. Furthermore, record keeping is possible and even easy in a MOO, in contrast with a web implementation.

A MOO contains all the capabilities of an Internet chat room. Thus, students are aware of one another's presence. If other students or instructors are present in the room, they may enter into a conversation. This conversation may be public, received by everyone currently in the room, or private, only heard by two participants. A person not in the room may be paged, that is, signaled that a conversation is desired and where the originating person is.

In a MOO, students (or teachers) may disguise their identity. This has the effect of freeing them to ask questions they might not be brave enough to ask if their identity was known. Two students at different physical locations thus may communicate and engage in collaborative work, which would be impossible on a web site. The students have all the control they had in the web implementation and substantially more. A MOO also may contain software agents. These are programs that occupy the MOO in approximately the same way as students. They may interact with the students in the form of a tutor or peer. They also may be invisible and perform clean-up or other automated tasks.

Record keeping in a web site is relatively difficult. A server may record what page was served but the identity of who received the page is usually only an IP address. In contrast, a MOO requires a real login and password. Because of this login process, a variety of record keeping is done automatically and more is available with special programming. It is therefore possible to track students' progress at a detailed level.

CONCLUSION

This chapter surveys the range of technologies we have employed and developed in order to build our worlds. This includes serve-side programming on the MUDs we have produced, and client-side programming to create the interfaces needed for students to play the games. It has also been necessary for us to invent a set of protocols for the server and the clients to communicate. We have described all this at a level we hope is useful to the technically inclined but short of overwhelming. We are hopeful we have achieved this slender goal.

Chapter 12

The Future
of Virtual Worlds

In this chapter, we embark on a somewhat laughable attempt at predicting the future.

However, we hedge our predictions by framing them as what we think should happen, and what we want to happen, instead of what actually might happen—the future we would like to see.

A few things are easy to predict. This "computer fad" seems to have turned into an ongoing thing, and the progression of computer technology seems to be proceeding apace. And the schools seem to be invested in computer technology as an educational tool. This provides an audience for the kinds of things we are trying to do.

Meanwhile, there are a large number of research questions to ask and answer. We enumerate a number of these and the trends we believe they will lead to.

The group writing this book lays no claims to being "media prophets" like Marshall McLuhan (1964), or prognosticators of any stripe. But we do have a vision for the future and a plan for venturing forth. So what follows is not claiming to predict the future, but describes what the future might be like—if we get our way.

There are several basic issues that need to be considered in all educational projects: content, delivery, and course support. Most projects innovate in only one of these, while in the systems described here, the three are totally interrelated. The idea is to attempt to contain the subject matter of a textbook, the interactivity of a computer game, the feedback of a teacher, and the information of an administrative database, and to make this available anytime, anywhere over the Internet, in a learner-centered style.

LARGE-SCALE EMPIRICAL ASSESSMENT STUDIES

We propose to conduct further large-scale studies over the next several years using the same basic protocol but varying the treatment variables in order to study the effect. There are several research questions we plan to explore.

We have noticed, particularly in the Geology Explorer studies, an interesting variance in student performance relative to the scenario. Some scenarios produce consistently higher scores than others, and this is correlated across coders, yet the scenarios are written to be similar in complexity and style. We will seek to understand what makes a "good" scenario and what factors within scenarios affect student performance through protocol analysis of interviews, both in-person and automated.

1. What are the features of goal-oriented scenarios that best promote co-operation? A key unexplored feature of these virtual environments is their multi-user nature. By pressing the role-based metaphor, we plan to set up experiments where students will be rewarded for collaboration. One such experiment will work on creating collaborative goals, and another on creating complementary instrument sets (so students will seek one another out for information not available to them with the tools they've been issued).
2. In these collaborative undertakings, what learning factors are influenced—depth? complexity? speed? We will seek to evaluate whether students are learning more things, or learning them faster, as a consequence of collaboration in virtual worlds.
3. What are the factors that influence student performance in scenario-based assessment? What scenario variability can be traced to question type or narrative style?
4. Most important, how can we explain the significance of our studies? To determine this, we plan to develop experiments where we vary
   - the similarity of the group tasks to separate role and immersion effects from low-level task specifics
   - the populations, by testing biology students with geology scenarios, for example
   - the experience level of the populations to compare, first-year students against seniors
   - the effects as we move to younger groups, to determine the age levels at which virtual environments begin to lose effectiveness.

DIRECTIONS FOR FUTURE RESEARCH

Role-based immersive virtual environments (IVEs) for education, and the assessment of role-based learning, will be the core activities of the future. These role-based, multi-user, content-laden systems are computerized educational games of a specific and particular design that emphasize immersion, exploration, and learning-by-doing (Slator, Juell et al., 1999). Based on the core competencies already established at NDSU, the mission will be to pioneer research and methods by extending the program in three directions: horizontally, vertically, and laterally.

Horizontal Expansion

Horizontal expansion is simply, but significantly, the mission to add content to existing systems. For example, the Geology Explorer (Saini-Eidukat, Schwert, & Slator, 2001) has modules for mineral and rock identification, site interpretation, and geologic mapping, and the Virtual Cell (White, McClean, & Slator, 1999) has modules for organelle identification, the electron transport chain, and photosynthesis. These modules represent several hours of student engagement but still only begin to provide experience with the many activities offered in the curricula. Each of the projects currently underway has a list of horizontal expansion plans (i.e., new modules) to pursue.

Vertical Expansion

The pedagogical goals of the NDSU systems have been centered mainly on undergraduate education—this is where the systems initially have been fielded and tested. The NDSU approach focuses on material that is traditionally most difficult for students to grasp from typical lecture-based presentation, and favors a more organic approach. For example, the Geology Explorer begins with a freshman-level activity (mineral and rock identification) and then builds on that experience by moving directly to an interpretive geologic mapping exercise (sometimes not covered until junior year in the traditional course sequence). In other words, these NDSU IVE systems build from one idea to another in the natural progression illuminated by the practice of working geologists in the field.

The idea of vertical expansion is to seek opportunities to extend the content both upward toward advanced levels and, just as important, downward to the public schools, the technical and community college arena, and the informal education opportunities of museums and other public education where there can be fewer assumptions about the prior experience of learners.

Lateral Expansion

Potentially the most important activity will be to identify the disciplines and subdisciplines that lend themselves to role-based learning-by-doing—and those that do not. For example, we have determined that geology and biology are natural fits with IVE pedagogical strategies. Practitioners in these sciences tend to practice in the field, which might be a hillside or a wet lab. Archaeology, cultural anthropology, botany, ecology, and paleontology might seem to be obvious extensions. However, what about psychology? Or economics? Perhaps these can be visualized within the framework. But then what about more fundamental pursuits like arithmetic and reading? Or mathematics and physics? These are not so obvious. Foreign language instruction might seem natural, since the immersive approach is central to that, and distance learning communities have already been created. But, language processing and understanding in computer-based systems present their own set of highly intractable problems. These are the confounding questions embedded in lateral expansion at the edges of our research and understanding. It seems clear there are a number of "-ologies" that will lend themselves to immersive role-based systems. But which are they? This is a central, global question we will seek to address. To explore these disciplines is to advance the science.

TECHNOLOGY

A future filled with technology seems fairly certain. Computers seem to get faster and cheaper at the same time, and it is not very risky to guess this will continue for a while longer. This is good news for researchers like ourselves who develop educational media that sometimes push the boundaries of the middle ground. We hope to make inroads across the "digital divide," and this leads to a funny balancing act. We want to implement advanced features, but we need to be accessible to a wide range of users. We do not want to be too far in front of the curve, because most schools in the world are behind the curve—some lagging very, very far behind the times.

You see the problem. If we push the envelope too far by, say, implementing a virtual world in high resolution 3D that requires cutting-edge video cards to render the scenes at acceptable frame rates, there will be a very small number of institutions that can use our materials. On the other hand, we need a certain degree of modern technology to work our magic. These systems are, after all, computer-based simulations of authentic environments—and this implies some degree of modern technology. We do not foresee much headway in implementing totally low-tech solutions—this has been done before, in the "page turning" educational applications of the past.

The hope and the plans for the future rely on the trend we have seen these past many years. While it takes a while for everyone to catch up, there is nonetheless an obvious upward arc, where remote rural schools, and destitute urban schools, find a way to upgrade their equipment. With the trajectory we have all witnessed in the recent past, the hope is that sooner, rather than later, everybody will be capable of experiencing virtual words for education as we are building them now, so we can go forward to the next level of implementation, whatever that turns out to be.

It would appear that computers are here to stay, and that computers in education are equally likely to stick around. The trick is to create educational software that is advanced and engaging, while still accessible to a range of schools, reaching, but not exceeding, their technical capabilities.

MATERIALS DEVELOPMENT

One of the critical needs is to ensure that virtual worlds make teaching easier, not harder. This means creating lessons and materials that are ancillary to the classroom.

We have created some lesson plans and the "Planet Oit Comic" in this regard, but there is clearly much more to do. Methodology for integrating IVEs into classroom instruction is an open issue.

DEVELOPMENT TOOLS

Creating virtual/visual worlds is an intensive process in terms of pedagogical design, knowledge engineering, and software development. Having gained experience in the handcrafting of these systems, we now envision an integrated library of software tools to substantially streamline the development of future worlds. These software tools will enable content experts to craft virtual worlds for instruction, with a minimum of intervention or oversight by computing professionals. They include software for building abstraction hierarchies, concept frames, object interfaces, virtual maps, agent attitudes, and others.

One good idea for application development would be to use the graphical user interface to construct the simulation builder itself. This way the people who design the simulations can do so from a graphical client. They would design the simulation by describing the interaction of discrete values. They then would create a user interface to do three things: affect the values of the simulation, reflect the state of the simulator, and convey other information like user interaction and tutoring.

The combination of a simulation, multiple players, and multimedia is not only an effective education and training tool, but a more compelling application all around.

DISSEMINATION

As of this writing, our virtual worlds are visible and available on the Internet for anyone to use. Teachers can register their classes using faculty pages, and their students can venture together onto our virtual worlds. This is great, and we encourage it, but there are some pitfalls to address.

The first pitfall is technical. When these systems get popular enough, there will be worldwide demand that will result in hitting our NDSU servers at all times of the day and night. This will be a fine thing; however, from a technical standpoint, it will create a bottleneck as all this traffic will be going in and out of our site. At some point, if this prediction is correct, the servers simply will not be able to handle the load.

The second pitfall is sociological. With servers visible and available on the Internet, there is the potential for predatory personalities to join schoolchildren as they explore the virtual world, and this is simply bad.

The answer is a "by cluster" dissemination scheme, where servers are hosted at remote locations, behind firewalls and security measures of that sort. In other words, the next step is to give teachers a copy of a virtual world so they can host it locally, on their own network, without fear of intrusion. Their students will explore the world together, with no possibility of outsiders entering the environment.

The way to do this is by developing an IVE "appliance"—a piece of hardware with a power cord and a network interface that can be plugged into a school's computer cluster and remain invisible to the outside world. This will guarantee that the only players students will meet in the world will be players from their own school, and not outsiders of any type.

CONCLUSION

The main goals of science education are to foster a scientifically literate public and to teach students a framework of basic principles and approaches that later can be used to solve science-based problems. The challenge for science educators is to employ educational methods that deliver both the basic principles and the important content material in a meaningful way.

Research in active learning environments includes implementing "live" simulations populated with interactive objects: artifacts and agents. These simulations are for exploration and discovery, to engage learners while treating them to a plausible synthetic experience. Simulated environments are valuable teaching tools because they can take learners to places they ordinarily would not experience, either because the places are too expensive, dangerous, or a physical impossibility.

Unfortunately, simulations are complex and difficult to build. The need is for research into the construction of such systems, so that appropriate tools can be developed to facilitate future constructions.

There is also need for research in the area of end-user interaction, which includes discovering better and more efficient ways of presenting information, supporting navigation, and delivering content. Client programs and browsing interfaces have moved through several generations within just the past few years, and there appears to be no end in sight.

Other issues also affect the science educator's choice of pedagogical methods. At the college level, the student body is more diverse than ever. The demographics of the student body suggest the average student age is older, with a greater percentage of students having simultaneously to support their education through outside employment. The students also have a different, more practical attitude toward their education. All of these factors require the educator to search for instructional methods to augment the lecture/laboratory approach to education.

Computer technology addresses some of these issues. For example, multimedia-based delivery of course materials offers multiple modes that reach students with different personal styles. Network-based instruction tools can relieve some of the place-bound and time-bound problems of the modern student. Finally, actively engaging students with unique visualizations and role-based simulations has the potential to engage in ways that lecture/laboratory approaches can never hope to.

The Common Sense of It

There is no doubt that children learn from parents, and parents learn from grandparents—whether there is literature supporting this or not, we all know it is true. Meanwhile, we are all raised in a culture, and we take that background and sensibility with us when we go to class. This affects how we experience school.

Culture is something we exist in, and something that forms us. We watch our elders and learn how they act; we watch our peers and learn how they act. Like a hockey player watching the professionals, we see how it is done—move left, stop, shoot, score—and we adopt these moves as our own.

Or, we go on a geology field trip, and we see how the van is packed, and how the day is scheduled, and how the students are directed, and when to call for lunch. Afterwards we have a notebook logging our experience, and we come away with an idea of how to run our own field camp.

Immersive virtual environments have the same key elements. The simulations demand participation and involvement, while the software tutors guide and teach, sometimes by giving hints, and sometimes by showing how are things are done. Afterwards we have a notebook logging our experience, and we come away with the knowledge of how to do it.

Final Words

Marshall McLuhan (1964), media prophet, maintained that 20th-century people did not want goals so much as they wanted roles. The authentic simulated environments described here enable learners to assume roles in particular contexts and have meaningful, virtual experiences as a consequence. When these experiences are structured and arranged, even loosely, so that playing a role in the environment can illustrate the important concepts and procedures of the simulated domain, then students are able to learn-by-doing.

Experience with problem solving in a context is what leads to intuition—that sensibility that mathematicians develop, allowing them to guess at a good path to a solution. However, most mathematicians will admit that intuition is a funny way to put it. Intuition implies knowing without reasoning—a mental leap to a conclusion, an extrasensory perception. But everybody knows that is not really what happens. What happens is, one solves a million problems, and that experience assists with knowing how to proceed with the next one. In other words, all that experience leads to expertise.

This is where we see things going. More and better experiences leading to learning that otherwise would not be possible for various reasons: cost, opportunity, or the laws of physics. This book is about learning and experiences. Virtual worlds can take us places, like the interior of a biological cell or the rolling plains of a long-forgotten history. This is where learning and experiences await.

Acknowledgments

These projects started at NDSU in 1996 and there is a dizzying swim of people who have contributed in various ways. This is an attempt at listing them. For anyone who is overlooked, please accept our apologies now, and be assured that if this book ever gets into a second printing, errors will be corrected.

Here goes.

A LITTLE HISTORY

Way back in the way back, there was a group on the NDSU campus in the early 1990s devoted to spreading the word about this new technology: the World Wide Web. This group called itself the World Wide Web Instructional Committee (WWWIC), and it helped people learn about the web, create web pages for their classes, and so forth. This group was funded internally by NDSU and was chaired by Dr. Paul Juell—and under his direction laid much of the groundwork for early adopters of web-based technologies in research and teaching at NDSU.

Starting in the fall of 1996, after these activities had been institutionalized, WWWIC devoted itself to research questions involving instruction and learning on the web, which quickly came to focus on research on learning in immersive virtual environments.

On the front lines were the faculty who invested themselves in these projects, which represented a new research direction and as such presented no small risk to faculty members' professional lives. Yet they saw the opportunities and jumped in.

The first among equals is Dr. Donald P. Schwert, who came to a talk and saw the possibilities, leading to the idea and design of the Geology Explorer. Shortly thereafter, Dr. Phil McClean, who was by then the chairman of WWWIC, proposed the Virtual Cell idea, and this created the critical mass that led to everything else. Dr. Bernhardt Saini-Eidukat and Dr. Alan R. White quickly were recruited to join the effort, and that formed the core of the group that persists to this day.

The World Wide Web Instructional Committee has now parlayed these research ideas into a $4 million battleship that employs more than 50 faculty, staff, and students on a routine basis.

Subsequently, Dr. Jeffrey Clark joined the group, adding an anthropology dimension with the Virtual Archaeologist project and a suite of efforts that would make its own book—such is the scope of the Archaeology Technology Lab. And, following that, Dr. Lisa Daniels in teacher education and Dr. Jeff Terpstra in statistics joined the group—which is where we are as of this writing.

Each and every one of the group has taken the step, reaching out to a new research paradigm in learning that draws on their expertise, and yet takes them out of their discipline and out onto the thin ice of interdisciplinary research in learning.

If you're young, you don't see the risk—but if you're old, you see what this means in professional terms. To have taken these steps back in 1996, well, that borders on courage.

BUILDING THIS BOOK

First, the confession—we thought this book would be easy to write, because we had so many conference and journal papers to draw on. We thought it would be a snap—easy-peasy. But it turned out to be anything but that. In the end, everything was rewritten, and nothing of those early papers has survived into this book.

If you are thinking about writing a book, and I don't advise it, be prepared to rewrite everything. It's a stone-cold drag, but there it is—it needs to be done, and there do not appear to be any shortcuts. Sadly.

SPECIAL THANKS

The work described in this book was primarily supported by grants from the National Science Foundation and the U.S. Department of Education FIPSE program. Profound gratitude is owed to Dr. Anthony Maddox and Dr. Harriet Taylor.

I am sad to say that I did not actually think of the title, "Electric Worlds"; John Bauer did. But I knew it was right the second I heard it. My thanks to Yorick Wilks and Louise Guthrie for their blessing on the allusion to "Electric Words." Thanks as well to Ruth Davis and Liz Macaulay, who picked me up when I needed it most.

Dayna Del Val and Justin Hawley, without whom this might never have appeared, provided the bulk of the editing, revising, and rewriting assistance leading to the publication of this book. Matthew Higdem and Audrey and Rita Slator provided earlier editorial assistance.

There are a very few who provided seminal inspirations in the early days.

John Bauer was a source of ideas, created a vision, and made early contributions to programming and graphical user interface development—we would not be here, except for that. Acey Olson developed the graphical backgrounds for the first version of Planet Oit, a vision that persists to this day.

Additional thanks are due to Mark Tinguely, who saved our world when its universe imploded; Kendall Nygard, who saw a good thing before anybody else; R. Craig Schnell, who bought us a disk drive in the very early days, when we really, really, needed it; and to Col. Dave Schmidt for the name Planet Oit.

It is one thing to get big grants, which is very satisfying, but it is another thing to get a little help when you are just getting started and need it the most. A little rhythm from the department, the college, and the administration—that is huge.

CONTRIBUTIONS TO THE PROJECTS

Throughout the years, a number of faculty, staff, and student employees have helped with the effort, sometimes for money, sometimes for credit. What follows is an impossible attempt to recognize them all.

Geology Explorer Planet Oit

Jon Abel, Kimberly Addicott. Bryan Bandli, John Bauer, Otto Borchert, Jill Bozovsky, Bob Cosmano, Rahul Devabhaktuni, Brent Alan Ellingson, Chris Fish, Brian Gietzen, Julia Arline Karst-Gray, Nathan Green, Sarah Gregor, Justin Hawley, Jill Hockemeyer, Guy Hokanson, Kim Jacobs, Yongxin "George" Jia, Kuo-Di Jian, Beau Kautzman, Tammy Kavli, Lucas Koehntop, Ned Krueger, Atif Majeed, Clark Markell, Bhaskar Marthi, Rose McKenney, Alan McQuarrie, Vidyalatha Nagareddy, Aparna Nandula, Acey Olson, Aric Olson, John Opgrande, Kishore Peravali, Rebecca Potter, Dan Reetz, Carson Rittel, Jennifer Thorstad, Leah Tilly, Shannon Tomac, Daniel Turany, Joy Turnbull, Dean Vestal, KC Vorthmann, Jane Willenbring, Bradley Vender, Mindy Sue Vogel, James Walsh, Jin Wang, Paul West, Shanhong Wu.

The Virtual Cell

Aaron Bergstrom, Rob Brantsig, Brady Brodsho, Kellie Erickson, Elisa Goldade, Jacob Halvorson, Lance Holden, Christina Johnson, Frances Lawrenz, Mei Li, Kellie Martindale, Kevin McClean, Ganesh Padmanabhan, Roxanne Rogers, Mark Rose, Naomi Roster, Daniel Small, Shannon Sorrells, Debra Tomanek, Bradley Vender, Erik Vossler, Hong Wu.

ProgrammingLand MOOseum

Justin Abel, Radha Balakrishnan, Yue Cui, Murali Dhandapani, Faye Erickson, Uma Kedla, Tom Lemke, Bryan McGowan, Martina Miteva, Satyanarayana Pasupuleti, Ge Peng, Sisir Ray, Mahesh Sharma, Hong Wu.

Dollar Bay

Jill Bozovsky, Matt Carlson (employee photos), Harold "Cliff" Chaput, Bob Cosmano, Ron Davis (casino images), Ben Dischinger, Chris Engel (fortune machine), Brian Gietzen (discount warehouse), Tim Hoke (the juggler), Rodney Holm (discount warehouse), Christopher Imdieke, Alan McQuarrie, Dale Muchow, Derrick Olson, Rebecca Potter, Ben Preisler, Patrick Regan, Mark Rose, Peter Schultz, Jaime Sebelius, Scott Sherman (vending vendor), Gary Steinhaus (the mail agent), Mark Trom (the Black Rat), Bradley Vender, James Walsh (the magician).

JavaMOO

Harold "Cliff" Chaput, Bob Cosmano, Ben Dischinger, Christopher Imdieke, John Opgrande, Bradley Vender.

Blackwood

Spencer Anderson, Jill Bozovsky, Joe Duncan, Chad Eddy, Jason Huck, Mohammed Elimarghary, Nathan Green, Justin Hawley, Jessica Mack, Doug Plante, Josh Stompro, Bradley Vender.

The Virtual Archaeologist

Marita Abe, Aaron Bergstrom, Nancy Boll, Wade Burns, Gary Clambey, Josh Dorothy, Derek Eichele, Kade Ferris, Shawn Fisher, Chad Forde, Naia George, Richard Frovarp, Emily Hagemeister, Justin Hawley, Bill Jockheck, Christina Johnson, Eunice Johnston, Ikania Kaale, Ryan Kravitz, James Landrum, III, Francis Larson, Chris Lindgren, William Perrizo, Sanjay Ramaswamy, Daniel Reetz, Tim Rousch, Stephanie Schrader, Douglas Snider, Lai Ong Teo, J. Liessman Vantine, Ryan White, Alan Woolworth, Melissa Zuroff.

DEDICATIONS

There are so many main authors on this book, we need to reserve a space for each of them to make his or her own dedication. Here goes.

Brian M. Slator

My mother, Isabel Slator (née Spencer) provided me with all the things I needed to get where I am right now—at a keyboard, typing a book dedication. From there, I turn to my wife, Rita, and my children, Adam, Audrey, and Megan, who have endured this book-writing process for far too long.

Richard T. Beckwith

To my wife, Olivia, and our children, Tallis and Ailsa.

Lisa Brandt

The students who inspire me, the colleagues who mentor me, the family and friends who succor me, to you I dedicate this work.

Harold Chaput

Love and gratitude to my husband, Kazuki.

Jeffrey T. Clark

For the years of patience, for lost evenings and weekends while I pursued my research goals, I dedicate my contribution to this book to my wife, Anna Marie, and my children, Todd and Kamaya.

Lisa M. Daniels

I would like to acknowledge with gratitude all those people I have been fortunate enough to have as students throughout the years. They have inspired me, increased my depth of understanding, and created in me a desire to continue exploring ways to improve learning experiences of future students, whether in my class or otherwise.

Justin Hawley

To my loving wife, Naia, and the countless number of faculty and friends from whom I have experienced and learned a great deal.

Curt Hill

To my wife, Loree; children, Travis, Libby, and Andy; and grandchildren, Maggie and Henry.

Phil McClean

You are who you are and able to think and do what you do because your parents found each other and created the environment that enabled you to be who you are. For that I dedicate this to my parents.

John Opgrande

I dedicate this to my family, friends, and mentors, who have stayed with me through the years of being the perpetual student. It's been a journey, but a fun journey at that!

Bernhardt Saini-Eidukat

To the women of my life: my mother, Frieda B. Eidukat; my wife, Anna Sígridur Arnar; and my daughter, Liv Margrét Kaur Eidukat.

Donald P. Schwert

To Charlene, who over these many years has patiently tolerated all of my probings into various avenues of science and of education, I make my dedication.

Bradley Vender

Dedicated to the memory of my mother, for whom this would have been a wonderful surprise, and to Charles, Jennifer, Mike, Maria, and little Gabriel, for whom it goes without saying. Also to Dr. Brian Slator and everyone else on the Virtual Cell and the other projects, without whom none of this would have been possible.

Alan R. White

I am deeply grateful to my Grandparents and my Mom and Dad for passing to me a long family tradition of appreciation for higher education and a love of teaching. Tristan and Caleb, my sons who are now fine young men, you make me swell with pride at your accomplishments. Bunny, my best friend and wife, thanks for sharing this ride with me. I dedicate my contributions to this book to family, past, present, and future. Oh yes, and to Don . . .

And let that be our last word—for now.

Glossary

3D organelle–A computer-generated, three-dimensional, differentiated structure within a cell, such as a mitochondrion, vacuole, or chloroplast, that performs specific functions.

AAAS–Advancing Science, Serving Society, the world's largest general scientific society, responsible for the Benchmarks for Science Literacy (see http://www.aaas.org/).

ACL (agent communication language)–Provides for the communication of such things as constraints, negations, rules, and quantified expressions.

Algorithm–A step-by-step, problem-solving procedure, most likely an established, recursive computational procedure for solving problems in a finite number of steps.

ANCOVA (analysis of covariance)–Predicts the grader's postscore (after treatment) using the group variable group (Oit, Alternative, Control) and the grader's prescores (before treatment) as the continuous covariate.

APD (average potential demand)–A variable in the Dollar Bay economic simulation.

Astro-VR–A social, virtual reality project for use by the professional astronomy community.

C++–An object-oriented computer programming language.

CAD–Computer-aided design.

CCI (chemical composition instrument)–An instrument found on the virtual Planet Oit.

CCLI-EMD–A National Science Foundation program, *Course, Curriculum & Laboratory Improvement*–Educational Materials Development.

CD–A small optical disc on which data such as music, text, or graphic images are digitally encoded.

CD-ROM–A compact disc that functions as read-only memory.

Ceilidh system–A system used for grading student computer programs (Foubister, Michaelson, & Tomes, 1997).

CGI (common gateway interface)–A standard for running external programs from a World Wide Web http server.

Cirque–A steep bowl-shaped hollow occurring at the upper end of a mountain valley, especially one forming the head of a glacier or stream.

CG (cluster groups)–Also called consumer groups, the psychographic description of consumer behavior used in the Dollar Bay game.

Code–To write or revise a computer program.

Command verbs–The English-like verbs typed into a text-based MUD, for example, on Planet Oit, the students' application of instruments ("streak," "scratch," "hit," etc.) and senses ("view," "taste," "touch," etc.).

Constructivist theory–The idea that individuals piece together their own understanding by reference to their own comprehension of materials and to their own individual experience.

CORBA (common object request broker architecture)–Object Management Group specifications that provide the standard interface definition between OMG-compliant objects.

CosmoPlayer–Downloadable plug-in that makes it possible to view VRML (Virtual Reality Modeling Language) files in a standard web browser.

Courseware–Educational software designed especially for classroom use.

Database–A collection of data arranged for ease and speed of search and retrieval.

EAI (external authoring interface)–A software system that allows external programs like the Virtual Cell to access data within a rendering engine like VRML.

Encore MOO (Haynes & Holmevik, 1997)–One of the more popular MOO systems that are freely and publicly available.

Enculturation–Process by which an individual learns the traditional content of a culture and assimilates its practices and values.

Ethnography–The branch of anthropology that deals with the scientific description of specific human cultures.

Expository text–Writing that is intended to give information.

FAQ–A list of frequently asked questions and their answers about a given subject.

Freebsd–A free operating system based on the BSD 4.4–lite release from Computer Systems Research Group at the University of California at Berkeley—see UNIX.

Geophysical–Relating to the physics of the earth and its environment.

Geoscientific–Relating to or employing the methodology of science of the earth.

GUI (graphical user interface)–An interface for issuing commands to a computer utilizing a pointing device, such as a mouse, that manipulates and activates graphical images on a monitor.

GUMI (graphical user-friendly MOO interface)–Software to connect with Planet Oit.

Heterogeneous–Consisting of dissimilar elements or parts.

Heuristic–A rule of thumb or educated guess.

HTTP–The hypertext transport protocol used to request web pages over the Internet.

Hypertext–A computer-based text retrieval system that enables a user to access particular locations in webpages or other electronic documents by clicking on links within specific webpages or documents.

Igneous–Describing rocks formed by solidification from a molten state.

Immersive–Something that surrounds or covers; engrossing.

Infrastructure–An underlying base or foundation especially for an organization or system.

IVN (interactive video network)–A network of meeting rooms for video conferencing.

Java–A trademark used for a programming language designed to develop applications, especially ones for the Internet that can operate on different platforms.

Java3D–Java language libraries supporting VRML (virtual reality modeling language) and other 3D formats.

Kimberlite–A rock formation in which diamonds are formed.

LambdaMOO–Freely available object-oriented MUD (Multi-User Domain).

LAN–Local area network.

Linux–A UNIX-based operating system.

Lisp–A programming language designed to process data consisting of lists.

Metamorphic–Changed in structure or composition as a result of metamorphism.

Microeconomics–The study of the operations of the components of a national economy, such as individual firms, households, and consumers.

MONSTER–Redesign of the second of the great early experiments in computer fantasy gaming (ZORK).

MOO–An object-oriented MUD (Multi-User Domain).

MSRP–Manufacturer's suggested retail price, common retailing concept employed in the Dollar Bay simulation.

MUD–Multi-user domain.

Multimedia–An application that can combine text, graphics, full-motion video, and sound into an integrated package.

MySQL–A structured query language database system commonly used in educational settings because of its robust software and free license for educational uses.

Neanderthal–An extinct human species or subspecies living during the late Pleistocene Epoch throughout most of Europe and parts of Asia and northern Africa and associated with Middle Paleolithic tools.

Network–A system of computers interconnected by telephone wires or other means in order to share information.

NodeStub–A class in basic VRML structure needed for an object in the scene graph and the ability to respond to changes in location, position, scale, and orientation.

NSES (National Science Education Standards)–Standards published and approved by the Governing Board of the National Research Council, whose members are drawn from the councils of the National Academy of Sciences, the National Academy of Engineering, and the Institute of Medicine.

OLE (object linking and embedding)–A distributed object system and protocol from Microsoft, also used on the Acorn Archimedes.

Oligopolistic–A market condition in which sellers are so few that the actions of any one of them will materially affect price and have a measurable impact on competitors.

PD–Abbreviation for public domain, applied to software distributed over Usenet and from Internet archive sites.

Pedagogical–Preparing, training, instructing, or teaching.

Perl–A high-level programming language, started by Larry Wall in 1987 and developed as an open source project.

PIs–Principal Investigators.

Port–To modify (software) for use on a different machine or platform; also the entryway or door through which a server receives requests on a computer.

PROC GLM–A function provided by the SAS statistical package.

Psychographic–A graphic representation or chart of the personality traits of an individual or group.

PVW (Polynesian Virtual World)–Where players meet and interact with a culture that is much divorced and foreign to their everyday experience.

RAM (random access memory)–A memory device in which information can be accessed in any order.

Scaffolding–Support usually employed to provide assistance to a student.

SceneRoot–Terminal end of a scene graph in a 3D rendering.

Sedimentary–Describing rocks formed by the deposition of sediment.

Showgoal–A command that shows students the different parts of an assignment.

SimCity–Maxis Software's simulation game that enables players to design and build their own city, which must be administered well if it is to thrive.

SLATE tool–Intended to integrate the "Ask System" and "WordNet" technologies into a single application.

Smalltalk–The pioneering object-oriented programming system developed in 1972 by the Software Concepts Group, led by Alan Kay, at Xerox PARC between 1971 and 1983.

Software–The programs, routines, and symbolic languages that control the functioning of the hardware and direct its operation.

Software agent–A program, typically autonomous and persistent, that performs a set number of known tasks.

TCP/IP (transmission control protocol, Internet protocol)–A protocol for communication between computers, used as a standard for transmitting data over networks and as the basis for standard Internet protocols.

Teleportation–A hypothetical method of transportation in which matter or information is dematerialized, usually instantaneously, at one point and recreated at another.

UDP (user datagram protocol)–A lightweight and efficient Internet protocol that is sometimes unreliable. Compare **TCP/IP**.

UNIX–A trademark used for a computer operating system developed at Bell Labs in the 1960s.

UQB (unit quality benefit)–A variable in the Dollar Bay economic simulation.

URL (uniform resource locator)–An Internet address (e.g., http://wwwic.ndsu .edu) usually consisting of the access protocol (HTTP), the domain name, and optionally the path to a file or resource residing on that server.

USB (universal serial bus)–An external peripheral interface standard for communication between a computer and external peripherals over an inexpensive cable using biserial transmission; also, Unit Service Benefit, a variable in the Dollar Bay economic simulation.

USC (unit search cost)–A variable in the Dollar Bay game.

UTC (unit transportation cost)–A variable in the Dollar Bay game.

Viewlogos–Objects in a platform's user interface.

Visual basic–A popular event-driven visual programming system from Microsoft Corporation for Microsoft Windows.

VMS (virtual memory system)–DEC's (Digital Equipment Corporation) proprietary operating system for its VAX minicomputer; one of the seven or so environments that loom largest in hacker folklore.

VRML (virtual reality modeling language)–A draft specification for the design and implementation of a platform-independent language for virtual reality scene description and rendering.

WebCT (web course tools)–An integrated package for higher education course delivery.

WWWIC (World Wide Web Instructional Committee)–An organization on the campus of North Dakota State University that specializes in virtual immersive worlds for education.

X3D–An alternative standard for 3D modeling and rendering (see **VRML**).

Xerox PARC–The famed Palo Alto Research Center. For more than a decade, from the early 1970s into the mid-1980s, PARC yielded an astonishing volume of groundbreaking hardware and software innovations.

Zelecon tool (Zelenak, 1999)–Predefined questions and answers that players can negotiate in the process of engaging in simulated conversation with software agents.

ZORK–The second of the great early experiments in computer fantasy gaming.

References

AAAS. (1993). http://project2061.aaas.org/tools/benchol/bolframe.html

Anido-Rifón, L., Llamas-Nistal, M., & Fernández-Iglesias, M. J. (2001, May). A component model for standardized web-based education. *Proceedings of WWW10*, Hong Kong.

Applebee, A. N., & Langer, J. A. (1983). Instructional scaffolding: Reading and writing as natural language activities. *Language Arts, 60*, 168–175.

Axelrod, R. (1996, Winter). Education and training [Course offered at the University of Michigan].

Bailey, F. G. (1983). *The tactical uses of passion: An essay on power, reason, and reality*. Ithaca, NY & London: Cornell University Press.

Bandura, A. (2001). Social cognitive theory: An agentic perspective. *Annual Review of Psychology*, Vol. 52, p. 1.

Barabasi, A. L., & Bonabeau, E. (2003). Scale-free networks. *Scientific American, 288*(5), 60–69.

Barcelo, J. A., Forte, M., & Sanders, D. H. (Eds.). (2000). "Virtual Reality in Archaeology." Computer Applications and Quantitative methods in Archaeology (Oxford: British Archaeological Reports International Series) (S843).

Bareiss, R., & Slator, B. M. (1993). From Protos to ORCA: Reflections on a unified approach to knowledge representation, categorization, and learning. In G. Nakamura, R. Taraban, & D Medin (Eds.), *The psychology of learning and motivation: Vol. 29. Categorization and category learning by humans and machines* (pp. 157–186). San Diego, CA: Academic Press.

Bartle, R. (1999, May). "How it really happened": Imaginary reality. http://imaginaryrealities.imaginary.com/volume2/issue5/really_happened.html

Bass, R., Clinch, B., Reeves, T., Slator, B. M., & Terhune, E. (1999, October 7). Exemplary models for web-based learning [PBS Adult Learning Service satellite videoconference].

Bates, R. L., & Jackson, J. A. (1984). *Dictionary of geological terms* (3rd ed.). Alexandria, VA: American Geological Institute.

Bateson, G. (1972). *Steps to an ecology of mind*. New York: Ballantine Books.

Batteau, A. W. (2000). Negations and ambiguities in the cultures of organizations. *American Anthropologist, 102*(4), 726–740.

Bell, B., Bareiss, R., & Beckwith, R. (1994). Sickle cell counselor: A prototype goal-based scenario for instruction in a museum environment. *Journal of the Learning Sciences, 3*(4), 347–386.

Berdan, F. F., Stark, E., & Van Loon, C. (1998). Multimedia development for cultural anthropology: Fieldwork simulation. *Syllabus, 12*(3), 54–57.

Bidney, D. (1947). Human nature and the cultural process. *American Anthropologist, 49*(3), 375–399.

Birman, B. F., Kirshstein, R. J., Levin, D. A., Matheson, N., & Stephens, M. (1997). *The effectiveness of using technology in K–12 education: A preliminary framework and review*. Washington, DC: American Institutes for Research, Office of Educational Research and Improvement.

Bishop, A. J. (1988). *Mathematical enculturation*. Boston: Kluwer Academic.

Blume, J., Garcia, K., Mullinax, K., & Vogel, K. (2001). *Integrating math and science with technology* (Master of Arts Action Research Project, Saint Xavier University and Skylight Professional Development Field-Based Masters Program). (ERIC Document Reproduction Service No: ED454088)

Bonvillain, N. (1997). *Language, culture, and communication* (2nd ed.). Upper Saddle River, NJ: Prentice-Hall.

Brandt, L. (2003, April). *Native Dancer, virtual learning, and anthropology: A discussion of potential outcomes*. Guest lecture, University of North Dakota, Department of Anthropology, Grand Forks. Contact: NVApaper@lisabrandtphd.com

Bransford, J. D., Franks, J. J., Vye, N. J., & Sherwood, R. D. (1989). New approaches to instruction: Because wisdom can't be told. In S. Vosinadou & A. Ortony (Eds.), *Similarity and analogical reasoning* (pp. 470–497). New York: Cambridge University Press.

Brown, D., & Clement, J. (1989). Overcoming misconceptions via analogical reasoning: Abstract transfer versus explanatory model construction. *Instructional Science, 18*, 237–261.

Brown, J. S., Collins, A., & Duguid, P. (1989). Situated cognition and the culture of learning. *Educational Researcher, 18*(1), 32–42.

Bruckman, A. (1993). MOOse-crossing. Thesis proposal, MIT.

Bruckman, A. (1997). Finding one's own in cyberspace. In C. Haynes & J. R. Holmevik (Eds.), *High wired: On the design, use, and theory of educational MOOs*. Ann Arbor, MI: University of Michigan Press.

Bruner, J. (1974). *Beyond the information given: Studies in the psychology of knowing* (pp. 75–79) (J. Anglin, Ed.). London: Allen & Unwin.

Brzezinski, D. (1989, December). M.U.L.E. A look at an 8bit classic. *Atari Interface Magazine*.

CafeMOO, University of California, Berkeley. Accessed February 11, 2002, http://moolano .berkeley.edu/, telnet://moolano.berkeley.edu:8888

Carlstrom, E. L. (1992). Better living through language: The communicative implications of a text-only virtual environment. Student paper, Grinnell College, Grinnell, IA.

Carrasquel, J. (1999, March). Teaching CS1 on-line: The good, the bad and the ugly. *Proceedings of SIG Computer Science Education Conference* (pp. 212–216), New Orleans, LA. New York: Association for Computing Machinery.

Carswell, L. (1997, August). Teaching via the Internet: The impact of the Internet as a communication medium on distance learning introductory computing students. *Proceedings of Innovation and Technology in Computer Science Education Conference*, Uppsala, Sweden.

Cell Biology. The biology project, University of Arizona (2001, August 9). Accessed March 2, 2002, http://www.biology.arizona.edu/cell_bio/cell_bio.html

Chinn, C. A., & Brewer, W. E. (1993). The role of anomalous data in knowledge acquisition: A theoretical framework and implications for science instruction. *Review of Educational Research, 63*, 1–49.

Clancey, W. J. (1995). Practice cannot be reduced to theory: Knowledge, representations, and change in the workplace. In S. Bagnara, C. Zuccermaglio, & S. Stucky (Eds.), *Organizational learning and technological change* (pp. 16–46). Berlin: Springer.

Clark, J. T., & Herdrich, D. J. (1993). Prehistoric settlement system in Eastern Tutuila, American Samoa. *The Journal of the Polynesian Society, 102*, 147–183.

Clark, J. T., Slator, B. M., Bergstrom, A., Fisher, S., Hawley, J., Johnston, E., Landrum, J. E., III, & Zuroff, M. (2003). Virtual archaeology as a teaching tool. In M. Doerr & A. Sarris (Eds.), The digital heritage of archaeology: Computer applications and quantitative methods in archaeology (pp. 29–35). Athens: Archive of Monuments and Publications, Hellenic Ministry of Culture.

Clark, J. T., Slator, B. M., Bergstrom, A., Larson, F., Frovarp, R., Landrum, J. E., III, & Perrizo, W. (2001, October 25–27). Preservation and access of cultural heritage objects through a digital archive network for anthropology. In *Proceedings of the 7th International Conference on Virtual Systems and MultiMedia* (pp. 28–38), Berkeley, CA. New York: IEEE Computer Society.

Clark, J. T., & Terrell, J. (1978). Archaeology in Oceania. *Annual Review of Anthropology, 7,* 293–319.

Clark, J. T., Slator, B. M., Perrizo, W., Landrum, J. E., III, Bergstrom, A., Frovarp, R., Ramaswamy, S., & Jockheck, W. (2002). The Digital Archive Network for Anthropology (DANA), A National Science Digital Library (NSDL) initiative. *Journal of Digital Information, 2.* Retrieved October 20, 2005 from http://jodi.esc.soton.ac.uk/Articles/v02/i04/Clark/

Clark, J. T., Wright, E., & Herdrich, D. J. (1997). Interactions within and beyond the Samoan Archipelago: Evidence from basalt geochemistry. In M. I. Weisler (Ed.), *Prehistoric long-distance interaction in Oceania: An interdisciplinary approach* (pp. 68–84). Auckland: New Zealand Archaeological Association.

Coley, R. J., Cradler, J., & Engel, P. K. (1997). *Computers and classrooms: The status of technology in U.S. schools.* Princeton, NJ: Policy Information Center.

CollegeTown, Buena Vista University. Accessed February 5, 2002, http://www.bvu.edu/ctown/, telnet://ctown.bvu.edu:7777

Collins, H. (1997). *Shedding the blinkers: A perspective on veterinary education.* Sydney, Australia: University of Sydney, Post Graduate Foundation in Veterinary Science.

Collins, H. (1998, November). Veterinary education and role-based learning. *Synergy* (9), Sydney, Australia: Centre for Teaching and Learning, University of Sydney. Retrieved November 10, 2005, from http://www.usyd.edu.au/ctl/Synergy/Synergy9/hcollins.htm

Computer Gaming World's Hall of Fame. (2001, June 1). *Computer Gaming World,* p. 80.

Cooper, B. C., Shepardson, D. P., & Harber, J. M. (2002). Assessments as teaching and research tools in an environmental problem-solving program for in-service teachers. *Journal of Geoscience Education, 50*(1), 64–71.

Coupland, D. (1995). *Microserfs.* New York: ReganBooks.

Curtis, P. (1992, April). Mudding: Social phenomena in text-based virtual realities. *Proceedings of the Conference on Directions and Implications of Advanced Computing* (sponsored by Computer Professionals for Social Responsibility), Berkeley, CA.

Curtis, P. (1997). Not just a game: How LambdaMOO came to exist and what it did to get back at me. In C. Haynes and J. R. Holmevik (Eds.), *High wired: On the design, use and theory of educational MOOs.* Ann Arbor: University of Michigan Press.

Curtis, P., & Nichols, D. (1993, May). MUDs grow up: Social virtual reality in the real world. Proceedings of *Third International Conference on Cyberspace,* Austin, TX.

Daly, C. (1999, June). RoboProf and an introductory computer programming course. *Proceedings of Innovation and Technology in Computer Science Education Conference,* Cracow, Poland.

D'Andrade, R. G. (1981). The cultural part of cognition. *Cognitive Science, 5,* 179–195.

D'Andrade, R. G. (1984). Cultural meaning systems. In R. A. Shweder & R. A. Levine (Eds.), *Culture theory: Essays on mind, self and emotion* (pp. 88–119). Cambridge: Cambridge University Press.

D'Andrade, R. G. (1987). A folk model of the mind. In D. Holland & N. Quinn (Eds.), *Cultural models in language and thought* (pp. 112–148). Cambridge: Cambridge University Press.

D'Andrade, R. G. (1989). Culturally based reasoning. In A. Gellatly, D. Rogers, & J. Slobada (Eds.), *Cognition and social worlds* (pp. 132–143). Oxford: Clarendon Press.

D'Andrade, R. G. (1992). Schemas and motivation. In R. G. D'Andrade & C. Strauss (Eds.),

Human motives and cultural models (pp. 23–44). Cambridge: Cambridge University Press.

D'Andrade, R. G. (1995). *The development of cognitive anthropology*. Cambridge: Cambridge University Press.

Daniels, S., & David, N. (1982). *The archaeology workbook*. Philadelphia: University of Pennsylvania Press.

Davidson, J. M. (1969). Settlement patterns in Samoa before 1840. *Journal of the Polynesian Society, 78*, 44–88.

Davis, R., & Smith, R. (1983). Negotiation as a metaphor for distributed problem solving, *Computer, 26*, 28–37.

Dean, K. L. (2000, December). Virtual explorer: Interactive virtual environment for education. *Teleoperators & Virtual Environments, 9*(6), 505–525.

Dede, C. (1996). The evolution of constructivist learning environments: Immersion in distributed, virtual worlds. In B. G. Wilson (Ed.), *Constructivist learning environments: Case studies in instructional design* (pp. 165–175). Englewood Cliffs, NJ: Educational Technology.

Dede, C., Salzman, M. C., & Loftin, R. B. (1996). ScienceSpace: Virtual realities for learning complex and abstract scientific concepts. In *Proceedings of the IEEE Virtual Reality Annual International Symposium* (pp. 246–252). Los Alamitos, CA: IEEE Computer Society Press.

de Jager, P. (1993, January 4). Oceanic views and a visit to the Holodeck. *Computing Canada, 19*, p. 20.

Dewey, J. (1900). *The school and society*. Chicago: University of Chicago Press.

Dibble, H. L., McPherron, S. P., & Roth, B. J. (2000). *Virtual dig: A simulated archaeological excavation of a middle paleolithic site in France*. Mountain View, CA: Mayfield.

Diversity University. Accessed February 12, 2002, http://www.du.org/, telnet://206.212.27.32:8888/

Dix, C. (2000). *Education, culture, and the transmission of identity: A case study in a central Illinois school*. Unpublished thesis, Illinois State University, Normal. http://www.soa.ilstu.edu/anthrothesis/dix/

Doppke, J. C., Heimbigner, D., & Wolf, A. L. (1998). Software process modeling and execution within virtual environments. *ACM Transactions on Software Engineering and Methodology, 7*(1), 1–40.

Doube, W. (1998, July). Multimedia delivery of computer programming subjects: Basing structure on instructional design. *Proceedings of Australian Computer Science Education Conference* (85–93), Brisbane, Australia.

Drake, J. (2001, April). Grading with a team. *Proceedings of Midwest Instruction and Computing Symposium*, Cedar Falls, IA.

Duffy, T. M., & Jonassen, D. H. (1992). Constructivism: New implications for instructional technology. In T. M. Duffy & D. H. Jonassen (Eds.), *Constructivism and the technology of instruction* (pp. 7–12). Hillsdale, NJ: Erlbaum.

Duffy, T. M., Lowyck, J., & Jonassen, D. H. (1983). *Designing environments for constructive learning*. New York: Springer-Verlag.

Duncan, D. B. (1955). Multiple range and multiple F tests. *Biometrics, 11*, 1–42.

Dunlap, J. C., & Grabinger, R. S. (1996). Rich environments for active learning in the higher education classroom. In B. G. Wilson (Ed.), *Constructivist learning environments: Case studies in instructional design* (pp. 65–82). Englewood Cliffs, NJ, Educational Technology.

Dupre, J. (1994). Against scientific imperialism. *Philosophy of Science Association Proceedings, 2*, 374–381.

East, J. P. (1999, April). Providing feedback to CS students: Some alternatives. *Proceedings of the Small College Computing Symposium*, La Crosse, WI.

Edelson, D., Pea, R., & Gomez, L. (1996). Constructivism in the collaboratory. In B. G. Wilson (Ed.), *Constructivist learning environments: Case studies in instructional design* (pp. 151–164). Englewood Cliffs, NJ: Educational Technology.

Eighteen Software. (1999). Eighteen Software products. Accessed February 20, 2002, http://www.18software.com/products.html

Environmental System Research Institute. (2002). ArcView product sheet. Accessed February 23, 2002, http://www.esri.com/software/arcgis/arcview/index.html

Faria, A. J. (1998, September). Business simulation games: Current usage levels—an update. *Simulation & Gaming, 29*(3), 295–308.

Farrell, G. (2001). *The changing faces of virtual education.* London: Commonwealth of Learning, British Department for International Development.

Ferguson, W., Bareiss, R., Birnbaum, L., & Osgood, R. (1992). ASK systems: An approach to the realization of story-based teachers. *The Journal of the Learning Sciences, 2*, 95–134.

Forte, M., & Siliotti, A. (Eds.). (1997). Virtual Archaeology: Re-Creating ancient worlds. New York: Harry N. Abrams, Inc.

Foubister, S. P., Michaelson, G. J., & Tomes, N. (1997). Automatic assessment of elementary standard ML programs using Ceilidh. *Journal of Computer Assisted Learning, 13*(2), 99–108.

Freeman, D. (1983). *Margaret Mead and Samoa: The making and unmaking of an anthropological myth.* Cambridge, MA: Harvard University Press.

Galbraith, J. K. (1967). *The new industrial state.* New York: Houghton Mifflin.

Geertz, C. (1983). *Local knowledge: Further essays in interpretive anthropology.* New York: Basic Books.

Genesereth, M., & Ketchpel, S. (1996). *Software agents* (Computer Science Tech. Rep.) Stanford: Stanford University.

Gerlach, L. P. (1991). Opportunity, liberty, ecology: Challenges of the post-cold war future. In R. B. Textor (Ed.), *The peace dividend as a cultural concept: Anticipating the possible benefits to American life from human effort released by the end of the Cold War* (Human Peace Monograph No. 9). Gainesville: University of Florida, International Union of Anthropological and Ethnological Sciences Commission on Peace, Department of Anthropology.

Getoor, L., Friedman, N., Koller, D., & Pfeffer, A. (2001). Learning probabilistic relational models. In S. Dzeroski & N. Lavrac (Eds.), *Relational data mining* (pp. 307–338). Heidelberg: Springer-Verlag.

Gick, M. L., & Holyoak, K. J. (1983). Schema induction in analogical transfer. *Cognitive Psychology, 15*, 1–38.

Gick, M. L., & Holyoak, K. J. (1987). The cognitive basis of knowledge transfer. In S. Cormier & J. Hagman (Eds.), *Transfer of learning: Contemporary research and applications* (pp. 9–46). Orlando, FL: Academic Press.

Gilman, C., & Schneider, M. J. (1987). *The way to independence: Memories of a Hidastsa Indian family (1840–1920).* St. Paul: Minnesota Historical Society Press.

Ginsparg, P., Gehrke, J., & Kleinberg, J. (2003). http://www.cs.cornell.edu/projects/kddcup/download/KDDCup-Overview.pdf

Gluckman, M. (1963). Introduction. In M. Gluckman (Ed.), *Essays on the ritual of social relations* (pp. 1–12). Manchester, UK: Manchester University Press.

Goldman, I. (1970). *Ancient Polynesian society.* Chicago: University of Chicago Press.

Goldman, S. R., Pellegrino, J. W., & Bransford, J. (1994). Assessing programs that invite thinking. In E. L Baker & H. F. O'Neil, Jr. (Eds.), *Technology assessment in education and training* (pp. 189–230). Hillsdale, NJ: Erlbaum.

Goodenough, W. H. (1957). Oceania and the problem of controls in the study of cultural and human evolution. *Journal of the Polynesian Society, 66*, 146–155.

Gormly, E. K. (1996). Critical perspectives on the evolution of technology in American public schools. *Journal of Educational Thought, 30*(3), 263–286.

Gott, S. P., Lesgold, A., & Kane, R. S. (1996). Tutoring for transfer of technical competence. In B. G. Wilson (Ed.), *Constructivist learning environments: Case studies in instructional design* (pp. 33–48). Englewood Cliffs, NJ: Educational Technology.

Guimarães, M. J. L., Jr. (2001). *Investigating physical performance in cyberspace: Some notes about methods.* Uxbridge, UK: Centre for Research into Innovation, Culture and Technology, Brunel University, Uxbridge. Online at http://www.brunel.ac.uk/depts/crict/vmpapers/mario.html

Haas, M., & Gardner, C. (1999). MOO in your face: Researching, designing, and programming a user-friendly interface. *Computers and Composition, 6,* 341–358.

Hagge, J. (1995). Early engineering writing textbooks and the anthropological complexity of disciplinary discourse. *Written Communication, 12,* 439–491.

Harris, M. (1968). *The rise of anthropological theory.* New York: Crowell.

Harris, M. (1979). *Cultural materialism: The struggle for a science of culture.* New York: Random House.

Hartman, J., & Wernecke, J. (1996). *The VRML 2.0 Handbook: Building moving worlds on the Web.* Reading, MA: Addison-Wesley.

Haydu, G. C. (1973). Psychotherapy, enculturation and indoctrination: Similarities and distinctions. *TIT Journal of Life Sciences, 3*(1), 25–27.

Haynes, C., & Holmevik, J. R. (Eds.). (1997). *High wired: On the design, use and theory of educational MOOs.* Ann Arbor: University of Michigan Press.

Heckman, C., & Wobbrock, J. O. (1999). Liability for autonomous agent design. *Autonomous Agents and Multi-Agent Systems, 2,* 87–103.

Herdrich, D. J. (1991). Towards an understanding of Samoan star mounds. *Journal of the Polynesian Society, 100*(4), 381–435.

Herdrich, D. J., & Clark, J. T. (1993). Samoan Tia 'Ave and social structure: Methodological and theoretical considerations. In M. Graves & R. C. Green (Eds.), *The evolution and organization of prehistoric society in Polynesia* (Monograph Series, pp. 52–63). Auckland: New Zealand Archaeological Association, New Zealand National Museum.

Herdrich, D. J., & Clark, J. T. (1996, April 10–14). *Spatial concepts in Samoa: Implications of a point field model for prehistory.* Paper presented at the annual meeting of the Society for American Archaeology, New Orleans, LA.

Higgins, T., Main, P., & Lang, J. (Eds.). (1996). *Imaging the Past. Electronic Imaging and Computer Graphics in Museums and Archaeology.* British Museum Occasional Paper, No. 114.

Hill, C., & Slator, B. M. (1998, April). Virtual lecture, virtual laboratory, or virtual lesson. *Proceedings of the Small College Computing Symposium* (pp. 159–173). Fargo–Moorhead, ND.

Hill, C., & Slator, B. M. (2000, June 26–July 1). *Computer science instruction in a virtual world.* Paper presented at the World Conference on Educational Media, Hypermedia and Telecommunications, Montreal.

Hinrichs, T. R., Bareiss, R., & Slator, B. M. (1993). Representation issues in multimedia case retrieval. In D. B. Leake (Ed.), *Proceedings of the AAAI-93 Workshop on Case-Based Reasoning* (AAAI Press Report Series) (pp. 35–40). Menlo Park, CA: AAAI.

Hitz, M., & Kögelar, S. (1997, August). Teaching C++ on the WWW. *Proceedings of Innovation and Technology in Computer Science Education Conference.* Uppsala, Sweden.

Hjarno, J. (1979–80). Social reproduction towards an understanding of Aboriginal Samoa. *Folk, 21–22,* 73–121.

Holmes, C. J. (1995). MUDBank project, Sonoma State University. Accessed March 6, 2002, http://www.sonoma.edu/projects/money.

Holmes, L. D. (1958). *Ta'u: Stability and change in a Samoan village* (Reprint No. 7). Wellington, Australia: Polynesian Society.

Hooker, R., & Slator, B. M. (1996, June 11). A model of consumer decision making for a MUD based game. *Proceedings of the Simulation-Based Learning Technology Workshop at the Third International Conference on Intelligent Tutoring Systems* (pp. 49–58), Montreal.

Huppert, J., Yaakobi, J., & Lazarowitz, R. (1998). Learning microbiology with computer simulations: Students' academic achievement by method and gender. *Research in Science & Technological Education*, pp. 231–245. Online via ProQuest.

Jacobson, M. J., & Archodidou, A. (2000). The knowledge mediator framework: Toward a design of hypermedia tools for learning. In M. J. Jacobson & R. Kozma (Eds.), *Innovations in science and math education: Advanced designs for technologies of learning* (pp. 117–162). Mahwah, NJ: Erlbaum.

Jacobson, M. J., & Spiro, R. J. (1995). Hypertext learning environments, cognitive flexibility, and the transfer of complex knowledge: An empirical investigation. *Journal of Educational Computing Research, 12*(4), 301–333.

Jerinic, L., & Devedzic, V. (2000, January). The friendly intelligent tutoring environment: Teacher's approach. *SIGCHI Bulletin, 32*(1), 83–94.

Jia, Y. (1998). *An abstraction tool for virtual reality.* Unpublished master's thesis, North Dakota State University, Fargo, ND.

Johnson, D., Ruzek, M., & Kalb, M. (2000). Earth system science and the Internet. *Computers & Geosciences, 26*, 669–676.

Johnston, E., Slator, B. M., Clark, J. T., Clambey, G. K., Fisher, S., Landrum, J. E., III, Martinson, D., Vantine, J. L., Hawley, J., Dorothy, J., Rousch, T., & Bergstrom, A. (2002, July/September). A historical virtual environment for archeology and creative writing students. *Computers in the Social Studies, 10*(3).

Johnston, W. (n.d.). *Computer-enhanced science education: The whole frog project.* Accessed February 27, 2002, http://www-itg.lbl.gov/ITG.hm.pg.docs/Whole.Frog/Whole.Frog.html

Johnstone, B. (2000). *Qualitative methods in sociolinguistics.* New York: Oxford University Press.

Jona, M. Y. (1995). *Representing and applying teaching strategies in computer-based learning-by-doing tutors.* Ph.D. dissertation, Institute for the Learning Sciences, Northwestern University, Evanston, IL.

Jones, G. (2001a, May 1). Sid speaketh—on dinosaurs, game design, and everything in between. *Computer Gaming World*, p. 66.

Jones, G. (2001b, February 1). The ultimate list. *Computer Gaming World*, p. 21.

Jorgenson, O., & Vanosdall, R. (2002). The death of science? What we risk in our rush toward standardized testing and the three R's. *Phi Delta Kappan 83*(8). Accessed October 22, 2005, from http://www.pdkintl.org/kappan/k0204jor.htm

Juell, P. (1999, March 1–4). Educational opportunities using VRML in the AI classroom. *International Conference on Mathematics/Science Education & Technology* (pp. 119–123), San Antonio, TX.

Kadobayashi, R., Nishimoto, K., & Mase, K. (2000). Immersive walk-through experience of Japanese ancient villages with the VisTA-Walk System. In J. A. Barcelo, M. Forte, & D. H. Sanders (Eds.), *Virtual reality in archaeology: computer applications and quantitative methods in archaeology* (BAR International Series 843, pp. 135–142). Oxford ArchaeoPress.

Katz, A. (1999, Spring). A computer-aided exercise for checking novices' understanding of market equilibrium changes. *The Journal of Economic Education, 30*(2), 148.

Kay, P. (1997). *Words and the grammar of context.* Cambridge: Cambridge University Press. (Reprinted from CSLI lecture notes (No. 40), Center for the Study of Language and Information, Stanford University, Stanford, CA.)

Kearsley, G. (1998). Educational technology: A critique. *Educational Technology, 4*, 47–51.

Keegan, M. (1995). *Scenario educational software: Design and development of discovery learning.* Englewood Cliffs, NJ: Educational Technology.

Keenan, C. (2002). Technology in English 015: Building low-cost, high-powered writing communities. Penn State, Allentown, PA. Accessed October 24, 2005 from http://cac.psu.edu/~cgk4/horizon.html

Kerendine, S. (1997). Diving into shipwrecks: Aquanauts in cyberspace: The design of a virtual maritime museum. *Curtin School of Design Journal, 4.*

Korniega, K. (2001, January 4). *ACM Tech News.* Online at www.acm.org/technews/articles/2001–3/0103w.html

Kramer, A. (1903). *Die Samoa-Inseln* (2 vols.). Stuttgart: Schweizerbartsche Verlag.

Kuhn, T. (1962). *The structure of scientific revolutions.* Chicago: University of Chicago Press.

Kulik, E. L. C., & Kulik, J. A. (1991). Effectiveness of computer-based instruction: An updated analysis. *Computers in Human Behavior, 7*, 75–94.

Kulik, J. A. (1994). Meta-analytic studies of findings on computer-based instruction. In E. L. Baker & H. F. O'Neil, Jr. (Eds.), *Technology assessment in education and training* (pp. 9–33). Hillsdale, NJ: Erlbaum.

La Velle, L. B. (2000, Spring). Cell biology web sites. *Journal of Biological Education, 34*(2), 105.

Lave, J., & Wenger, E. (1991). *Situated learning: Legitimate peripheral participation.* Cambridge: Oxford University Press.

Learning In Motion. (n.d.). Accessed February 27, 2002, http://www.learn.motion.com/lim1.html

Lesgold, A. (1994). Assessment of intelligent training technology. In D. L. Baker & H. F. O'Neil, Jr. (Eds.), *Technology asssessment in education and training* (pp. 97–116). Hillsdale, NJ: Erlbaum.

LeVine, R. A. (1984). Properties of culture: An ethnographic view. In R. A. Shweder & R. A. LeVine (Eds.), *Culture theory: Essays on mind, self, and emotion* (pp. 67–87). Cambridge: Cambridge University Press.

Liffick, B. W., & Aiken, R. (1996, June). A novice programmer's support environment. *Proceedings of Innovation and Technology in Computer Science Education Conference,* Barcelona, Spain.

Linn, M. C. (1995). Designing computer learning environments for engineering and computer science: The scaffolded knowledge integration framework. *Journal of Science Education and Technology, 4*(2), 21–27.

Lockyear, K., & Rahtz, S. P. Q. (Eds.). (1991). Computer Applications and Quantitative Methods in Archaeology 1990 (Oxford: British Archaeological Reports) International Series 565.

Lookatch, R. P. (1996). The ill-considered dash to technology. *The School Administrator, 53*(4), 28–31.

Losh, C. L. (2000). *Using skill standards for vocational-technical education curriculum development* (Information Series No. 383). (ERIC Document Reproduction Service No. ED440295)

Low, G., Lomax, A., Jackson, M., & Nelson, D. (2003). *Emotional intelligence: A new student development model.* Paper presented at the National Conference of the American College Personnel Association. Minneapolis, MN. Online at http://www.tamuk.edu/college1/New Folder/EI Report/emotional_intelligence.htm

MacDougall, D. (1997). The visual in anthropology. In M. Banks & H. Morphy (Eds.), *Rethinking visual anthropology* (pp. 276–295). New Haven, CT: Yale University Press.

MacUser. (1989, December). Best 18 Education Products. *MacUser, 5*(12), 120.

Mahoney, D. P. (1998, May). A NICE way to learn. *Computer-Graphics-World, 21*(5), 16.

Mateas, M., & Lewis, C. (1996). A MOO-based virtual training environment. *Journal of Computer-Mediated Communication, 2*(3), http://jcmc.indiana.edu/

Mayfield, J., Labrou, Y., & Finin, T. (1995). *Desiderata for agent communication languages* (Tech. Rep.). University of Maryland, Baltimore.

McArthur, R. H., & Wilson, E. O. (1967). *The theory of island biogeography*. Princeton, NJ: Princeton University Press.

McClean, P. E., Schwert, D. P., Juell, P., Saini-Eidukat, B., Slator, B. M., & White, A. (1999, March 1–4). Cooperative development of visually-oriented, problem-solving science courseware. Proceedings of *International Conference on Mathematics/Science Education & Technology* (pp. 486–491), San Antonio, TX.

McClean, P., Saini-Eidukat, B., Schwert, D. P., Slator, B. M., & White, A. R. (2001, April 17–21). Virtual worlds in large enrollment biology and geology classes significantly improve authentic learning. In J. A. Chambers (Ed.), *Selected papers from the 12th International Conference on College Teaching and Learning* (pp. 111–118). Jacksonville, FL: Center for the Advancement of Teaching and Learning.

McCluhan, H. M. (1994). *Understanding media: The extensions of man*. Cambridge, MA: MIT Press.

McGee, S., Howard, B., & Hong, N. (1998, April). Cognitive apprenticeship, activity structures, and scientific inquiry. In S. McGee (Chair), *Changing the game: Activity structures for reforming education*. Symposium conducted at the annual meeting of the American Educational Research Association, San Diego, CA.

McLellan, H. (1994). Virtual reality goes to school. *Computers in Schools*, 9(4), 5–12.

MCLI. (1992). About the games and simulations evaluations. Maricopa Center for Learning and Instruction (MCLI) and Maricopa Community Colleges. Accessed March 2002, http://www.mcli.dist.maricopa.edu/proj/sw/games/simlife.html.

McLuhan, M. (1964). *Understanding media*. New York: McGraw-Hill.

Mead, M. (1929). *Coming of age in Samoa*. London: Cape.

Mead, M. (1930). *The social organization of Manu'a* (Bulletin 76). Honolulu, HI: Bernice. P. Bishop Museum.

Mead, M. (1957). Introduction to Polynesia as a laboratory for the development of models in the study of cultural evolution. *Journal of the Polynesian Society, 66*, 145.

MediaMOO. (1999). Accessed October 22, 2005 from http://www.cc.gatech.edu/fac/Amy .Bruckman/MediaMOO/. MediaMOO, College of Computing, Georgia Tech., Atlanta, GA.

Meir, E. Biology education software FAQ. Accessed October 22, 2005, http://www.beakerware .com/bioedusoft/index.html

Meleisea, M. (1987). *The making of modern Samoa*. Suva, Fiji: Institute of Pacific Studies of the University of the South Pacific.

Mestre, J. P., Dufresne, R. J., Gerace, W. J., Hardiman, P. T., & Tougher, J. S. (1992). Enhancing higher-order thinking skills in physics. In D. F. Halpern (Ed.), *Enhancing thinking skills in the sciences and mathematics* (pp. 77–94). Hillsdale, NJ: Erlbaum.

Mikropoulos, T. A. (2001). Brain activity on navigation in virtual environments. *Journal of Educational Computing Research, 24*(1), 1–12.

Moerman, M. (1987). A little knowledge. In S. A. Tyler (Ed.), *Cognitive anthropology* (3rd Ed., pp. 449–469). Prospect Heights, IL: Waveland Press.

Moore, M. G., & Thompson, M. M. (1990). *The effects of distance learning: A summary of the literature* (ACSDE Research Monograph No. 2). University Park, PA: American Center for the Study of Distance Education, College of Education, Pennsylvania State University.

MOOVille. (2004). Networked writing environment. University of Florida, Gainesville, FL. Accessed February 5, 2002, http://web.nwe.ufl.edu/writing/

Morris, B. (1994). *Anthropology of the self: The individual in cultural perspective*. Boulder, CO: Pluto Press.

Morris, R. (2000). Virtual field geology. California State University, Long Beach. Accessed February 25, 2002, http://seis.natsci.csulb.edu/VIRTUAL_FIELD/vfmain.htm

MundoHispano, University of St. Louis–Missouri. Accessed February 1, 2002, http://www.umsl.edu/~moosproj/mundo.html, telnet://admiral.umsl.edu:8888

Nadis, S. (1999, March). Immersed in science. *Computer-Graphics-World*, 22(3) 42–43.

Naidu, S., Ip, A., & Linser, R. (2000). Dynamic goal-based role-play simulation on the web: A case study. *Educational Technology and Society*, 3(3), 190–202.

National Academies Press. (1995). National Science Education Standards—Contents. Accessed October 22, 2005 from http://www.nap.edu/readingroom/books/nses/html/

Nooteboom, B. (1999). The triangle: Roles of the go-between. In A. Grandori (Ed.), *Interfirm networks: Organization and industrial competitiveness* (pp. 91–119). The Netherlands: Groningen University.

Nooteboom, B. (2000). Learning by interaction, absorbitive capacity, cognitive distance and governance. *Journal of Management and Governance*, 4, 69–92.

Norman, D. A. (1988). *The design of everyday things*. New York: Doubleday.

Norman, D. A. (1993). *Things that make us smart: Defending human attributes in the age of the machine*. Reading, MA: Addison-Wesley.

Norr, H. (1989, March 21). Designing the city of your dreams. *MacWEEK*, 3(12), 16.

Novak, G. (2000). Geology labs online. California State University at Los Angeles. Accessed February 25, 2002, http://vcourseware3.calstatela.edu/GeoLabs/index.html

O'Meara, T. (1990). *Samoan planters: Tradition and economic development in Polynesia*. Fort Worth, TX: Holt, Rinehart and Winston.

O'Neil, J. (1995, October). On technology and schools. *Educational Leadership*, 53(2), 6–7.

Opgrande, J. E., Slator, B. M., Bergstrom, A., McClean, P., Vender, B., & White, A. R. (2002, November 18–20). Coordinating pilot studies for distributed learning environments with web-based support tools. *Proceedings of the International Conference on Information and Knowledge Sharing* (pp. 83–88). St. Thomas, VI.

Ortner, S. B. (1984). Theory in anthropology since the sixties. *Comparative Studies in Society and History*, 26(1), 126–166.

Ortuno, M. M. (1991). Cross-cultural awareness in the foreign language class: The Kluckhohn model. The *Modern Language Journal*, 75(4), 449–460.

Owen, P. (2002). The year of the phoenix: Using anthropology as the core of an interdisciplinary freshman class. *Public Anthropology: The Graduate Journal*. East Lansing: Michigan State University. Retrieved November 10, 2005, from http://www.publicanthropology.org/Journals/Grad-j/MichiganState/MichiganStateTOC.htm

Patterson, T. C. (1994). *The theory and practice of archaeology: A workbook* (2nd ed.). Englewood Cliffs, NJ: Prentice-Hall.

Pea, R. (1993). Practices of distributed intelligence and design for education. In G. Salomon (Ed.), *Distributed cognition: Psychological and educational considerations* (pp. 47–87). Cambridge, MA: Cambridge University Press.

Peacock, J. L. (1986). *The anthropological lens: Harsh light, soft focus*. New York: Cambridge University Press.

PennMOO, University of Pennsylvania. Accessed October 23, 2005, http://ccat.sas.upenn.edu/PennMOO/, telnet://ccat.sas.upenn.edu:7777

Petre, M., & Price, B. (1997). Programming practical work and problem sessions via the Internet. *Working Group Reports and Supplemental Proceedings of Innovation and Technology in Computer Science Education Conference*.

Phipps, R., & Merisotis, J. (1999). *What's the difference? A review of contemporary research on the effectiveness of distance learning in higher education*. http://www.ihep.com/difference.pdf (p. 42).

Piirto, R. (1990, December). Measuring minds in the 1990s. *American Demographics*,

Piringer, N. T. (2001). Viewpoint: Internet2. *Going the Distance*, 1(2). Warrensburg: Missouri Distance Learning Association. Also available online at http://www.modla.org/about/newsletters/Jan2001_news.pdf

Poirer, J. R. (1995). Interactive multiuser realities: MUDS, MOOs, MUCKS and MUSHes. In *The Internet unleashed* (pp. 1126–1127). Indianapolis, IN: Sams.

Preston, J. A., & Shackelford, R. (1999, June). improving on-line assessment: An investigation of existing marking methodologies. *Proceedings of Innovation and Technology in Computer Science Education Conference*, Cracow, Poland.

Price, T. D., & Gebauer, A. B. (1997). *Adventures in Fugawiland: A computer simulation in archaeology* (2nd ed.). Mountain View, CA: Mayfield.

Purcell, P. (1996). Museum 2000: A multimedia prospect. In T. Higgins, P. Marin, & J. Lang (Eds.), Imaging the past, (Occasional Paper No. 114, pp. 119–125). London: British Museum.

Raghavan, K., & Katz, A. (1989, August). Smithtown: An intelligent tutoring system. *Technological Horizons in Education, 17*(1), 50–54.

Reeves, T. (1999, June 19–24). *Pseudo-science talk*. Presented at World Conference on Educational Media, Hypermedia and Telecommunications, Seattle, WA.

Regan, P. M., & Slator, B. M. (2002, October 1–3). Case-based tutoring in virtual education environments. ACM Collaborative Virtual Environments (pp. 2–8), Bonn, Germany.

Regian, J. W., & Shute, V. J. (1994). Evaluating intelligent tutoring systems. In E. L. Baker & H. F. O'Neil, Jr. (Eds.), *Technology assessment in education and training* (pp. 79–96). Hillsdale, NJ: Erlbaum.

Reid, T. A. (1994, December). Perspectives on computers in education: The promise, the pain, the prospect. *Active Learning, 1*(1).

Reimer, T. C., & Edelson, D. C. (1998). Addressing the challenges of a social simulation with computer supported collaborative learning (CSCL) tools. In A. S. Brickman, M. Guzdial, et al. (Eds.), *Proceedings of ICLS 98: International conference on the Learning Sciences* (pp. 345–347). Charlottesville, VA: Association for the Advancement of Computing in Education.

Reimer, T. C., & Edelson, D. C. (1999). Using a CSCL tool to support a legislative role-playing simulation: Hopes, fears, and challenges. In C. Hoadley & J. Roschelle (Eds.), *Proceedings of the Computer Supported for Collaborative Learning Conference* (pp. 466–474). Mahwah, NJ: Erlbaum.

Reuss, R., & Gardulski, A. (2001, March). An interactive game approach to learning in historical geology and paleontology. *Journal of Geoscience Education*, pp.

Rice, B. (1988, March). The selling of lifestyles: Are you what you buy? Madison Avenue wants to know. *Psychology Today*, 46–50.

Rieber, L. P., Smith, L., & Noah, D. (1998). The value of serious play. *Educational Technology, 38*(6), 29–37.

Roblyer, M. D. (1989). The impact of microcomputer-based instruction on teaching and learning: A review of recent research. *ERIC Digest* [EDO-IR-89-10], p. 4.

Rogers, E. M. (1962). *Diffusion of innovations*. New York: Free Press.

Rogers, E. M., & Shoemaker, F. F. (1971). *Communication of innovations: A cross-cultural approach*. New York: Free Press.

Rogoff, B. (2003a, June 30). *Culture and learning: An overview of research strands*. Address to National Academy of Science workshop (Committee on Research in Education). Online at http://216.239.41.104/search?q=cache:Jmol4nSOwokJ:www7.nationalacademies.org/core/BRogoff.pdf+%22culture+and+learning%22&hl=en&ie=UTF-8

Rogoff, B. (2003b). *The cultural nature of human development*. New York: Oxford University Press.

Russo, A. (1998, April). *Object immersion: Database-driven VRML and Robocam technology in the virtual museum*. Paper presented at Museums and the Web: An International Conference, Toronto, Ontario. Online at http://www.archimuse.com/mw98/abstracts/russo.html

Saikkonen, R., Malmi, L., & Korhonen, A. (2001, June). Fully automatic assessment of programming exercises. *Proceedings of Innovation and Technology in Computer Science Education Conference*, Canterbury, UK.

Saini-Eidukat, B., Schwert, D., & Slator, B. M. (1998). Text-based implementation of the Geology Explorer: A multi-user role-playing virtual world to enhance learning of geological problem-solving. *Geological Society of America Abstracts with Programs, 30*(7), 390.

Saini-Eidukat, B., Schwert, D. P., & Slator, B. M. (1999, April 7–9). Designing, building, and assessing a virtual world for science education. *Proceedings of the 14th International Conference on Computers and Their Applications* (pp. 22–25). Cancun, Mexico.

Saini-Eidukat, B., Schwert, D. P., & Slator, B. M. (2001). Geology Explorer: Virtual geologic mapping and interpretation. *Journal of Computers and Geosciences, 27*(4).

Salomon, G., & Globerson, T. (1987). Skill may not be enough: The role of mindfulness in learning and transfer. *International Journal of Educational Research, 11*, 623–638.

Sapir, E. (2002). *The psychology of culture: A course of lectures* (2nd ed.). Berlin: Mouton de Gruyter.

SAS Institute Inc. (1985). *SAS user's guide: Statistics* (version 5). SAS Institute Inc., Cary, NC.

Saunders, M., Sierant, J., Downey, G., & Blevis, E. B. (1994, June). *The role of content specialists in the design, use and transfer of a multi-media tool-set that features believable interactive characters*. Workshop presentation at American Association for Artificial Intelligence, Menlo Park, CA.

Schank, R. (1991). *Case-based teaching: Four experiences in educational software design* (ILS Technical Report No. 7). Northwestern University, Evanston, IL.

Schank, R. (1994). *Engines for education*. http://www.ils.nwu.edu/~e_for_e/

Schilling-Estes, N. (1998). Investigating "self-conscious" speech: The performance register in Ocracoke English. *Language in Society, 27*, 53–83.

Schlumberger Information Solutions. (2002). Inside reality product sheet. Accessed February 23, 2002, http://www.sis.slb.com/content/software/virtual/.

Schmidt, W. H., McKnight, C. C., & Raizen, S. A. (Eds.). (1997). A splintered vision: An investigation of U.S. science and mathematics education [Third International Mathematics and Science Study (TIMSS)]. Dordrecht, Germany: Kluwer Academic.

schMOOze University, Hunter University. Accessed February 2, 2002, http://members.tripod.co.jp/schmooze/

Schwert, D. P., Slator, B. M., & Saini-Eidukat, B. (1999, March 1–4). A virtual world for earth science education in secondary and post-secondary environments: The Geology Explorer. *International Conference on Mathematics/Science Education & Technology* (pp. 519–525), San Antonio, TX.

Sebesta, R. W. (1996). *Concepts of programming languages* (3rd ed.). Reading, MA: Addison-Wesley.

Shi, H., Shang, Y., & Chen, S-S. (2000, July). A multi-agent system for computer science education. *Proceedings of Innovation and Technology in Computer Science Education Conference*, Helsinki, Finland.

Shore, B. (1982). *Sala'ilua: A Samoan mystery*. New York: Columbia University Press.

Shute, V. J., & Glaser, R. (1990). A large-scale evaluation of an intelligent discovery world: Smithtown. In *Interactive Learning Environments* (R. Roda & B. Scott, Eds.) (Vol. 1, pp. 51–77).

Shute, V. J., & Psotka, J. (1995). Intelligent tutoring systems: Past, present, and future. In D. Jonassen (Ed.), *Handbook of research on educational communications and technology* (pp. 570–600). New York: Macmillan.

Sidorkin, A. M. (2002). *Learning relations: Impure education, deschooled schools, and dialogue with evil*. New York: Peter Lang.

Simmons Market Research Bureau. (1993). *Simmons 1993 Study of Media and Markets*. New York: Author.

Slator, B. M. (1999, June 24–26). Intelligent tutors in virtual worlds. *Proceedings of the 8th International Conference on Intelligent Systems* (pp. 124–127). Denver, CO.

Slator, B. M. (with the members of CsCI345). (2001, August 13–16). Rushing headlong into the past: The Blackwood simulation. *Proceedings of the Fifth IASTED International Conference on Internet and Multimedia Systems and Applications* (pp. 318–323), Honolulu, HI. Complete author list at http://lions.cs.ndsu.nodak.edu/~mooadmin/papers/imsa-final.htm

Slator, B. M., & Bareiss, R. (1992). Incremental reminding: The case-based elaboration and interpretation of complex problem situations. *Proceedings of the 14th Annual Conference of the Cognitive Science Society* (pp. 1122–1127), Bloomington, IN.

Slator, B. M., & Chaput, H. (1996, June 12–14). Learning by learning roles: A virtual role-playing environment for tutoring. *Proceedings of the Third International Conference on Intelligent Tutoring Systems* (C. Frasson, G. Gauthier, & A. Lesgold, Eds.) (pp. 668–676). Montreal: Springer-Verlag.

Slator, B. M., Clark, J. T., Daniels, L. M., Hill, C., McClean, P., Saini-Eidukat, B., Schwert, D. P., & White, A. R. (2002). Use of virtual worlds to teach the sciences. In L. C. Jain, R. J. Howlett, N. S. Ichalkaranje, & G. Tonfoni (Eds.), *Virtual Environments for Teaching and Learning* (pp. 1–40). Singapore: World Scientific.

Slator, B. M., & Farooque, G. (1998, November 11–13). The agents in an agent-based economic simulation model. *Proceedings of the 11th International Conference on Computer Applications in Industry and Engineering* (pp. 2–9), Las Vegas, NV.

Slator, B. M., & Hill, C. (1999, June 19–24). Mixing media for distance learning: Using IVN and MOO in Comp372. World Conference on Educational Media, Hypermedia and Telecommunications, Seattle, WA.

Slator, B. M., Juell, P., McClean, P., Saini-Eidukat, B., Schwert, D. P., White, A. R., & Hill, C. (1999). Virtual worlds for education. *Journal of Network and Computer Applications*, *22*(4), 161–174.

Slator, B. M., & MacQuarrie, S. D. (1995). Case-based reasoning: Multi-media learning environments and tools for AI. *International Journal of Microcomputer Applications*, *14*(3).

Slator, B. M., Schwert, D. P., & Saini-Eidukat, B. (1999, May 6–8). Phased development of a multi-modal virtual educational world. *Proceedings of the International Conference on Computers and Advanced Technology in Education* (pp. 92–96). Cherry Hill, NJ.

Slator, B. M., Schwert, D. P., Saini-Eidukat, B., McClean, P., Abel, J., Bauer, J., Gietzen, B., Green, N., Kavli, T., Koehntop, L., Marthi, B., Nagareddy, V., Olson, A., Jia, Y., Peravali, K., Turany, D., Vender, B., & Walsh, J. (1998, April). Planet Oit: A virtual environment and educational role-playing game to teach the geosciences. *Proceedings of the Small College Computing Symposium* (pp. 378–392), Fargo-Moorhead, ND.

Slator, B. M., Schwert, D., Saini-Eidukat, B., McClean, P., Abel, J., Gietzen, B., Green, N., Kavli, T., Koehntop, L., Marthi, B., Nagareddy, V., Olson, A., Jia, K., Peravali, K., Turany, D., Vender, B., & Walsh, J. (1998). Planet Oit: A virtual environment and educational role-playing game to teach the geosciences. *Proceedings of the Small College Computing Symposium* (pp. 378–392), Fargo-Moorhead, ND.

Smith, G. H. (1972). *Like-A-Fishhook Village and Fort Berthold, Garrison Reservoir, North Dakota* (Anthropological Papers 2). National Park Service, U.S. Department of the Interior, Washington, DC.

Smith, S. M. (2001). *Ethical enculturation: A nursing concept for the education of baccalaureate nursing students*. Arkadelphia, AR: Academic Forum Online, Henderson State University.

Snowman, J. (1995). Computer-based education: More hype than help? *Mid-Western Educational Researcher*, *8*(1), 32–36.

Spindler, G. (1955). *Sociocultural and psychological processes in Menomini acculturation* (Publications in Culture and Society No. 5). Berkeley: University of California Press.

Spindler, G., & Spindler, L. (2000). *Fifty years of anthropology and education (1950–2000): A Spindler anthology*. Mahwah, NJ: Erlbaum.

Spiro, R. J., Feltovich, P. J., Jacobson, M. J., & Coulson, R. L. (1991, May). Cognitive flexibility, constructivism, and hypertext: Random access instruction for advanced knowledge acquisition in ill-structured domains. *Educational Technology*, pp. 24–33.

Spradley, J. P. (1987). *Culture and cognition: Rules, maps, and plans*. Prospect Heights, IL: Waveland Press.

Stair, J. (1897). *Old Samoa, or flotsam and jetsam from the Pacific Ocean*. London: Religious Tract Society.

Stancic, Z., & Veljanovski, T. (Eds.). (2001). Computing Archaeology for Understanding the Past, CAA 2000: computer applications and quantitative methods in archaeology. Proceedings of the 28th Conference, Ljubljana, April 2000. Edited by Oxford, Archaeopress.

Stea, R. (2001). A virtual field trip of the landscapes of Nova Scotia. Accessed February 28, 2002, http://www.gov.ns.ca/natr/meb/field/start.htm

Steiner, S. (2002, March). M.U.L.E. game of the week. *Classic Gaming*. Online at http://www.classicgaming.com/rotw/mule. shtml

Street, S., & Goodman, A. (1998). Some experimental evidence on the educational value of interactive Java applets in web-based tutorials. *Proceedings of the Australian Computer Science Education Conference*, Brisbane, Australia.

Suzie, J. (1995). Donut: Starknet campus of the future. *The Journal of Virtual Reality in Education*, *1*(1), 46–47.

Swanson, D. B., Norman, G. R., & Linn, R. L. (1995). Performance-based assessment: Lessons from the health profession. *Educational Researcher*, *24*(5), 5–11, 35.

Swidler, A. (1986). Culture in action: Symbols and strategies. *American Sociological Review*, *51*, 273–286.

Swoyer, C. (2003). The linguistic relativity hypothesis. In E. N. Zalta (Ed.), *Stanford encyclopedia of philosophy* [Supplement to *Relativism*]. Online at http://plato.stanford.edu/archives/spr2003/entries/relativism

Tam, E. K., Badra, F., & Marceau, R. J. (1999, August). A web-based virtual environment for operator training. *IEEE-Transactions-on-Power-Systems*, *14*(3), 802–808.

Tamosaitis, N. (1995, March). Online MUDs mold new worlds: Ultimate hangout or refuge from reality? *Computer Life*, pp. 155–157.

Tapped In. Accessed February 12, 2002, http://www.tappedin.org/

TeleEducation NB. (1995). Is distance learning any good? http://tenb.mta.ca/anygood/

Terras, M. M. (1999). A virtual tomb for Kelvingrove: Virtual reality, archaeology and education. *Internet Archaeology*, 7. http://intarch.ac.uk/journal/issue7/terras_toc.html

Tesfatsion, L. (1995), A trade network game with endogenous partner selection. In *Computation approaches to economic problems* (H. Amman, B. Rustem, & A. B. Whinston, Eds.) (249–269). Kluwer.

Thagard, P. (1989). Explanatory coherence. *Behavioral and Brain Sciences*, *12*, 435–467.

The Cell. Think Quest. Accessed March 2002, http://library.thinkquest.org/3564/

The Cognition and Technology Group at Vanderbilt. (1997). *The Jasper project: Lessons in curriculum, instruction, assessment, and professional development* (p. 185). Mahwah, NJ: Erlbaum.

Thomas, P., & Logan, K. (2001). *Observational studies of student errors in a distance learning environment using a remote recording and replay tool*. Proceedings of the 6th annual conference on Innovation and technology in computer science education (pp. 117–120). New York: ACM Press.

Thomas, R. P. (1981). *Microeconomic applications: Understanding the American economy*. New York: Wadsworth.

Tishman, S., Jay, E., & Perkins, D. N. (1993). Teaching thinking dispositions: From transmission to enculturation. *Theory Into Practice, 32*, 147–153.

Trotter, A. (1998). A question of effectiveness. *Education Week, 18*(5), 6–9.

Turing, A. (1950). Computing machinery and intelligence. *Mind, 65*(236), 433–460. (Reprinted in *Computers and thought*, 1963, by E. Feigenbaum & J. Feldman, Eds., New York: McGraw-Hill)

Turner, G. (1986). *Samoa: A hundred years ago and long before*. Apia, West Samoa: Commercial Printers. (Original work published 1884)

Turner, V. (1977). *The ritual process: Structure and anti-structure*. Ithaca, NY: Cornell University Press.

Turner, V. (1987). *The anthropology of performance*. New York: PAJ Publications.

UkeU. (2002, November). *Principles and practices in electronic courseware design*. London: UKeUniversites Worldwide, UK Higher Education Funding Council, UK Secretary of State for Education and Employment.

Universities Space Research Association. (2002). Earth science systems online. Universities Space Research Association. Accessed February 25, 2002, http://www.usra.edu/esse/essonline/

Unkel, C. (1997). WinMOO. http://www-personal.engin.umich.edu/~cunkel

U.S. House of Representatives. (1997, May 6). Technology in the classroom: Panacea or Pandora's box? Hearing before the Committee on Science, Subcommittee on Technology, U.S. House of Representatives, One Hundred Fifth Congress, first session, Washington, DC, GPO, p. 108. [Document Y4.SCI 2: 105/13]

User Guide—SimCity. (1999). *Atelier software and electronic arts*. Accessed March 6, 2002, http://atelier.iside.net/ateliersoftware/palm/manuals/ english/simcity-manual-eng.pdf

Van Haneghan, J., Barron, L., Young, M., Williams, S., & Bransford, J. (1992). The Jasper series: An experiment with new ways to enhance mathematical thinking. In D. F. Halpern (Ed.), *Enhancing thinking skills in the sciences and mathematics* (pp. 15–38). Hillsdale, NJ: Erlbaum.

Vaupel, J., & Sommer, M. (1997). Multimedia education, distance learning, and electronic commerce applications. In *Proceedings of the International Conference on Virtual Systems and Multimedia* (P. Storms, Ed.) (p. 174). Los Alamitos, CA: IEEE Computer Society.

Venner, A. (1999, May). Factory training—military style. *American-Machinist, 143*(5), 60.

Vestal, A. (2002, March). The history of console RPGs. *CNET Network*. http://www.videogames.com/features/universal/rpg_hs/

Viadero, D. (1997). A tool for learning. *Education Week, 17*(11), 12–18.

Vidal, J. M., & Durfee, E. H. (1996). Building agent models in economic societies of agents. http: //ai.eecs.umich.edu/people/jmvidal/papers/amw/amw.html

Video Discovery. (2002). Understanding earth product overview. Accessed February 28, 2002, http://www.videodiscovery.com/view_product.asp?product_id=94&view=1

Voget, F. W. (1975). *A history of ethnology*. New York: Holt, Rinehart and Winston.

Voss, J. F. (1987). *Education and learning to think*. Washington, DC: National Academies Press.

Vye, N. J., Goldman, S. R., Voss, J. F., Hmelo, C., & Williams, S. (1997). Complex mathematical problem solving by individuals and dyads. *Cognition and Instruction, 15*(4), 435–484.

Wade, V. P., & Power, C. (1998, July). Evaluating the design and delivery of WWW based educational environments and courseware. *Proceedings of Innovation and Technology in Computer Science Education Conference*, Dublin, Ireland.

Warschauer, M. (2003). Demystifying the digital divide. *Scientific American, 289*(2), 42.

WebCT. (2002). WebCT software and services. Accessed March 5, 2002, http://www.webct.com/products

Weizenbaum, J. (1966). ELIZA—a computer program for the study of natural language communication between man and machine. *Communications of the ACM, 9*, 36–45.

White, A. R., McClean, P. E., & Slator, B. M. (1999, June 19–24). The Virtual Cell: An interactive, virtual environment for cell biology. World Conference on Educational Media, Hypermedia and Telecommunications, Seattle, WA.

Wiederhold, G. (1989). *The architecture of future information systems.* Stanford: Stanford University, Department of Computer Science.

Williams, J. (1984). *The Samoan journals of John Williams* (R. M. Moyle, Ed.). (Pacific History Series No. 11). Canberra: Australian National University Press.

Williamson, T. (2001, November–December). Millions mull social utopia—but within limits. *Dollars & Sense*, p. 40.

Wilson, J. (1998, October). She saw farther! *Computer Gaming World, 171*, 21.

Winn, W. (1999). Learning in virtual environments: A theoretical framework and considerations for design. *Educational Media International, 36*(4), 271–279.

Woit, D. M., & Mason, D. V. (1998, July). Lessons from on-line programming examinations. *Proceedings of Innovation and Technology in Computer Science Education Conference*, Dublin, Ireland.

Wolcott, H. F. (1985). On ethnographic intent. *Educational Administration Quarterly, 21*(3), 187–203.

Wolcott, H. F. (1991). Propriospect and the acquisition of culture. *Anthropology and Education Quarterly, 22*(3), 251–273.

Woolworth, A. R. (1969). *An ethnohistorical study of the Mandan, Hidatsa, and Arikara tribes of Indians from prehistoric times to 1915 A.D.* St. Paul: Minnesota Historical Society.

Wu, Y. (1998). Simulation of the biological process of steroid hormones with VRML. Master's thesis, North Dakota State University, Fargo.

Young, M. F., Nastasi, B. K., & Braunhardt, L. (1996). Implementing Jasper immersion: A case of conceptual change. In B. G. Wilson (Ed.), *Constructivist learning environments: Case studies in instructional design* (pp. 121–133). Englewood Cliffs, NJ: Educational Technology.

Zelenak, J. (1999). *Zelecon: A tool for building conditional conversational networks for software agents.* Master's thesis, North Dakota State University, Fargo.

About the Authors

Richard T. Beckwith is a Senior Researcher at Intel. His Ph.D. is from Teachers College at Columbia University in Developmental and Educational Psychology.

Lisa Brandt is a Research Affiliate with the Department of Sociology-Anthropology at North Dakota State University. Her research program, An Anthropology of Troubles, lies at the intersection of cultures and performance, learning, identity, environment, health, conflict, and change.

Harold Chaput is a member of the development team at Electronic Art. His Ph.D. is from the University of Texas at Austin in Computer Science.

Jeffrey T. Clark is an archaeologist in the Department of Sociology and Anthropology at North Dakota State University (NDSU), where he has been teaching since 1983. He began his career in archaeological fieldwork in 1973 and eventually went on to earn his doctorate in 1987 at the University of Illinois. His regional expertise is in Oceania (particularly the Samoan islands in Polynesia), although he has also worked extensively in North America. His publications dealing with those regions have covered a range of topics, including sea-level and landscape change, geochemical studies of artifacts, human settlement patterns, the impact of malaria on Pacific colonization, and historical archaeology. In 1998, Clark founded the Archaeology Technologies Lab (ATL) at NDSU to pursue technology applications in archaeology.

Lisa M. Daniels is an assistant professor in the School of Education at North Dakota State University (NDSU). She is a member of a cross-departmental research team that investigates the use of virtual environments in the teaching of science. Other research projects include working with regional science teachers to design lesson plans and assessments effective for diverse learners, evaluating the effect of dispositions on teaching, and determining the effectiveness of federal education reforms. She teaches courses in educational foundations, and the societal implications of and on schools. Daniels serves as associate director of the Center for Science and Math Education at NDSU.

Curt Hill is an Associate Professor in Mathematics and Computer Science at Valley City State University. His interests include Computer Science Education, Programming Languages, Antiquated Computing Devices and the generation of fractal images.

Phil McClean is a Professor of Plant Sciences at North Dakota State University with teaching responsibilties in genetics and plant molecular genetics. He received the Excellence in Teaching—Early Career from the North Dakota State University College of Agriculture in 1994 and the Peltier Award for Innovation in Teaching from NDSU in 1998. Dr. McClean was also honored in 1999 with an Innovative Excellence in Teaching, Learning and Technology Award at the 10th International Conference on College Teaching, Learning and Technology.

John Opgrande works in the private sector as a developer and consultant. His M.S. is from North Dakota State University in Computer Science.

Bernhardt Saini-Eidukat is Associate Professor of Geology and Chair of the Department of Geosciences at North Dakota State University.

Donald P. Schwert is Professor of Geology and Director of the Center for Science and Mathematics Education at North Dakota State University. As a geologist, Schwert has been responsible for teaching courses centered on surficial geology (e.g., environmental geology, glacial geology, geomorphology). Aside from his work on virtual worlds for earth science education, Schwert also studies ecosystem change over time, and he has published extensively on ice age climates and human impact on ecosystems.

Brian M. Slator graduated with a Bachelors in Computer Science (with a second major in English), from the University of Wisconsin–La Crosse in 1983. He attended graduate school at New Mexico State University, where he studied with Yorick Wilks and received a Ph.D. in Computer Science in 1988. After serving 6 years as a research scientist at the Institute for the Learning Sciences at Northwestern University he joined the Computer Science department at North Dakota State University in 1996, where he is currently a professor and engaged in research dealing with learning in role-based simulations.

Bradley Vender is a programmer/analyst on the staff at North Dakota State University. His M.S. is from North Dakota State University in Computer Science.

Alan R. White is a plant cell biologist who studies the synthesis of plant cell wall polysaccharides and the structural and functional organization of the plant Golgi apparatus. In addition to his plant cell wall research, Dr. White has a long-standing interest in improvement of science education. In recent years, he has been actively involved in development of the Virtual Cell program, a virtual environment for teaching cell biology. Dr. White served as the Dean of the College of Science & Mathematics at North Dakota State University from 2000–2005. He is currently Dean of the Thomas Harriot College of Arts and Sciences at East Carolina University.

Index